PRICING OF NEW ISSUES IN INDIAN CAPITAL MARKET

PRICING OF NEW ISSUES IN INDIAN CAPITAL MARKET

By

S.K. Singh

ANMOL PUBLICATIONS PVT. LTD.
NEW DELHI - 110 002 (INDIA)

ANMOL PUBLICATIONS PVT. LTD.
4374/4B, Ansari Road, Daryaganj
New Delhi - 110 002

Pricing of New Issues in Indian Capital Market

First Edition, 2001

ISBN 81-261-0849-5

PRINTED IN INDIA

Published by J.L. Kumar for Anmol Publications Pvt. Ltd., New Delhi - 110 002 and Printed at Mehra Offset Press, Delhi.

Contents

Foreword

Indian economy is experiencing the waves of change due to liberalisation and globalisation of markets and capital market is no exception. With the establishment of Securities and Exchange Board of India (SEBI), the Indian capital market has been freed from controls on capital issues. As a result, the scenario in the Indian market has significantly changed over the past one decade. Capital market has emerged as a major source of finance for the corporates. For a stable growing economy like India, a healthy and vibrant capital market is the need of the hour. The health of a capital market can be judged by how correctly it values various securities so as to infuse faith in the investors to invest in proposed ventures.

With the abolition of Controller of Capital Issues (C.C.I.), the market forces have come to determine the optimal price of new issues. As a result, a study of pricing of new issues was necessary for helping the corporations and merchant bankers to formulate a strategy for mobilising necessary finance. The present study entitled, "Pricing of New Issues in Indian Capital Market" by Dr. S.K. Singh is timely and relevant to provide an insight into the technicalities of pricing of new issues.

This study has tried to analyse the factors behind the pricing of new issues and provide a methodology to price new issues. Dr. Singh has tried to analyse the methodology of pricing of new issues before the abolition of C.C.I. and has identified the factors which went into the pricing of new issues. He has pointed out the difficulties faced by the corporates and merchant bankers to price new issues and used analytical tools of statistics to suggest a methodology to price new issues. He has provided case studies in which he has used his methodology to show how the free pricing of issues is being practised by the companies. He has also suggested a methodology to estimate premium on new issues because this component is necessary for valuation.

The book is most relevant for corporates, merchant bankers and students who intend to have a perspective on pricing of new issues.

Professor T. N. Kapoor
Former Vice-Chancellor
Panjab University, Chandigarh

New Delhi
January 13, 2001

Preface

In the capital markets both the segments viz. the primary market and the secondary market are equally important while not being mutually exclusive. As a rule, only when a country's primary market is alive; it is possible to ensure a good degree of activity in secondary market because it is the primary market which will ensure a continuous flow of securities to the secondary market, more so in developing economies. On the contrary, if a country's secondary market is only active but not transparent and disciplined, the cult of equity and related investment in the primary market will be difficult to be continuously developed and sustained. This is because the liquidity which the secondary market imparts to such investments in the hands of the investors will be adversely affected.

The scenario in the Indian Capital market has changed very fast over the past decade or so. It has emerged as a major source of finance for the corporate sector. A healthy and vibrant capital market is therefore, an imperative for a stable economy. The health of a capital market can be judged by the efficiency with which it values various securities as this alone can ensure the long term faith of investors which determines success or failure of a capital market. With the changing economic scenario and the problems associated with conservative pricing by Controller of Capital Issues (C.C.I.) a need was felt to allow the market forces to determine what is an optimal price for a new issue. It was for this basic reason that price determining mechanism of Indian capital market was selected as the subject of this study.

The study of pricing of new issue; in India is done with a view to explore the variables to be used by merchant bankers in pricing the issues and to suggest a proper methodology in pricing the issues. The study is broadly organised into five chapters as follows.

Chapter first provides an overview of the entire study. Chapter II deals with CCI methodology of pricing the issue. Suitable examples have been taken at relevant places to make the things more understandable. The chapter also reveals the limitations associated with the CCI methodology of pricing the issues. The theoretical aspect of valuation of equity shares is dealt in Chapter III of the study. Various security pricing models have been explained to highlight the factors determining the price of an equity share. Chapter IV is the core of the study. The chapter deals with the development in free pricing era and also discusses the limitations in the free pricing period. In order to overcome the limitations and problem associated with the present practice of merchant bankers, a suitable methodology has been suggested using statistical tools, techniques and data of seventeen companies operating in textile industry. The case studies of seventeen companies has helped in developing a suitable methodology for pricing the new issues which has finally enabled me in obtaining statistically justifiable results. The chapter also deals with pricing in case of further issues. The case study of five companies operating under textile industry has been done to display misutilization of free pricing in case of further issues and also to develop a methodology to evaluate proper quantum of premium on further issues. Chapter V of the study summarizes the entire study and also finally suggest the appropriate methodology of pricing the issues. The chapter also highlights the suggestions made for achieving the best price using the methodology obtained through study coupled with book building method of price, keeping in view the interest of companies as well as the investors.

In bringing this study into its present shape, I have received valuable assistance, guidance and encouragement from many quarters. The main intellectual stimulus for conducting the present Doctoral research was provided by my revered supervisor Dr. K.M. Upadhyay, Professor and Head, Department of Commerce and Business Studies, Jamia Millia Islamia, Central University, New Delhi. I express my sincere and heart felt gratitude to him for his initial motivation as well as subsequent guidance throughout the study. He has been all through an unfailing source of encouragement. Despite his preoccupations, he spared a lot of time for me for which I am deeply indebted.

My interest in the present work got further stimulated by privileged discussions with Shri S.K. Awasthi, Managing Director, PNB Capital Services Ltd., Delhi.

I am grateful to Shri Deepak Malhotra, Principal, Dyal Singh College (E), University of Delhi who has been a source of constant inspiration to me in pursuing my research work.

I would also like to express my sincere thanks to Dr. V.K. Mehta, I.E.S., Deputy Advisor, Planning Commission, who was kind enough to read the entire manuscript. Discussions on the research methodology with him enlightened me to make improvements in my work.

Collection of data is always an uphilltask. The present study involves interaction with various primary market intermediaries to view the entire subject microscopically. I am deeply indebted to all the merchant bankers for their co-operation for sparing their valuable time to fill up the questionnaires, which helped me in conducting this research. I would like to thank Mr. Shankaran and Mr. J.K. Singh for the help they provided in data validation and computer processing. My thanks are also due to the staff members of Delhi Stock Exchange for the cooperation and information provided by them during the course of this study and my numerous visits to the Exchange. The library staff of Delhi Stock Exchange also deserves a special mention for their cooperation in providing past annual reports of various companies and other data during my visit to their Stock Exchange. I am also highly indebted to the library staff of Ratan Tata library, Delhi School of Economics, University of Delhi and to the library staff of Jamia Millia Islamia for their kind and willing assistance.

I owe also to my wife Rini and sons Pragyan and Sugyan who were deprived of their due share in my time during the preparation of this book.

Last but not the least I am deeply beholden to Prof. T.N. Kapoor, Former Vice Chancellor, Panjab University, Chandigarh for writing Foreword to this book.

Finally, I am obliged to Shri Ashok Kumar, who so willingly and cheerfully typed and arranged the manuscript.

Dr. S.K. Singh

1

Introduction

The Indian Capital Market has undergone significant changes and developments, after the initiation of liberalisation and reform process by the Government of India. The Capital Market is an important element of the economy as it helps in mobilisation of savings and their channelisation in the productive investments thereby facilitating in capital formation. The step towards liberalisation and deregulation of market forces received overwhelming response from the market as the number of companies approaching capital market as well as amount of funds raised from the capital market has shown increasing trend during the period 1991-92 to 1995-96. The increasing trend is an outcome of the announcement made by Dr. Man Mohan Singh, the then Finance Minister, while presenting budget for 1992-93 regarding elimination of Government controls over capital issues including fixation of premium. The Finance Minister opined that companies should directly approach the Capital Market provided the Issues are in conformity with published guidelines relating to disclosure and other matters relating to investor protection. The Finance Minister admitted in his Budget Speech of 1992-93 that "the pricing of issues has lost its relevance in the changed circumstance of today". The CCI Methodology of pricing the issues was critically viewed and it was felt by the market that CCI pricing relied totally on historical facts and ignored the future potential of a company while pricing the issues. The conservative approach of CCI had very often resulted in heavy over subscription of issues. It is pertinent to mention here that the issue of Tata Timken over subscribed more than 4000 times. Such massive oversubscription not only reflected inadequate pricing but also display locking up of large amount of funds. The task of bankers to the issue and the registrars also gets overstretched. Thus, pricing methodology of CCI has led to multiple problems not only for the companies approaching capital market and investors but also for other primary market intermediaries and investors.

The decision of the Government to abolish CCI met the much awaited demand of Industry that they should be allowed to price their shares as they faced tremendous problems in dealing with CCI. The abolition of CCI flooded the primary market with issues, both right and new. Many projects which were held in abeyance due to want of funds, hit the market in the year 1992-93. Entrepreneurs, realising the ways with which the funds could be raised from the primary market rushed in to take the advantage of the long awaited opportunity. Equities became the most attractive and profitable instrument of saving. The number of shareholders increased from 1.5 millions in the beginning of 1970 to 15 million in 1993. It is estimated that capital raised through public and rights issue during 1992-93 could be around Rs. 15, 000 crore to Rs. 17, 000 crore.

In fact, there was an opinion favouring total deregulation but some market analyst were of the opinion that market based approach should prevail but a totally irregulated freedom for issues in the present market conditions of Indian secondary market marked by inefficiency and lack of transparency may not be in the interest of investors. It is in this context that SEBI has announced its guidelines. SEBI guidelines for issue pricing provides detailed direction for new companies but it has not given much directions for the existing companies. SEBI has required companies to justify the premium on their issues but the requirements of SEBI in this regard are not very impressive. SEBI has argued that it did not want to unnecessarily interfere in the free play of market forces. It has left the decision on investors to find out good and bad issues on the basis of Information given in the prospectus of a company SEBI non-interfence in the free pricing era would enable investors in educating themselves and making them competent enough to evaluate their investment proposals in the primary market. In such an environment, the merchant bankers and companies would also be required to play a responsible role as their irresponsibility in playing proper role would affect their reputation in the market and their survival may become very difficult.

Free pricing clashed with investor expectation. The greed of the corporate sector got exposed as many companies entered the market with unjustifiabily high premium and finally resulted in heavy loss to the investors, it seems investors have been taken for granted by promoters in the post free pricing period. The merchant bankers have failed to perform the role expected from them. No doubt, SEBI has put the onus of justifying the premium on merchant bankers but justification being the subjective assessment, merchant banker can easily escape their responsibilities. Moreover there is no specific model for pricing of issues which further enables merchant banker to take full liberty in over pricing the issues. However, this has not continued for long and now investors have become over cautious which has resulted in undersubscription of various rights and public issues. In words of the then Chairman of SEBI "The market is adjusting to the new regime of free pricing. Investors have also reacted to the changes by rejecting the issues if prices do not suit them. Their reaction will become more mature as merchant bankers and underwriters take their role more seriously. I expect to see more realistic pricing in the future." This indicates that the role of Merchant bankers, Companies, investors and all other intermediaries has completely changed in the free pricing scenario and they should not stick to their traditional role if free pricing is to be made successful in India. The process of free pricing is initiated and the market is undergoing through transitionary phase. Various modifications may be done in the time to come so as to weed out the deficiencies in the present system and finally reaching to the state of perfection.

Among all the financial instruments, equity shares are being widely used by Indian Corporates to raise funds from public and therefore, the study is concentrated on the pricing of equity shares. The study of pricing of new issue in India is done with a view to explore the variables to be used by merchant bankers in pricing the issues and to suggest a proper methodology in pricing the issues.

The methodology of pricing issues can be properly developed only after getting familiar with the objective of its introduction. The Control of capital Issues, which was introduced for the first time during second world war, tried to optimise the use of funds by channelising them in the most desirable sector from the economic growth point of view. The provisions of the Act were for regulating flows of fund not only within India but also outside India. Any company incorporated in India could not make issue of capital outside India without the consent of CCI. No guidelines were issued by the Controller of Capital Issues for calculation of premium on the shares. The CCI estimated the fair values of shares with the help of net asset values, price earning capitalisation value and market value of the share. All these variables are quantitative in nature therefore it was felt that CCI methodology was not fair enough to decide the premium on issues. Consequently, many corporate bodies having good track record of promoters and other qualitative factors could not avail the benefit of them because of purely mathematical methodology of pricing the issues by CCI.

The oversubscription of issues was a common phenomenon during the time of CCI. The disadvantages associated with oversubscription such as blocking of funds, manifold increase in the task of registrars and bankers to the issue, came to the notice of the participants of the market. It was realised that the objective of setting CCI has been defeated because of its illogical framework of pricing securities and finally free pricing of issue was announced as a part of liberalisation process in India during the year 1992-93. The basic objective of free pricing is to provide securities at a price which are optimum from the investor as well as issuer point of view. This price can be achieved only after determining the requirement of investors from equity investments. The task of determining the price has been laid down on merchant bankers in the free pricing era. The Securities and Exchange Board of India has laid down certain guidelines for disclosure and investor protection within the framework of which merchant bankers have to duly perform their role of pricing the securities. SEBI has divided the entire merchant banker community under four broad categories depending upon their networth position and accordingly assigned the duties to them.

The merchant bankers in India very rarely consider theoretical basis of equity valuation while fixing premium on issue. The models of equity valuation such as capital asset pricing model, present value method, Markowitz Model etc. have been developed on the assumption of perfect market conditions which do not hold good in Indian Capital market. But these should not be ignored completely by merchant bankers. The merchant banker should make use of these concepts while pricing an issue. The present value model is based upon dividend and stock price. According to this concept a stock's price rise if the projected dividend growth increases and the investors required rate of return from a stock decreases or some combination of a change in the dividend growth rate and investors required rate of return occurs. The simplest definition of investor's required rate of return is defined as the rate available from risk-free investments plus a risk premium necessary to compensate the investor for assuming the added risk of owning the stock. The risk free rate is usually defined as the AAA corporate bond interest rate. The size of the premium depends on the level of certainty associated with the projected future dividend stream. As the level of certainty declines, the risk premium increases. Present value models are used by those who believe that theoretical price for an individual stocks can be computed. In practice, the theoretical price is compared with the actual price to find out whether the stock is undervalued or overvalued. In contrast to present value model, the proponents of relative value model reject- the idea that a stock's theoretical price can be computed. Rather, they maintain that individual stock have value only relative to other stocks and this relative value is a function of the relationship between certain key company characteristics that are representative of the relative risk return relationship of a given stock. The Markowitz Model further enlightens about the expectations of investors. He proposed that investors do not maximise the returns in absolute terms but this return maxmisation is seen in the context of risk associated with the return. In other words an investor tries to maximise the return given a certain risk or minimise the risk given a certain return.

An important advancement was made by Sharpe (1963) who suggested that the return on any security can be considered to be related to the performance of some index of business activity. The Capital Asset Pricing Model (CAPM) tried to relate the returns of a particular security with the associated risk of security and return on market portfolio for the same period. The utility of these models become ineffective in the light of stringent assumptions on which these models have been based. But, these models can be used to fairly, assess the expectations of investors from equity investments. The interaction with various primary market intermediaries revealed that the premium subjectively estimated using broad quantitative factors such as issue size, promoter's stake, book value per share, earning per share and projected profitability of a company. The merchant bankers do not properly quantify the variables determining the premium. The merchant bankers are not duly performing their role as expected of them by SEBI in the free pricing era. The prices evaluated by the merchant bankers were found to be significantly different from fair prices of securities.

Keeping in view the inadequate pricing by merchant banker due to nonavailability of any specific techniques to derive an optimum price of issue, the study has been done and the statistical tools have been used to arrive at a suitable model that could be utilised to generate the optimum price of issues.

The results yielded by the model have been statistically tested for corrections and a positive result was obtained.

It is expected that the study would considerably help the merchant bankers in pricing the issues and would also overcome various problems associated with unfair pricing mechanism such as heavy over subscription of issues, origination of grey market, blocking up of large quantum of fund etc. Thus, it would help in the economic growth by smoothening the circulation of money and channelisation of adequate quantity of funds towards desired sectors.

2

Emergence of Free Pricing in India

The control of capital issues was introduced for the first time in India during the World War II. The main aim of CCI was to prevent the diversion of scare resources to activities that made little or no contribution to the prosecution of the war. The secondary purpose was to maintain the production of essential goods and services of mass consumption. The control over capital issues continued even after the war and the Capital Issues (Continuance of Control) Act was passed in April 1947.

Some of the main objectives of capital issues control are listed below.

(i) To channelise capital investment to priority sectors and thereby ensure resource availability to achieve the national development objectives.

(ii) To ensure that the enterprise develop a sound capital structure by avoiding over capitalisation or under-capitalisation, and maintain a proper debt equity ratio.

(iii) To avoid undue congestion of offers for public subscription during any part of the year.

MAIN PROVISIONS OF THE ACT

The Act provided that:-

(i) The consent of the Central Govt. is necessary to make an issue of capital outside India by any company incorporated in India.

(ii) Any company whether incorporated in India or not, requires the consent of the Central Govt.

  a) To make an issue of capital in India.

  b) To make in India any public offer of securities for sale.

  c) To renew or postpone the date of maturity or repayment of any security maturing for payment in India.

(iii) No person shall issue in India any prospectus or other document offering for subscription or publicly offering for sale any securities which does not include a statement that the consent or recognition of the Central Govt. has been obtained to the issue of offer of securities.

(iv) No person shall accept or give any consideration for any securities in respect of an issue of capital made or proposed to be made in India or elsewhere unless the consent or recognition of the Central Govt. has been accorded to such issue of capital, and

(v) No person shall sell or purchase or otherwise transfer or accept transfer of any securities issued by a company in respect of any issue of capital made in India unless such issue has been made with the consent of the Central Government.

RIGHTS ISSUE

In case of rights issues, the capital issues control act provided that a company issuing right shall send a circular to all the existing shareholders before applying for permission to the controller of capital issues. This circular shall contain information on how the additional funds will be used, and their effect on the earning capacity of the company. Thus, when a company offers a right issue, all the existing shareholders shall be given an opportunity to apply for additional shares. If the rights are not fully taken up, the balance shall be equitably distributed among the applicants for additional shares. Any balance still left over after making such allotment is required to be disposed of by the company in the market at the ruling price or the issue price.

ISSUE OF BONUS SHARES

The Companies Act and the Capital Issue Control Act allow the capitalisation of profits or free reserves of a company by the issue of bonus shares to shareholders. Bonus shares are allotted to share holders in proportion to their respective shareholding under the capital issues Control Act, all companies require the approval of the Union Government through the Controller of Capital issues for the issue of bonus shares.

C.C.I. method of estimating values of share and fixation of premium

No guidelines were issued by the Controller of Capital issues for calculation of premium on the shares. The CCI estimates the 'fair value' of share with the help of the following values.

a) NAV (Net Asset Value)
b) PECV (Price Earning Capitalisation Value)
c) MV (Market Value)

I. Calculation of NAV

The NAV defined as =

$$\frac{\text{Net Worth+ Fresh Capital Issue}}{\text{Number of shares including the fresh capital issue.}}$$

While calculating net worth figure, the following points must be taken into account, (i) Intangible asset are not considered. (ii) Depreciation is calculated as per a consistent basis. (iii) Contingent liabilities which are likely to unfair the net worth are duly considered. (iv) A reserve not created out of genuine profits or out of cash will not be considered. (v) Revaluation of fixed assets will ordinarily not be taken into account. (iv) Adequate provision is made for liabilities like arrears of preference dividends, unclaimed dividends, and bad debts.

*Calculation of Net Worth:

Net Asset Value (NAV)

Rs. Lakhs	Rs. Lakhs
Total Assets	Share holders funds—
Deduct all liabilities:	
1. Preference capital—	1. Equity capital
2. Secured and unsecured borrowings—	2. Free reserves
3. Current liabilities —	Total-
4. Contingent liabilities -	Deduct Contingent liabilities:

Net worth:

Add (1) Fresh capital issue (Face value)

Total Net worth / Number of shares, including fresh and bonus issues

= Net asset value (NAV) per share

Net asset value (NAV) according to the company's auditors.

II. Calculation of Profit Earning Capitalisation Value (PECV)

The PECV is defined as:

$$\text{PEVC} = \frac{\underset{\text{(After Tax)}}{\text{Average Profit}} + 1/2 \times \dfrac{\text{Fresh capital issue}}{\text{Existing net worth}} \times \text{Existing Profit After Tax}}{\text{Number of shares, including the fresh capital issue/capitalisation rate}}$$

Calculation of Average Profit after Tax

Profit Earning Capacity value (PECV)

Year	*Profit before tax*	*Profits after Tax*	*Dividend declared*
1			
2			
3			
4			
5	—	—	—

Average profits before tax (on the basis of simple or weighted average as the case may be)	:	______
Deduct	:	______
Provision for taxation at	:	______
Average profits after tax	:	______
Deduct: Preference dividend	:	______
Net Profit after tax	:	______
Add: Contribution to profits	:	______
by fresh issue, if any	:	______
Total profits after Tax	:	______
Number of equity shares, including	:	______
fresh and bonus issue	:	______
Earning per share (EPS)	:	______
Profit earning capacity value at 15%	:	______
Capitalisation rate (i.e. by multiplying EPS by 6.66)	:	______
PECV according to the company's auditors	:	______

While calculating average profit after tax, the following points must be taken into account.

(i) Provision for taxations should be made at the current statutory rate under the Income Tax Act.

(ii) The profits shown in the audited accounts are adjusted so as to exclude non recurring miscellaneous income of an abnormal nature and write back of provisions.

(iii) Normally, the average of profits is done for the latest three year but for Industrial subject to cyclical up and downs, it is advisable to consider the profits of latest five year.

The capitalisation rate is chosen as follows:

(1) 15 per cent in the case of manufacturing companies.
(2) 20 per cent in the case of trading companies.
(3) 17.50 per cent in the case of intermediate companies.

III. Calculation of 'Market Value' (MV)

The market value is calculated as the average of

(i) The high and low of the preceding two years, and

(ii) The high and low of each month in the preceding 12 months. While calculating it, appropriate adjustment are made to.' bonus issues and dividend payment.

Formulae for calculation of Market Value.

Average Market Price

	High	*Low*	*Remarks*
1 year	—	—	—
2 year			
3 Latest year			
4 Month -wise			

(i)

(ii)

(iii)

(for preceding 12 months)

Average market price on the above basis.

IV. Determination on Fair Value

First of all, determine average of NAV and PECV based on 15% capitalisation rate. If the average so obtained is less than market value by a margin of about 20%, it is regarded as the Fair Value (FV). If the average of the NAV and PECV is less than the MV by a margin of over 20 per cent, the PECV may be reworked by lowering the capitalisation rate. The capitalisation rate should not be taken be low 8%.

Case Study: Pricing of Premium Issues

"X CO. LTD."

Calculation of Premium

The following calculations were submitted by the company to CCI requesting a premium of Rs. 20 per share but CCI allowed a premium of Rs. 8 per share for the "X Co. Ltd." in 1990.

a) Break-up value of shares (on existing capital base)

	As on 30.9.1989	*For the year ended 31.3.1989*	*For the year ended 30.9.1987*
No. of shares	1300000	1200000	600000
Share Capital (Rs)	15000000*	12000000	6000000
Add: Reserves	52000000	39732658	317773504
Net Worth	67000000	51732658	37773504
Break-up value per share	Rs. 45	Rs. 43	Rs. 63
Average break-up value per share	Rs. 50		

* Share capital of Rs. 150 lacs as on 31.9.1989 includes Rs. 15 lacs for

share application money

After expanded capital base as on 31.3.1991

Share Capital	67000000
Share Premium	100000000
Reserve	100000000
	267000000

No. of shares 6700000

Break-up value per share Rs. 40 per share

b) Profit earning method

	For the year ended 31.3.1990 (12 months)	*For the year ended 31.3.1989 (18 months)*	*For the year ended 31.3.87 (12 months)*
Profit (after depreciation but before tax and after providing investment allowance reserve)	150.000	63.97	69.00
Add:			
i) Investment allowance reserve	—	34.88	—
ii) Interest and commitment charges on term loan	80.00	72.14	11.45
	230.00	170.99	80.45
LESS:			
i) Excess provision	—	—	0.81
ii) Profit on sale of investment	—	39.43	—

	230.00	131.56	79.64
Pre-tax profit for 12 months	230.00	87.71	79.64
Less: Tax	24.00	19.00	16.00
	206.00	68.71	63.64
Profit after tax			

Average profit 112.78

Capitalisation @ 12% 939.86

Value per shareRs. 28.00 per share

C. Premium $\frac{\text{Rs. } 28+50}{3}$ = Rs. 39 per share

Calculation of Premium

	31.3.1989	*31.3.1987*	*31.3.86*
Equity Reserve	258.66	188.87	128.91
Less: Liabilities			
Misc. Exp.	0.20	0.24	—
Debit balance of Profit & Loss A/c	—	—	—
Depreciation Net provided	—	—	—
Income tax liabilities			
Contingent liabilities	0.20	0.24	—
	258.46	188.63	128.91

Net Worth 172.31 (Ann.)

	31.3.1989	*31.3.1987*	*31.3.86*
A. Value of share (Net Worth)	28.72 (Ann)		
B. Valuation of share based on yield			
i) profit after tax	53.23	53.00	3.67
Average profit after tax	36.63		
ii) Average profit	6.105- value/no. of shares		
Value x 6.66	40.66		

Premium $\frac{A + B}{2} = \frac{28.72+40.66}{2} = 34.69$

Premium calculation

The following calculation has been made on the basis of audited balance sheet as at 30th November, 1989 and after considering four months results.

A. Net worth method of share valuation after expanded capital base as on 31.03.1991

Share Capital	33750000.00
Reserve & Surplus	35025657.00
	68775657.00

Divided by 3375000 equity shares = Rs. 20.38

* value capitalised @ 15% or 6.105 x 100/15 = 40.66

B. Valuation of shares based on yield (Rs. in lacs)

Profit before tax for the year 1989-1990 (101 lac for 8 months)		151.50
Annualised basis less tax		23.00
Profit after tax		127.50
Number of shares		3375000
Value per share	3.77	
Capitalised value 3.77 x 6.66	25.10	
Premium: 25.10 / 20.38 = 45.48/2	22.74	
Premium	12.74	

By capitalising at 15% return

$$\frac{127{,}50{,}000 \times 100}{15} = 8{,}50{,}00000$$

$$\text{Value per share } \frac{85000000}{3375000} = 25.18$$

Premium Calculation as per CCI

In the above case CCI had allowed premium at Rs. 8 per share and had calculated the premium as under:

Share Capital		135	
Reserve			
Resreve		299	
		434	
Less: Excise liability		1	
		433	
Divided by No. of shares		33.75	= 18.88 (A)
Average profit	85		
Less: Tax	20		
	65		
Add Profit by deploying additional funds	19		
	84		
Divided by No. of shares		33.75 = 2.49	
Capitalised @ 15%		2.49 x 6.66	17.00 (B)

$$\text{Average} \quad \frac{18.88 + 17}{2} = 18$$

Premium allowed Rs. 8 against 18 per share calculated by CCI.

DRAWBACKS OF CCI APPROACH

The CCI approach for calculating the prices of new issues has certain limitations associated with it due to which it was abolished and the companies are made to fix premium on their shares themselves subject to certain restriction. *The various drawbacks of CCI approach which led to it abolition are listed below:-*

1. Computation of Net Asset Value (NAV)

a) Adjustment for the Proposed Issue

The CCI method require that in computing the book

value or NAV, the effect of the proposed issued of capital should be taken into account by adding the face value of the fresh issue of capital to the net worth as at the latest balance sheet date and by dividing the resulting net worth by the enlarged capital base including the fresh issue. As long as the unadjusted book value is above face value, the effect of the adjustment prescribed by the CCI method will be to reduce the book value.

The very notion of adjusting book value to reflect the dilution caused by a fresh issue is based on a total misconception. If the fresh issue is to be made at a premium, the net worth after the issue should include the proposed premium in addition to the face value. There is no reason to exclude the proposed premium while adjusting the book value. It is readily seen that the post-issue book value is given by either of the following formulas in terms of the unadjusted book value.

$$\text{Unadj. BV} - \frac{\text{Fresh issue}}{\text{Enlarged Capital}} (\text{Unadj. BV} - \text{Issue Price})$$

$$\text{Issue Price} + \frac{\text{Old Capital}}{\text{Enlarged Capital}} (\text{Unadj. BV} - \text{Issue Price})$$

It is clear that if a new issue is made at below the old (unadjusted) book value, the post issue book value will be:

i) below the old book value, and
ii) above the issue price.

Such an issue will, therefore, leave the old shareholders with a book value below that of the value before the issue. It will also give the new shareholders a book value exceeding what they paid in. The CCI formula is, therefore, unfair to existing shareholders and more than fair to new shareholders.

The above formulas make it very clear that the book value should not be adjusted for "dilution" at all, this will ensure that the new book value including the new share premium will be equal to both the old book value as well as to the issue price.

(b) Revaluation of Assets

The CCI approach do not recognize revaluation of fixed assets unless this has taken place "long ago, say nearly 15 years ago". In the absence of revaluation, the balance sheet values of assets are far divorced from the current market price, especially when the assets including large blocks of land and building acquired decades ago. Any "fair" valuation should reflect altogether, fairness demands that all companies which come to CCI for valuation should be compelled to revalue all their assets especially land and buildings.

Similarly, it is well known that many large companies carry investments in their balance sheets at original cost which is a small fraction of their current market value. There is no reason why such investments should not be valued realistically for the purpose of share valuation. It is also common for many companies to carry at cost intercorporate investments in all loans to associate companies whose net worth has been fully eroded. In such cases, the investments/ loans should be written off or written down for purposes of valuation.

The CCI method also require that "any reserve which has not been created out of genuine profits or out of cash will be taken into account, e.g. amalgamation reserve". In India, amalgamation requires clearance by various agencies including the High Courts which examine the fairness of the terms of amalgamation. Since amalgamation reserve has arisen from a duly approved fair valuation process, there is no justification for ignoring it in a subsequent share valulation.

(c) Depreciation

The CCI approach recognizes straight line method (SLM) or written down value (WDV) method of depreciation provided

TABLE 2.1

A comparison of SLM and WDV method of depreciation

	SLM Method			*WDV Method*		
	Yr1	*Yr2*	*Yr3*	*Yr1*	*Yr2*	*Yr3*
Income summary						
Profit before Depreciation*	120	120	120	120	120	120
Depreciation	34	34	34	90	63	44
Net Profit	86	86	86	30	57	76
Balance Sheet Summary						
Gross fixed assets	300	300	300	300	300	300
Cumulative Dep.	34	68	102	90	153	197
Net fixed assets	266	232	198	210	147	103
Net current assets	300	300	300	300	300	300
Total	566	532	498	510	447	403
Share capital	200	200	200	200	200	200
Retained profit	86	172	258	30	87	163
Net worth	286	372	458	230	287	363
Borrowings	280	160	40	280	160	40
Total	566	532	498	510	447	403
NAV per share (Rs. 100/-per share)	143	186	229	115	144	182

* Depreciation calculated at 11.31% SLM and 30% WDV as per schedule XIV of the Companies Act, 1956.

the company has consistently followed that method. For any fair valuation, it is more appropriate to use SLM depreciation on replacement cost as this is most likely to reflect the true economic value of the assets. Failure to insist on the uniform depreciation policy can lead to an anomalous situation where a company which follows WDV depreciation is valued lower than a comparable company which follows SLM depreciation. This is illustrated by a simple example (TABLE 2.1).

The CCI approach disallows any changeover from WDV to SLM unless the changeover had taken place before five years. In other words, where there has been a change in the depreciation policy from WDV to SLM within the last five years, the guidelines seek the rework the depreciation on WDV basis and ignore the SLM depreciation provided in the books. For this purpose, companies are required to furnish the depreciation claims for income tax purposes to enable the CCI to determine the WDV depreciation. Under the Companies Amendment Act, 1988, the rates of SLM and WDV depreciation to be provided in the books have been specified in Schedule XIV; these rates are now totally delinked from the income tax rates. As such, recomputing depreciation on the basis of income tax claims in anomalous.

2. Profit Earning Capacity Value (PECV)

a) Capitalization Rate

As per the CCI method, "The Profit earning capacity value (PECV)" will be calculated by capitalizing the average of the after tax profits at the following rates:-

i) 15% in the case of manufacturing companies;

ii) 20% in the case of trading companies, and

iii) 17.5% in the case of 'intermediate' companies that is to say, companies whose turnover from trading activities is more than 40%, but less than 60% of their total turnover."

The CCI's method of determining the capitalization rate is peculiar. Finance theory suggests that principally the capitalization rate is a function principally of the degree of risk of the profit stream, i.e. the more risky business should be capitalized at a higher rate. On the other hand, the factor to which the CCI attaches greatest importance is whether the company is in trading or manufacturing. The implicit suggestion that trading companies are more risky than manufacturing companies is devoid of theoretical or empirical support. Very often, an established trading company carries for less risk than a relatively new manufacturing company Again, the CCI's demarcation of intermediate companies in terms of percentage of sales from trading activity is also unsound: percentage of profits is obviously the more relevant criteria.

Finance theory asserts that companies with substantial leverage (high [debt/equity] ratio) should be capitalized at higher rates reflecting higher degree of risk. The CCI's formula does not explicitly consider leverage at all in determining the capitalization rate.

It is also not at all clear how finance, leasing and investment companies will be fitted into the valuation scheme. The distinction between finance and non finance companies is more important than the putative distinction made by the CCI between trading and manufacturing.

Moreover, within manufacturing or trading, different lines of business have totally different risk profiles, the CCI uses omnibus rates of capitalization, ignoring these variations completely

The guidelines provide for relaxation of the normal capitalization rate only for a manufacturing company under the following circumstances:

i) When the market price of its share is substantially

above the average of NAV and PEVC at 15% capitalization.

ii) Where a company has a "high profitability rate as revealed by the percentage of after tax profits to the equity capital of the company".

iii) Where the company has diversified its activities and is a multi-unit company as a result of which it would be in a position to sustain its overall profits even if any one part of its operations runs into difficulties".

The CCI's proposal to measure the profitability in terms of return on equity capital instead of the widely used return on net worth is erroneous. Furthermore, since, for a profitable company high leverage has the effect of magnifying the profitability rate, the CCI formula would end up granting a lower capitalization rate to highly levered companies. In fact, a higher capitalization rate is appropriate for such companies consistent with their higher risk pronness.

The assumption in the CCI method that diversified and multi-unit companies have greater capacity to sustain overall profits is not borne out by empirical work. It is fairly well established that companies which stick to their knitting or undertake only related diversification have shown greater consistency in long term performance. Moreover, finance theory tells us that if the relevant measure of risk is systematic (non diversifiable) risk, then diversification should not make a difference, as shareholders themselves have the freedom to diversify their respective portfolios.

b) Computation of Average Profits

The CCI method state that "The use of estimating the profit earning capacity value lies in the assessment of the future maintainable earnings of the business. While the past trends in profits and profitability would serve as a guide, it should not be overlooked that valuation is for the future and that it is the future maintainable stream of earnings that is of great significance in the process of valuation. All relevant factors that have a bearing on the future maintainable earnings of the business must, therefore, be given due consideration. However, the computational methodology propounded in the guidelines bears no relation to these lofty ideals. Infact, the entire concept of the future maintainable earnings would appear to be only an obiterdictum. The operative part of the guidelines largely confines itself to the average of the last three to five years profits as per audited accounts. There is an implied assumption that the recent past will replicate itself into perpetuity

The CCI approach propose greater weightage for the most recent year's performance when past profits show a steadily increasing or decreasing trend. Where it has been determined that profits shows a steady trend, one would have expected the future maintainable profits to be estimated by extrapolating the trend.

The CCI approach assert that "'if a business has sustained looses in all the three years or even in the latest two years, the PECV will have to be regarded as nil because it would not then be realistic to assume that the business would earn profits in the near future". This assertion is outrageous. Indeed, if it were true that the business would earn no profits in the near future, there is no justification for allowing it to raise scarce capital, and perhaps, there is every justification for winding up the company under the just and equitable clause (section 433 (i) (f) of the Companies Act, 1956). Unlike the CCI. the stock market values a company realistically on the basis of its future prospects despite past losses.

(c) Taxation

In computing the average profit provision for the taxation, with some exceptions, is to be "assumed at the current statutory rate under the income tax". This assumption ignores the actual tax position of a given company which may be considerably lower for the foreseeable future due to unabsorbed capital allowances or losses or various reliefs and concessions. 'in the case of export oriented units and investment/leasing companies, the tax benefit could be indeed significant, and to ignore them would be grossly unfair.

3. Other Adjustments

While, in computing the NAV, adjustments are required to be made in respect of depreciation changes and gratuity and other liabilities not provided for in the books, no such adjustment are prescribed for computing the average profits. In addition to these adjustments, it is also necessary to restate, at least for this purpose, the profit and loss account by incorporating various items charged directly to reserves by creative accountants.

The CCI method propose to estimate the profitability of fresh issue of capital as follows:

i) "Where the fresh issue of capital is for the purpose of financing expansion or new projects, it could be assumed that the fresh capital would contribute to the profits up to a maximum of 50% of the existing rate of profitability. This will be added to the existing profits after tax and the total will be divided by the enlarged capital base to arrive at the future maintainable earnings per share."

ii) "Where the fresh capital is sought to be raised for general reasons like modernization and replacement of assets, it would not be advisable to assume that the fresh capital will contribute to the profitability of the business in any tangible manner in the near future. In such cases, while the fresh issue of capital will be taken into account, no additional profits will be assumed."

In the case of expansion or new projects, the CCI ties the return expected from the fresh capital to the existing profit rate. It would have been more correct to estimate that the fresh capital would earn the benchmark rate of return, i.e. 15 per cent. In normal conditions, the factor of half is a grossly conservative and unfair assumption. On the other hand, a company which has just wiped out its accumulated losses can have an astronomical profitability rate simply because its net worth base is extremely small. It would be quite incorrect to assume that the fresh capital can earn half of this rate of return. Similarly, as a recent experience shows a small company with an excellent profitability record, raising large amounts of capital for mega projects totally out of preparation to its current scale of operations would be granted an absurdly high premium on the basis of its past record. Infact, the mega project may not only be much less profitable than the existing business, but it may also drastically increase the riskiness of the company.

Again, the proposal in the CCI approach to ignore future profitability of new issues made for financing modernization is contrary to the well known fact that returns from such project are more assured and less risky than returns from new projects. It may also be noted that if a new issue is made even without any specific project in mind, it is necessary to give effect to the saving in interest cost arising from the supplanted borrowings.

4. Market Price

The CCI approach state that the average market price (based on high-low of the previous three years) "will be kept in the background as a relevant factor while settling the Fair Value (FV) unless there are reasons to believe that the market price is vitiated by speculative transactions and manipulative practices". One may be pardoned for suggesting that, in the absence of the "vitiations" referred to by the CCI, the market price should be kept in the foreground, and that the figures obtained by various accounting calculation should be relegated to the background. In any event, it is a moot point as to how the CCI would be able to establish the incidence of "vitiation". The guidelines are somewhat naive in suggesting that a high market price vis-a-vis the FV computed in the normal course is an indication inter-alia of "good reputation for the quality and integrity of (the company's) management". Given the current regulatory failure in the area of insider trading, high market price could, if anything, be a reflection of lack of integrity.

The CCI method seek to revise the FV by recomputing the PECV at a lower capitalization rate whenever the original FV is significantly below the average market price. The method of carrying out this adjustment in the fair value is inappropriate. If the market price exceeds the fair value by more than 20 per cent, CCI approach reduce the capitalization rate to 12 per cent from 15%, there by increasing the capitalized value (PECV) by 25 per cent. This could lead to a situation where the new FV exceed both the original FV and the average market value as shown in the example (Table 2.2).

TABLE 2.2

	Original (15% capitalization)	*Revised (12% capitalization)*
NAV	24	24
PECV	176	220
FV (Average of NAV)		

ABOLITION OF CCI

According to the Dr. Manmohan Singh the practice of government control over Capital issues as well as pricing of issues has lost its relevance in the changed circumstances of today and he therefore proposed to do away with the government's control over the capital issues including fixation of premium. His intention to abolish the capital issue control act was announced in his budget speech of Feb 29, 1992. The office of CCI was abolished in May, 1992, the companies were allowed to approach the market directly provided the issues are in conformity with published guidelines relating to disclosures and other matters related to investor protection.

A critical analysis of the performance of the CCI reveals that the office never had any expertise to determine what should be the appropriate amount of capital needed for the project. The market forces were set in motion by the New Industrial policy 1991. Market demand should determine where the investment is to be channelised and priorities will not be decided by the pundits of Yojana Bhawan, or of Udyog Bhawan or of North Block. In the light of new policy parameters, it was obvious that size of the capital should not be left to be determined by a government agency.

The CCI could not decide appropriate capital structure which would be in the best interest of the issuing company as it did not have any expertise to determine which security i.e. whether equity, preference, CCP, debentures would serve the best interest of the company issuing them. Thus not only its office had no expertise to determine the size of the issue but they could also not decide which is the best security. The issue price calculated the book value of the share, EPS, average dividend declared and market quotation. These had to be determined by the CCI office which was regarded as the custodian of investors interest. In fact for quite sometime CCI office was guided by the twin criteria of book value of the share and comparison of the average dividend were reasonable expectations. It was assumed that 12% dividend declared is a normal return on investment and was considered to be reasonable. Thus, the company declaring 18% dividend will be allowed to charge premium of Rs. 5 on the equity share of Rs. 10 each provided book value consideration did not require lower price fixation. Afterwards, the market quotation was introduced when it was discovered that even before the security was listed unofficial quotations were obtained from Jaipur, Rajkot and other dons of speculation and brokers made these quotations known to the investors by means of private and confidential news letters. This generated a lot of artificially created speculation in the primary market. The company could not reap the benefit of the demand as the price was fixed already. The CCI, therefore, started basing his pricing decision on average market pricing in addition to the aforesaid twin criteria.

If the issuer is left with the freedom to fix the price for a security he will be able to get the benefit of the reputation built by him. Investor confidence is built by consistent performance and honesty of the promoters in their dealings. Share premium account is a capital account. If the company gets a handsome premium it would be able to raise its funds more economically

CCI used to be criticised on account of underpricing of the issues i.e. fixing share premium at low level. Such criticism had the support. For example, take the cases of Mideast India, the second highest ever subscribed issue amongst premium issues in 1991 -92 which was allowed a premium of Rs.20 for a Rs.10 whereas the share was quoted at Rs.280 having been listed at Bombay & Delhi stock exchanges. Similar were the cases of Tata Timken, Mangalore refineries and Petrochemicals. There have been likewise many issues which were opened on premia and were over subscribed 50 to 70 times as the investors had viewed them as underpriced. There is long list of such issues but most celebrated of these were Kotak Mahindra Finance, Ahmednagar Forgings, Altas India, etc. Contrary to above, there had been many cases where CCI had allowed higher premia on issues than the market could support. For example, the mega issues of Usha rectifier and Bindal Agro were allowed premia by CCI for convertible debentures which put to a loss to investors as the market quoted lower prices than the prices at which conversion was done by the companies.

With the abolition of CCI, the companies are free to fix up the premium on their issues by themselves and with the help of the merchant bankers. Merchant Banker is the most critical link between a company raising funds and the investors. His reputation goes a long way in the making or breaking of a public issue. He is also the only player who can pass on the buck without any qualms and today he rides the high horse in the capital market. In today's free pricing environment his role is more important than even before. Nearly 600 merchant bankers, half of whom are authorised by the SEBI, have raised Rs. 18600 crore last year and in the next few months 200 of these bankers based in Bombay will raise over Rs. 10,000 crore. They play with high stakes and it is time to applaud their contribution to the Indian economy.

Merchant banking in India can be categorised in four broad sections:-

1) To provide long-term source of funds required by industries/trade/commerce, for investment. The merchant banker primarily came into being as corporate counsellors for restructuring base of capital, thereafter for issue management and underwriting of the same.
2) Project counselling which includes credit syndication and the working capital.
3) Capital structuring.
4) Portfolio management.

The year 1985 was an epoch making year in the history of merchant banking when a large number of issues were over-subscribed by several times and the importance of merchant banking activities was made evident in managing issues and their underwriting. Finance has presently gone 'hi-tech'. The deregulation and liberalisation of the industry in India has been accompanied by changes in the financial sector. With the passage of time merchant banking activities have changed in performance in line with the changing need-pattern of the enterprises and the economic environment.

Since August, 1990, merchant bankers engaged in issue-management, corporate advisory service, underwriting and portfolio management have to secure authorisation from the SEBI after meeting the requirements related to capital adequacy and other formalities. A code of conduct has also been formulated by the SEBI for merchant bankers. Further, the Association of Merchant Bankers of India (AMBI) has three SEBI representatives to oversee the functioning of the AMBI and the industry in particular.

Merchant Bankers are accountable for activities connected with an issue right up to the allotment of shares. They have to certify the statements in the prospectus to the SEBI. Penalty points are awarded to MBs who do not comply with the stipulated conditions.

Merchant Bankers now have an important role to play in capital and debt structuring too. Due to the proposed reduction in debt/equity ratio from 2: 1 to 1.5: 1, merchant bankers have been identified as the prime intermediaries between the capital market and the investors. The opening up of the FERA rules has seen the financial service also going global. Indians are now moving out into foreign markets. The Dunkel proposals gives an indication that merchant banking is transcending the national boundaries.

The merchant banker today also has to take care of his future strategies and management of duties and functions in the dynamic market conditions.

The mood of the merchant banker is in tandem with that of the investor and national index. Thus, he is wary of financial scandals (or scams as they are called) because it dampens the spirit of both the investors as well as the underwriters.

Liberalisation has been the main cause for the jump in the number of companies going public. It also paved the way for the abolition of the office the Controller of Capital Issue (CCI).

In the changing environment of specialized functions, the future is likely to see the merchant bankers focus on the marketing of issues on inherent strengths. Experts concede that private merchant bankers will do better than the public sector merchant bankers. But whatever the outcome of the debate, one has to understand that the premium on a script is dependent upon factors like the financial strength of the company brand equity of products, technological strengths, price quoted in the market, etc. The risk faced by the investors has to be studied and appropriate safety-nets assured. But the laws have prevented merchant bankers from providing excessive safety-nets because that might give a wrong impression to the small investor.

The Reserve Bank of India (RBI) has allowed the merchant banking subsidiaries of banks to resume issue management functions of other leasing and hire purchase finance companies. Merchant banking, a major intermediary activity in the capital market, has been statutarily brought within the regulatory framework of the Securities and Exchange Board of India (SEBI) under new regulations SEBI (Merchant Bankers) Regulations, 1992 announced by the Government on 22nd December, 1992.

The new regulations are expected to result in greater transparency in the operations of merchant bankers and make them more accountable. The regulations stipulate that no person can act as a merchant banker without obtaining a certificate of registration from SEBI which will be granted subject to the merchant banker abiding by the regulations.

The comprehensive regulations provide for the registration of four categories of merchant bankers. Under the first category, bankers can act as an issue manager, adviser, consultant and in the fourth category he can act only as an adviser or consultant to an issue.

The merchant bankers are required to fulfil the capital

adequacy requirements which are Rs. 1 crore, Rs. 50 lakhs, Rs. 20 lakhs for the first three categories of merchant bankers, respectively. As category four, merchant bankers are authorised to act as consultants or advisers to an issue, no capital adequacy requirement has been prescribed.

To ensure transparency and accountability SEBI has advised merchant bankers to enter into agreements with corporate body setting out their mutual rights, liabilities and obligations relating to an issue particularly on disclosures, allotment and refund, maintenance of books of accounts, and submission of half. yearly report to SEBI.

The regulations stipulate that all issues should be managed by at least one merchant banker functioning as a lead manager. The lead merchant banker is responsible for verification of the contents of a prospectus or the letter of offer in respect of an issue and is required to submit to SEBI a due diligence certificate conforming that the disclosures made in the draft prospectus are true, fair and adequate to enable the investor to make a well informed decision,

The regulations provide for a procedure for inspection of merchant bankers by SEBI. Under these regulations, SEBI will be empowered to suspend a registration of merchant banker in case he furnishes wrong or false information, fails to resolve the complaints of investors, indulges in price rigging or fails to maintain capital adequacy requirement. Merchant bankers are supposed to evaluate and appraise a company's proposal for the issue of shares. Having satisfied about the financial and economical soundness of the proposal, the merchant bankers are expected to price the rights and further issues.

The merchant bankers differ over their responsibility of over pricing of issues. Some are of the view that it is more due to greed than the incapacity of the merchant bankers to price the issue reasonably They point out to the fact that companies are moving to merchant bankers to find someone who can offer higher premium on their shares. They admit that "the rush of companies in entering the capital market and raising capital at high premia had killed the golden goose".

Of course, share premium is a low cost fund for the company and it can collect huge amount through over pricing of issue but, things are not supposed to continue for long. Since the underwriters, appraisers and even investors are capable of differentiating between frauds and genuine merchant bankers. Hence, merchant bankers have to exercise their full diligence, prudence, expertise and experience while pricing an issue so that their credibility and reputation can be built up and maintained in the capital market. They should spare themselves from offering higher premiums, simply to get business. Instead, their decisions should be based on financial and technical analysis of the company as well as industry, and general environment of the company This will lead to reasonable and fair pricing of issues which will generate investors confidence in a particular merchant banker.

On the other hand problems of the merchant bankers are also worth considering. It is important to point out that the procedure involved in the issue of shares is very lengthy Only after three months of the ratification of the company's decision of premium by the share holders at the annual general meeting, or extra-ordinary general meeting, a rights issue can be opened. Similarly, in the case of public issues, the duration is two months. It is very difficult to forecast the movements of share prices at India's imperfect stock market, three months in advance.

The SEBI guidelines stipulate that in appropriate cases, companies will be allowed to raise fresh capital by freely pricing their capital issues. The guidelines also state that such issue price will be determined by the issuer in consultation with the lead managers to the issue.

The free pricing of the capital issues has placed the responsibility upon the issuer company for fixing premia on the issues which is to be decided by its shareholders and in consultation with the concerned lead manager. Companies are keen on higher premia to get more capital at cheap rates reducing over all cost of capital but SEBI guidelines require the issues company to provide justification for the price in the offer documents. There is complete freedom, now for the companies to raise funds to meet their various types of business requirements, not limited to financing of the project cost or meeting overruns or working capital requirements. The companies are raising funds for other purposes like repayment of high debt borrowings or to meet normal capital expenditure. There is no restriction on companies for raising funds for meeting their different requirements provided adequate information to safeguard the interests is made available in offer documents.

According to SEBI guidelines on free pricing of capital issues only the following categories of the companies have been permitted to price their issues freely viz:-

(A) First Issues of New Companies

There could be two options for such issues.

Option One

A new company i.e. a company without a track record of profitability set up either by a first generation entrepreneur or a established promoter with a track record, may be allowed to freely price its first issue and list the securities on main stock exchange.

In this case there is no historic yard stick i.e. a track record of profitability for the market as well as the investor on which the investment decision could be based. Evaluation of investment may thus become difficult às the judgement has to be based only on the future perception. The feasibility of free market pricing for such issues needs to be examined in this light.

It may be noted that in countries where free pricing mechanism is allowed, only companies with a consistent track record of profitability of 3 to 5 years are allowed to be listed on the stock exchanges.

Some of the issues in this catergory, depending on the size of the issues, could however opt for the OTC exchange where they can have the advantage of a lower requirement for minimum issue capital and minimum public offer compared to the other stock exchanges, the sponsor determining the price of shares offered to public members and dealers of OTC, compulsory market making by sponsor and another member dealer for one year, and an undertaking by the sponsor to offer and allot the securities to public in a fair manner. The above mechanism also takes care of the interests of the issuers, sponsors as well as the investors,

Option Two

Allows option two these companies to go to the market with public issue at par. This is the prevailing procedure. The advantage here is the investor is not asked to take an additional amount of risk than what is inherent to any investment decision.

Hence he may feel more comfortable with a par issue of such companies. The feasibility of continuing the practice of issues at par for such companies, needs to be examined in the light of the difficulties faced by the investor for evaluating an issue mentioned in the first option.

(B) First Issue by Existing Private Companies Going Public

There could be a number of existing private companies with a track record of profitability. For these companies, there could be three options.

Option One

Allow these companies to freely price their first issues and list the securities on the main stock exchanges. The merit for this option is that the market as well as the investors have a track record for these companies to base the investment decision. The evaluation process is not based entirely on future perception of the performance of the companies. The disclosure and investor protection angles in relation to free pricing of such issues would need to be considered and these are by and large identical to those discussed for companies in category C given below. The feasibility of allowing such companies to freely price their issues would have to be examined in the light of the above considerations. One other question that needs to be examined is whether there should be some condition about the minimum track record of consistent profitability as is the prevailing practice in international markets.

Option Two

These companies be allowed to go to the market only at par. This would not be any different from the existing practice for new companies. But restricting such companies to go to the market only at par, would imply depriving the deserving issuers from taking advantage of the market particularly when they have a sound track record.

Option Three

For this type of issues the OTC Exchange may also provide an option and the issuers may make a public issue on this exchange depending on the size of the issues. The OTC Exchange can provide these issuers with listing conditions different from those of the other exchanges which would include a lower requirement for minimum issue capital and minimum public offer compared to the other stock exchanges, sponsor determining the price of shares offered to public members and dealers of OTC, compulsory market making by sponsor and another member dealer for one year, and an undertaking by the sponsor to offer and allot the securities to public in a fair manner. The disclosure and investor protection angles would be taken care by the OTC Exchange.

C. Public Issue by Existing Listed Companies

These companies could be allowed to raise fresh capital by freely pricing their issues subject to their conforming to certain guidelines. These guidelines would not be for getting prior clearance or approval but only for the disclosure and investors protection. The determination of the price should be left to the lead managers and principal underwriters in consultation with the issuers themselves. But this would call for a far greater degree of responsibility, high standards of diligence and competence of the merchant bankers and underwriters, for they would not only have to be competitive amongst themselves but also to take into account the interests of the issuers as well as the investors.

Certain boundary conditions by way of guidelines for ensuring adequate investor protection that could be considered are:

a) While market pricing will be completely free, full underwriting should be mandatory
b) There could be a minimum of three principal underwriters for every issue.
c) Disclosures of the net worth limits of each of the underwriters as well as their upto date exposure would have to be made.
d) While these principal underwriters would have to take up the development liability they could distribute their risk by sub-underwriting their underwriting quota.
e) There could be usual contractual arrangements between the issuers and the principal underwriters and between the principal underwriters and sub-underwriters to be filed with SEBI.

f) Failure to meet the underwriting liability or sub-underwriting liability would attract penal provisions under the regulations for underwriters by the regulatory body while the contractual obligations for financial liability could be settled in the courts.

g) The principal underwriters may provide a safety net for investors for a certain period of the time say upto 6 months after the closure of the issue when they should be prepared to buy back from the original investors upto the limit of their underwriting in case the market price falls below say 20% to 40% of the issue price depending upon the extent of the premium. This would help distribute the risk associated with the market pricing between the underwriting lead manager and the original investor. This could be a transitional arrangement before the market gets familiar with free market pricing of issues and would also confer greater care and discipline among lead managers in pricing their issues. This is particularly relevant for an inefficient market where possibilities of price rigging and market manipulation prior to the issue cannot be ruled out.

The safety net arrangement was used in the privatisation issues in U.K.

h) Besides the principal underwriters and the sub-underwriters, there could be a set of secondary underwriters in the case of very large issues and their contracts would be directly with the issuers and not via, the principal underwriters.

i) Issue of FERA companies could also come under this arrangement.

D. Right Issues and Composite Issues

a) If there is a Rights Issue without a public issue coming within a period of three months following a rights issue, the price for the issue would be determined as now through AGM by the shareholders. If public issues comes within 3 months it will be treated as a composite issue.

b) If there is a composite issue, there is a case for allowing the existing shareholder the benefit for having stayed with the company and giving him shares at a price lower than the price for the public issue.

c) The public issue could- be at a market price as in the case above.

The aforesaid paragraphs deal primarily with the considerations involved in equity issues. In the case of issues of debentures there are certain additional consideration. These are discussed below:

E. Conditions for Fully Convertible Debentures

Some of the considerations for free market pricing of FCD issues could be as follows:

i) Compulsory credit rating would be necessary if conversion is to begin before six months.

ii) Premium amount on conversion at various stages to be determined at the outset and stated in the prospectus.

iii) Redemption amount to be indicated at the time of the issue in the prospectus.

iv) The names of the debentures trustees would have to be mentioned in the prospectus and the trust deed would have to be executed within six months of the closure of the issue.

v) There should be no cap or collar on interest rate.

E. Conditions for Partially Convertible Debentures

Some of the considerations for free market pricing of PCD issues could be as follows:

i) Compulsory credit rating of the debenture would be necessary.
ii) Premium amount and the terms of conversion should be stated at the outset in the prospectus.
iii) Redemption amount and period to be indicated at the time of the issue in the prospectus.
iv) The names of the debentures trustees would have to be mentioned in the prospectus and the trust deed would have to be executed within six months of the closure of the issue.
v) There should be no cap or collar on interest rate.
vi) The discount on 'Khokas' or the non convertible portion of the PCD in case they are traded and the procedure for their purchase on spot basis must be disclosed on the prospectus.

G. Conditions for Non-Convertible Debentures

Some of the considerations for free market pricing of NCD issues could be as follows:

i) Issues should be credit rated
ii) The interest rate should be free.
iii) Redemption amount to be indicated at the time of the issue in the prospectus.
iv) The names of the debentures trustees would have to be mentioned in the prospectus and the trust deed would have to be executed within six months of the closure of the issue.

Other Guidelines

Besides the considerations mentioned in the paragraphs above, in the interest of investor protection the guidelines for allowing free market pricing could also include:

1) The promoters' contribution to the capital to be brought in at the same market price as other investors.
2) Preference capital shall not exceed one third of equity
3) Filing of letter of offer/prospectus, for ensuring compliance with the guidelines.
4) It should also be ensured that there is no default in servicing of debentures already issued and debenture certificates for previous issues have already been despatched.
5) All intermediaries including debentures trustees appointed for the issue must hold an authorisation *on that behalf by SEBI.*
6) Merchant bankers to enure fair and timely allotment of issues within the limits prescribed in the Companies Act.
7) Equity capital subscribed privately by the promoters, directors and their friends should not be less than fifteen per cent of the total issued equity capital, if it does not exceed Rs. 1 crore, 12.5 per cent if it does not exceed Rs. 2 crores and 10% if it is in excess of Rs. 2 crores in case of first issues by new companies.
8) Promoters' to make their subscription in advance before public issues.
9) Promoters' shares to have a minimum lock in period of three years.
10) Employees' quota not to exceed 200 shares per individual and unallotted shares to be allotted on equitable basis to the remaining employees who have applied.
11) Subscription list to be kept open for at least two working days and disclosed in the prospectus.
12) Rights issues not be kept open for more than 60 days.

13) The gap between the closure dates of various issues should not exceed 40 days.

14) In case the minimum subscription of 90% of the issued amount is not received, the entire subscription will be refunded to the applicants within 90 days from the date of closure of the issue. A delay in refunds by more than 10 days will attract penal interest at 15% for the delayed period and this has to be disclosed in prospectus and all publicity material associated with the issue.

15 Within 15 days of the closure of the issue a report in a format to be prescribed together with a compliance certificate by a Chartered Accountant should be forwarded to SEBI by the lead managers.

16) SEBI should have the right to issue further guidelines for compliance by companies.

IMPLICATIONS OF THE SEBI GUIDELINES

1(a). 50% participation in equity by promoting companies in the case of first issue by a new company will have grave implications on the issuer's cost of funds as the servicing cost of part of the capital will be magnified to the extent of the premium which effectively would ensure the shares will often not get the premium they deserve. However, this will have a positive impact on the investors since price rigging will act against the interest of the issuer. At this preliminary stage of the evolution of capital markets such a step, taken by SEBI is understandable.

(b) Similarly, a contribution of a minimum of 25% of the total issue of equity upto Rs. 100 crores and 20% of issues above Rs.100 crores for existing listing companies are basically investor protection measures.

(c) For PCDs and FCDs one third of the total convertible part has to be subscribed by the promoter. This would effectively, make at least, FCDs a less palatable instrument than equity, because of excess cost of funds implications, to the issuer. In fact, the expectation is, FCD issues will dwindle in the coming years.

(d) In all the above cases, the lock in period of 5 years of promoter's contribution would further ensure investor protection.

2. The virtual ban on private placement of promoter's quota of a new company and minimum contribution of Rs. 1 lakh by director's friends and relatives for shares of exiting companies might well prove the death knell of the private placement market of the promoter quota. Like in the west, private placement will now have to be made to big institutional players or brokers who are more apt at valuing a share and are less likely to be taken for a ride.

3. SEBI has asked for justification of the issue price. However, it is often impossible to quantify such subjective factors like quality of management etc. Further, in the case of first issue of a new company, with no existing track record, the process of issue price determination is bound to be more subjective than objective, because of the numerous imponderation that an issuing investment bankers has to look at. In fact, the method generally applied world wide is the tender method in such cases, to overcome these uncertainties. But new guideline implies that issue prices will have to be fixed well in advance of such determining the issuer to know the possible investor's response to the issue. The rigidity imposed by any mechanistic formula in determining the issue price objectively might well act against the interests of the both the issuer`and the investor in the long run. To add to this, there can be a million different ways of pricing an issue each yielding a different result and comparing such varying pricing mechanism objectively is impossible.

4. The compulsory commitment which an issuer has to get from an underwriter would imply that the lead manager/underwriter will have added responsibility to price the issue and make adequate disclosures objectively and fully to ensure full subscription. This will also mean a compulsory underwriting fee, to be paid by the issuer which would proportionately inflate the cost of funds to the issuer in the form of higher floatation costs.

5. The specification, in case of issue size exceeding Rs.250 crore, to call up only a maximum of 25% of the total quantum of issue in each call at a predetermined in the actual performance of the company from those of the projected figures between the calls, will not be reflected in issue price. Further more, by making the issuer get only 25% of issue per call. the SEBI is making a simplistic assumption that high capital cost project, will necessarily require funds at regular intervals of time, which is quite debatable.

6. Since, the issuer/underwriter has no option to retain the over subscribed portion to a certain maximum limit (15% call the greenshoe option in U.S.A.) as it was the case earlier any cost 'overruns' cannot be funded through a single issue. Furthermore, the lead manager/underwriter will in no way, be able to support the 'aftermarket' with oversubscribed portion to ensure against lack of liquidity in the scrip etc. especially in the case of a newly established company with no track record.

7. Although the guidelines do not allow any bonus issues to be made within 12 months of a fresh issue of capital; the period of 12 months can be covered both by the period prior to the issue and the period after it. Hence, the issuer may issue a bonus few months within a public rights issue, rig the prices of its shares upwards and hence the issue price, and get away with it.

8. The holding period yield on a common equity is defined as:-

$$\frac{(P_1 - P_0) + D_1}{P_0}$$

Where

P_1 = Price of the share at the end of the holding period.
P_0 = Share price at the time of issue.
D_1 = Dividend stream during the holding period.

Here $\frac{P_1 - P_0}{P_0}$ is the capital gain component.

and $\frac{D_1}{P_0}$ is the dividend yield component

Till recently, in the Indian New Issue market, as well as in secondary market, the capital gain component used to be principal forms of returns to the investor and hence the appeal for common stock. However, in the event of premiums being determined by the market forces and future expectations, the capital gain component will dwindle and dividend, hitherto inconsequential in share price behaviour, will play a more significant role. The issuer, to ensure full subscription, will thus have to balance the capital gain factor with future dividend to lend support to the aftermarket performance of the public/ rights issue. Theoretically speaking, the price of an issue after some holding period should be:-

$$P_1 = \frac{P_0[1+\{(P_1 - P_0) + D_1/P_0]^{tH}}{(1+K)^{tH}}$$

Where, 'k' is the minimum required rate of return on the stock and tH the holding time period. Hence, the excess returns in real terms to the investor will eliminate from the excess holding period yield over the minimum rate of return. So, the issue price can be a maximum of the expected aftermarket price as discounted by the minimum required rate of return. Thus logically, an investor's response to a new issue will be dependant on the excess return on the fresh issue of capital.

The investor base in India consists of a considerable number of small players in the new issue market who used to be attracted to it primarily due to its high rate of return. When this return will dwindle, so will the interest of the common folk in the primary market. As in the West, the "mutual funds and other institutions will gradually have to play a more dominant role in financing common stock equity, especially of new companies. These investors being sophisticated, would buy an issue, based primarily on its fundamentals and hence create a market place which will react to risk-return characteristics of any issue positively Pricing, thus in the long run, would depend on both the fundamentals as well as the supply-demand functions of an issue.

By and by as return on common stock will lessen, thanks to free premium fixation, the debt market will grow in significance as return on it, match its risks. One, of the primary irritants of debt instruments to the common investor is the lock of liquidity in these instruments—one of the reasons being, that, returns on debt instrument is simply not comparable to that of common stock when the return on the latter dwindles, the debt market will emerge to take their rightful place in both the primary and secondary capital market.

9(a). Hitherto, companies issuing bonus shares were required to ensure that the total amount to be capitalized for bonus shares, should not exceed total amount of paid-up equity capital of the company except in the case of closely held non-FERA companies which have been: in existence for more than 10 years, or which have been making profits for the last 5 years, and are desirous of seeking listing under securities contracts (Regulation) Rules 1957. This condition has not been adopted by SEBI. In view of this, companies can now issue bonus shares in excess of 1: 1 so long as such companies ensure compliance of residual reserve test and profitability test. The capital market may thus well witness companies with huge reserves coming out with liberal bonus proposals, in days to come.

b) The other measures regarding issuance of bonus taken by SEBI are generally investors protection measures.

10. The guidelines regarding compulsory credit rating of debt instruments with maturity of more than 18 months, is a welcome step. Added to this, is the freeing of the interest rates, which will mean that the interest rate on debentures must necessarily be linked to its risk characteristics, otherwise investors will not subscribe to these.

The ban on issue of FCDs with conversion period of more than 36 months unless conversion is made optional with 'put' and 'call' option is in keeping with the trend worldwide.

The guidelines also provide, that in case, non-convertible portions of PCDs/NCDs are to be rolled over with/without change in the interest rate a compulsory option has to be given to those debenture holders who want to withdraw and encash from the debenture programme. Further, before roll-over of any NCD on non-convertible portion of PCDs, fresh credit rating has to be obtained within a period of 6 months, prior to the due date of redemption and communicated to the debenture holders before roll-over and fresh 'trust deed' has to be executed. While, the option of roll-over of PCDs/ NCDs being left to the shareholders is in their interest without being unduly biased towards the issuer—however, the same cannot be said of companies, which have issued NCDs, and have already provided for 'trustees' in their issue documents, which includes, their right to keep debentures alive for the purpose of reissue in terms of section 121 of the Companies

Act 1956. Such companies intending to roll-over the debentures will have to pay stamp duty not only for creation of security on the debentures, but also on the debentures certificates to be issued, if applicable. This will imply higher floatation costs to the issuer; SEBI can make this stipulation optional at the discretion of the "trustees'.

11. The guideline regarding protection of the interests of the debenture holders are more or less in tune with those issued by CCI formerly The primary differences are, with respect to Debenture redemption reserve (DRR), which now, is permissible after 10% of the debenture liability has been actually redeemed by the company as against the limit of 40% earlier (fixed by CCI) which means, that companies will have access to DRR as soon at 10% of the debenture liability is redeemed. The other difference is in respect of security for debenture which have to, now, be created within 6 months from the date of issue of debentures as against 12 months, earlier.

12. The penal interest of 2% to be paid to debenture holders; if the company is not in a position to create security within 12 months, from the date of issue of capital will go someway in activating the debt market.

13. Although, the minimum time limit for keeping the public issue open has been stipulated by SEBI, no maximum time limit has been specified. This might result in administrative delays. Conversely, for rights issue, the maximum time limit has been specified (60 days) not the minimum, which is rather ad-hoc.

The stipulation of having the issued share capital fully paid-up within 12 months of the opening of the issue, implies that 'self registration' a practice commonly followed in the West as elucidated in Part II will take some years to germinate, in India.

14. To conclude, the SEBI guidelines have placed the maximum onus on the lead manager/underwriter to ensure that all issues of capital meet the disclosure standards and investor protection criterion. His/her job, from now on, will not merely be restricted to look into the legal paraphernalia of these issue and structuring FCDs and PCDs under the 'simplifying' contraints of CCI, but will entail playing an active role, in pricing, structuring and also ensuring a good after market performance of the issue it undertakes because it is finally the lead manager/underwriter who will put his/her reputation on the line.

It is a world of free equity issue pricing. The free pricing of equity offers is coming to a full circle. The Securities and Exchange Board of India (SEBI) has made it obligatory for companies to indicate the premium on their shares computed on the basis of the formula followed by the erstwhile.

Commenting on the prospectus submitted by companies to SEBI for clearance for public offers, the Board has observed. "It would also be necessary to indicate the premium amount as per CCI formula by way of a note". This is to give some indication of the value of their investments to the public.

While the companies are still free to charge whatever premia they want, the difference between the premium charged by a company and the premium as it works out on the basis of the CCI formula should give an insight into the worth of the shares. In addition, companies charging higher premium should also be expected to justify why they are charging more. If one looks at the provisions of section 78 of the companies Act, the share premium can be utilised for (i) issuing fully paid bonus shares, (ii) to provide for premium on redemption of redeemable preference share/debetures, (iii) to write off preliminary expenses and (iv) to write off brokerage/commission/discount incurred on issuing share/debentures.

However, companies would not prefer to resort to item (iii) and (iv) on account of tax implications. These items will be treated as deferred revenue expenditure for income tax deductions. Of the items in (i) and (ii), companies would like to use them firstly for item (ii) and then the residue for item (i). This leads us to the most important question as to why premium should be ever charged?

In the mid 80s and early 90s companies were interested to issued convertible debentures. As the issue of CDs requires rating formalities and above all fixed cost of servicing the convertible debentures, companies with even moderate track record go in for higher issue prices than the intrinsic value of such shares (there by higher premium). This does not require rating formalities to be gone through and need for servicing a fixed portion is also eliminated. Hence shift to premium on shares. Latently the size of membership is reduced enabling better control by the promoters with relatively less investment if promoter's do not subscribe to the present issue as shown below:

Cost of the project	Rs. 100
Debt/Equity	Rs. 1 : 1
Equity	Rs. 50
Debt	Rs. 50

Promoters' contribution 25 per cent of the total issued capital Rs.12.5.

This company, we will assume, is an existing company with good track record and closely held. The promoters have already subscribed to the shares and in the last one year they have not raised equity capital. This enables the promoters to work out the premium in such a way that the total equity holding can be pegged to less than Rs. 50, say at a premium equivalent to 100 per cent of the par value and the resultant equity capital will look as follows:

Total equity needed	Rs. 50
Held by Promoters	Rs. 12.5
Balance	Rs. 37.5
Issue to Public shares	Rs. 18.75
Premium	Rs. 18.75
Total equity	Rs.31.25

In this case, the promoters have not brought in fresh investment. This is true only if the promoters have not contributed to the equity within one year of the current issue as the SEBI guidelines require offer for public should be at the same price at which the promoters had contributed equity within one year of the current issue.

The latest innovation by merchant bankers relating to the fixing of premia is the introduction of "layered Premia" issue which is being proposed by several progressive companies. The salient features of this new instrument are:

1. Fixing a Floor Rate for the Premia

It is necessary for the Board of Directors to obtain permission from the general body of shareholders merely to fix the "floor price" i.e. the minimum amount of premium which the company should charge. In the past, shareholders were always requested to resolve in favour of a "maximum" premia to be fixed leaving it open to the Board to fix a lesser amount. The basis of this enabling resolution was the presumption that the general body of shareholders are not capable of deciding exactly what was best possible for the company whereas the Board with the help of experts can do this. However, there was need for an outer limit so that the shareholders can safeguard their own interest if they wanted to go in for further investment in the company But with the maturing of the new issue markets the shareholders have become more aware of the nuances of public issues and so are in a position to know the intrinsic worth of their company

So in the case of new instruments, shareholders decide the minimum amount the Board of Directors should receive from the new investors. However, to ensure that their own interest are not affected, they are at liberty to fix the minimum premia which the company should collect so that their own additional investment are worthwhile.

2. Underwriting

As a corollory, underwriters too will be given the option of underwriting from the highest premia to the lowest. In fact, those underwriters who are witling to underwrite at higher premia will be preferred to those who are willing to do so at the floor price.

3. Auctioning of the Issue

The next stage involves in actually "Auctioning" the issue to the investor. Those who offer the maximum premia are allotted the share first and the allotment is continued by accepting offers which provide the best possible premia upto the floor. To ensure operational convenience, the premia is fixed in multiples of say Rs. 5 so an issue of Rs. 10 paid up share will have a floor premium of Rs. 10 and a maximum of Rs. 50. Within this there can be slabs of *Rs. 5* each i.e. the issue can be sold at any price beginning from Rs. 20, 25 and so on upto Rs. 60.

The new investment offers advantages to the issuing company, to the merchant banker and also to the underwriters. Structuring the issue as stated above with premia being charged in layers will provide tremendous flexibility to the issue. First of all, the need to fix the premia by merchant bankers or by the issuers is virtually removed.

It is easier to fix the ceiling and floor and permit the market forces to find their own level. By fixing the floor sufficiently low, the merchant banker can ensure that he never goes wrong! It is however not possible in the normal circumstances to find out now much the premia an investors is willing to pay. Since the new instrument is so structured as to virtually auction the shares to the highest bidder downwards it is automatically ensured that the maximum amount is collected. Thus the issue is intrinsically market driven.

The flexibility enables the same issue being offered at different prices to different investors. Since different classes of investors may preceive the prospects of the company differently, maximum collection can be made from those who have a positive opinion on the company. There is no question of over-subscriptions involved. As soon as the shares are subscribed the issue doses. Excessive demand is, thus converted into realisation of maximum premia which is very ideal for the company.

Another inherent advantage is that the "closed bid" auction provides element of uncertainty, ensuring that those who are really interested will put in a bid which is slightly bigger than what they are willing to offer.

Since the new instrument offers to the underwriter an option to offer the premium which according to him the shares could have fetched, he can, depending on his exposure, decide his underwriting commitment.

Apparently, therefore, the new instrument offering layered premia seems to be an ideal solution to many of the difficulties presently being faced by the issuers and the merchant bankers. However, there are several rough edges which need to be smoothened by the SEBI.

Since the beginning of free pricing era beginning from June, 1992, it has been observed that the issuer companies have fixed the prices of right issues or convertible debenture issues nearer to the market price prevailing at the time or just few months before the opening of the Issue whereas in the post-issue period, on listing of the securities, the market price fell below the issue price putting the investors in situation of capital losses. For examples, IPCL, Nagarjuna Fertilisers, Mc-Dowell, Finolex Pipes, and many more were the companies falling under the above category. With the result, investors have now learnt to discriminate between the good and bad and fairly priced issues. No doubt, investors, so far, had to advantage of obtaining securities at prices much below the market price with maximum difference between the par value and market price. Fixation of pricing of issues nearer to the market value did not motivate investors whose enthusiasim was depressed due to bearish trends in the secondary market.

The Tables 2.3 and 2.4 present the illustrative list of companies which had brought their right issues at high premium near the market value and on post issue listing their price tumbled down.

TABLE 2.3

Companies	*Issue Price*	*Market Quote CR Price*	*Post Issue Price*
Garware shipping	80	105	18
Bharat Forge	160	575	175
Simplex Mills	80	175	75
Gujarat Ambuja Cement	200	375	225
HEG	40	120	45
Hindustan Textronics	50	150	57
Shivaji Works	75	360	81
Sonu Synthetics	15	130	28

CR=Current Rate

TABLE 2.4

Equity	*Lead Managers*	*Issue Price*	*Date of opening*	*Post-issu price*
Nagarjuna	JMF	30	9.9.92	25
Rathi Alloys	ANZ/HB Port.	30	11.9.92	26
Finolex Pipes	ICICI/IMF/SBI/BOB	40	11.9.92	38
Adarsh Chemicals	SBI	30	16.9.92	24
Premier Housing	INDB/BOB	25	16.9.92	25
Pateja Forgings	ICICI/PNB	90	23.9.92	87
Visaka Industries	SBI	35	12.10.92	30
Kakatiya Cement	ICICI	50	16.10.92	47
Synthetics	ICICI/IFCI/PNB	75	24.10.92	64
Gujarat Lease Fin.	Cr.Lyn/SCICI/BOB	80	30.10.92	72
Kaveri Engg. Ind.	Ind.GL/SAFE	35	4.11.92	27
Debentures				
Reinz Talbros (PCD)	ANZ	35	24.8.92	52
ECOS Piramal Spg. (PCD)	DSP	53	7.9.92	50 ECOS
Nagarjuna Fert.	JMF/SBI/IDBI	18	7.10.92	15 ECOS

ECOS = Effective cost of shares.

3

Valuation of Equity Shares: Theoretical Concepts

Security analysis examines and evaluates individual securities to estimate the result of investing in them. The aim of all investors is to earn a satisfactory return for his preferred level of risk. This requires their acquiring assets that are at least fairly priced or preferably under priced. Should such assets become overvalued the investor is to recognize the fact and to dispose them off in order to earn maximum returns one has to value a share. It is only then he is able to figure whether the share is under priced or not. Valuation of a share can be done by taking various aspects into consideration. Since valuation relates to unknown future events, its accuracy may depend as much on the economic, capital market, sector and industry factors at work as on specific company performance. Valuation takes into account all the characteristics of a company and it sbusiness to determine the suitability of a security for a particular portfolio structure. Comparative selection among alternative investment opportunities requires appraisal of securities so that their relative attractiveness in terms of return and risk can be judged at any time. This purpose can be accomplished only if consistent analytical procedures are employed and industry and company forecasts are based on an internally consistent set of economic and capital market projections. Isolated analysis and evaluation of an individual security is impractical and inappropriate. One security cannot be effectively appraised apart from other securities or apart from the general investment climate.

In analyzing and valuing companies, security analysts have always sought to appraise risk factors such as product obsolescence, intensity of competition, operating leverage, financial leverage and earnings volatility In anticipating future price behaviour, one begins with an examination of the history of the fluctuations and cycles which have occurred in the returns on common stocks. The past requires interpretation as a starting point for formulation of expectations as to the future, *but* expecting any mechanical extrapolation of the past as a forecast of the future is extremely hazardous and inadvisable. Consideration should also be given to existing and emerging social, political and economic forces of changes that can be expected to affect the level and variability of common stock returns.

To provide perspective and assist in anticipating the future, two movements of common stock should be seen:

(i) Secular trend in annual prices.
(ii) Amplitude of price cycles using monthly average data.

The term investment and speculation are used to refer to different approaches to investment process. Investment is viewed as the process of purchasing securities or property for which stability of value and level of expected return are somewhat predictable. Speculation is the process of buying similar media in which the future value and lever of expected earnings are highly uncertain. Therefore speculation is very dangerous. Hence, one should make investments on the basis of analysis of a security. There are mainly two approaches for security analysis:

(a) Technical Analysis and
(b) Fundamental Analysis

Technical Analysis

Technical analysis is the method of predicting the appropriate time to buy or sell a stock used by those believing building castle in the air from view of stock pricing. (The castle in the air theory of investing concentrates on psychic values i.e. the professional investors prefer to devote their energies not to estimating intrinsic values, but rather to analyzing how the crowd of investors is likely to behave in the future and how during periods of optimism they tend to build their hopes into castles in the air).

Technical analysis is essentially the making and interpreting of stock charts. Hence, a study of both the movements of common stock prices and volume of trading for made. The direction of future change reflected and interpreted by examining charts tell only what the other players have been doing and it is believed that the crowd is likely to do the same in the future.

Technical analysts do not take factors like earnings, dividends and future performance of a company as they believe that all the information is automatically reflected in the company's past market price.

Drawbacks

(1) Since sharp reversal in the market may occur quite suddenly, the technical analyst will often miss the boat.

(2) Such techniques must ultimately be self defeating. As more and more people use it, the value of any technique depreciates.

(3) No buy or sell signal can be worthwhile if everyone tries to act on it simultaneously

Fundamental Analysis

Fundamental analysts takes the opposite stand, believing the market to be 90% logical and 10% psychological. Caring little about the particular pattern of past price movement, fundamentalists seek to determine an issues proper value. Value in this case is related to growth, dividend payout and risk. By estimating such factors as growth for each company the fundamentalists arrive at an estimate of a security's intrinsic value. If this is above the market price then the investor is advised to buy. Fundamentalists believe that eventually the market will reflect accurately the security's real worth.

Drawbacks

Despite its plausibility and scientific appearance there are three potential flaws in fundamental analysis:

(1) The information and analysis may be incorrect.

(2) The security analysts estimate of "value" may be faulty

(3) The market may not correct its "mistake" and the stock price might not converge to its value estimate. Important factors on which Investment decisions are based

Investment according to William Sharpe is "the sacrifice of certain present value for (possibly uncertain) future value".

A distinction is often made between investment and savings. The latter is defined as foregone consumption while the former restricted to real investment of the sort that increases national output in the future.

Investment vehicles can be broadly classified as securities viz. common stock, bonds, calls, warrants etc. and other vehicles viz. mutual funds, real estate, gold and other tangible investments.

Investment decisions are mainly based on two important factors.

Risk and Return

Return is a key variable in the investments decision because this measure allows us to compare the amount of actual and expected gain provided by various investments. Returns can be viewed as the reward for investing. Risk on the other hand is the chance that the actual return from an investment may differ from its expected value.

Return

Return can be defined as the reward for investing. Return reflects both payments received in cash and any change in the value of investment. The various components of return are:

(a) *Current income:* Which is received periodically, it may take the form of interest, dividends, rent and so on.

(b) *Capital gain:* The second component of return is concerned with the change, if any, in the market value of an investment.

Investors pay a certain amount for an investment from which they expect to receive not only current income but also the return of invested funds sometime in the future.

Return is a key variable in the investment decision because this measure allows us to compare the amount of actual or expected gain provided by various investments.

Risk

Risk can be defined as the chance that actual return from an investment may differ from its expected value.

The major sources of risk include:

(a) *Business risk* - is the variability in operating earnings before interest and tax (EBIT). A firm's business risk depends largely on its operating leverage (proportion of fixed costs to variable costs). The decision to become more capital intensive generally leads to an increase in the proportion of fixed costs within the cost structure. In turn increase in operating leverage leads to greater variability in operating earnings.

(b) *Financial risk* - It is associated with debt and equity financing used to finance a firm or property.

(c) *Purchasing power risk* - i.e. the risk of inflation. With the rise in inflation the purchasing power of rupee decreases.

(d) *Interest rate risk* - As interest rates change, the prices of these securities fluctuate, decreasing with increasing interest rates and vice versa.

(e) *Liquidity risk* - It is the risk of not being able to liquidate an investment conveniently and at a reasonable price.

(f) *Market risk* - depends on factors like political, economic, social events etc.

Beta is a market measure of risk. It shows how the price of security responds to market forces, and is found by relating the historical returns on a security with the historical returns for the market. There is a trade off between risk and return while making an investment decision. For accepting greater risk, an investor must receive an increased return. In order to analysis a security the following factors are taken into consideration.

(1) *PIE ratio* : It is the current market price divided by the previous year's per share earning. It is believed to reflect the investors' expectations concerning a firm's future activities i.e. higher the ratio, more confident the investors are about the future. The P/E ratio of any company that is fairly priced will equal the growth rate of the company's earning per share. In general, a P/E ratio that is half the growth rate is worth buying and one that is twice the growth rate is not worth considering.

(2) *Product:* The profitability of a company depends on the product to some extent. Factors like the demand of the product, its quality its uses, its popularity, etc. play an important role in deciding the turnover of the company Thus the product of the company is a significant factor to be considered while making a buy/sell decision on the company's securities.

(3) *Industrial growth rate:* The industrial growth rate is an important factors in security analysis, but more important is the company's market share. If a company belongs to an industry which has as low a growth rate of 2% then the growth prospects of the company per se are low. 'If the company continuously increases its market share then it can grow although the industry growth rate is low.

(4) *Dividend yield:* Stocks that pay good dividends are often favoured over stocks that pay less or no dividend by investors who desire extra income. One strong argument in favour of companies that pay dividends is that companies who do not pay dividends have a sorry history of blowing that money on a string of stupid diversification (i.e. diversify to worsen the company's position). Also the presence of the dividend can keep the stock, the price from falling as far as it would if there were no dividends. Then again, smaller companies that don't pay dividend are likely to grow fast because of it. They are plowing that money into the expansion.

(5) *Book value:* It represents the amount of stock holder's equity in a firm. Book value is determined by subtracting the firm's liabilities and preferred stock from the amount of assets it holds. It indicates the amount of stock holder funds used to finance the

firm. The flow is that the stated book value often bears little relationship to the actual worth of the company It often understates or overstates reality by a margin. Overvalued assets on the right side of the balance sheet are especially treacherous when there is a lot of debt on the left.

(6) *Earnings per share (E.P.S.): E.P.S.* basically translates total corporate profits into profits on a per share basis and provides a convenient measure of earnings available to stockholders.

(7) *Hidden assets:* Companies that own natural resources—such as land, timber, oil or precious metals carry those assets on their book at a fraction of the true value. In that case the book value understates the true worth of the firm. Hence by investing in such firms one can get more value for the investment. For examples if a company shows assets worth Rs. 200 lacs debts of Rs. 300 lacs resulting in a negative value of Rs. 100 lacs. But, if the Rs. 200 lacs assets bring Rs. 400 lacs in bankruptcy sale then the actual book value is a positive Rs. 100 lacs. Hence when a buy decision is to be made one has to have a detailed understanding of what those real values are.

(8) *Replacement Cost:* It gives an estimate of the cost of starting a new company In short, if the firm is to be replaced then what will be the cost of replacement. If the replacement cost is very high then it acts as a barrier to entry and thus the firm is protected from competition.

(9) *Management:* It plays a vital role in the well being of the company. A sound management would mean that the company has bright future prospects provided there are no other calamities. It can make optimum utilization of its resources.

Riskiness of An Investment

As a tool for understanding the fundamental meaning of risk, consider two prospective investments, A and B. The possible rates of return for investment A and the corresponding probabilities for each return are found below:

Investment A		*Investment B*
Probability	*Return*	*Treasury Bill*
15%	0%	100% certain
20%	10%	Return® 12%
30%	20%	
20%	30%	
15%	40%	

Investment A could conceivably provide a return on investment as high as 40% if all went well or no return on investment (0%) if the project did not develop as planned. With the information given above and from equation (1) the expected rate of return, R, for investment A is calculated to be 20%:

$$R = (.15)\ (0\%) + (.20)\ (10\%) + (.30)\ (20\%) + (.20)\ (30\%) + (.15)\ (40\%) = 20\%$$

In contrast to this security, investment B is a treasury bill, offering a 'certain' rate of return of 12%. Investment A has a higher expected rate of return than investment B, 20% vs 12%. However, investment A is more 'risky'- that is, investment A has greater uncertainty as to the final outcome. This is reflected in the greater variation of possible rates of return earned on the investment. Therefore the greater the potential variability in returns, the greater the risk. Although the eventual return for investment A is clearly less certain than for investment B, a measure of risk is useful when the difference between two investments is not so evident. The statistical measure of variability is the standard deviation (a) and can be computed as follows:

$$\sqrt{\sum_{z=1}^{N}(R_i - \overline{R})\, P(R_z)}$$

where

N = the no. of possible outcomes or different rates of return on the investment,

R_i = the value of the ith possible rate of return,

R = the expected value of the rates of return,

$P(R_i)$ = the probability that the ith outcome of return will occur.

For investment A, The standard deviation would be 12.65%, determined as follows:

$$\sigma = [(0\% - 20\%)\,(.15) + (10\%\text{-}20\%)\,(.20) + (20\%\text{-}20\%)\,(.30) + (30\%\text{-}20\%)\,(.20) + (40\%\text{-}20\%)\,(.15)\,]^{1/2}$$

$$\sigma = \sqrt{160\%} = 12.65$$

Therefore, now we have a measure of the risk of investing in asset A. However, for an interpretation as to the measure/rating is good or bad, an answer is possible only by comparing another opportunity against investment A.

The investor's required rate of return:-

In general, the investor's required rate of return can be defined as the minimum rate of return necessary to attract an investor to purchase or hold a security. In other words, an investor who examines an investment opportunity does so with the intention of achieving a rate of return sufficient to warrant making the investment. Thus, the investment will be made only when the purchase price is low enough related to the expected future cash flows to provide a rate of return greater than or equal to the investor's required rate of return.

The required rate of return is a function of:

(1) The time value of money,

(2) The variability in returns of the asset (risk), and,

(3) The Investor's attitude towards risk.

The first element, the time value of money is represented by a riskless or risk-free rate of return. As the level of risk increases investors in the market place begin to require additional expected returns to induce them to acquire a security Thus, the required rate of return, R, is equal to the risk free rate, R,

plus a premium, P:

$R=R_f+ p$

Riskiness of an investment has been defined in terms of the variability of its anticipated returns, as measured by the standard deviation. *However, total variability can be divided into two components:*

(1) The **unsystematic risk**, which is the variability of returns unique to the security, and

(2) The **systematic risk**, which is the variability of the security's return resulting from variations in the general market. Thus, the total risk or variability of a given security's return can be represented as follows:

Total Risk = Unsystematic (unique security) risk+ systematic (relative to the market) risk.

By investing in the portfolio of securities (a number of different securities), that is, by diversifying, an investor can minimize the impact of the unique security risk. Source of variation unique to a security could include variability resulting from labour strikes, errors in judgement by a firm's management regarding a capital expenditure decision, or court decision. Diversification, however, cannot eliminate all risk from an investor's portfolio of stocks. Specifically, it is not possible to eliminate the variations in portfolio returns resulting from general, economic, political and sociological changes that affect all firms simultaneously Thus, the investor who owns a well-diversified portfolio must still contend with the variation in security returns common to all securities. Therefore, the relevant risk for an investor is that portion of the variability of returns that is non diversifiable, that being the systematic risk.

In measuring a security's systematic risk, we need an indication of the relationship between the security's returns and the general market returns. We can calculate this relationship statistically by determining the regression coefficient between a security and the general market returns. This coefficient frequently called beta, β_j, is measured as follows:

$$\beta_j = \sigma_j + m / \sigma_m^2 \qquad (1)$$

where

b_j = the systematic risk of security j

σ_{jfm} = the covariance of the return of the security with the market returns.

σ_m^2 = the variance of the market returns.

The variance of security's returns is a measure of the variability of security's returns by itself. The covariance of security's returns with general market returns is a measure of the variability of the security and the market taken together. The covariance is calculated as follow:

$$\sigma_{j+m} = r_{j+m} \sigma_j \sigma_m$$

where,

r_{j+m} = the correlation coefficient for measuring the relationship between security j returns and the market returns,

σ_j, σ_m = the standard deviation of the security j returns and the standard deviation of the market returns respectively.

In equation (1), if beta equals one, then a security's expected returns will vary in direct proportion with the market's expected returns, that is a 10% market return should produce a 10% security return. If the market return then increases from 10% to 15%, the security's return should likewise rise from 10% to 15%. Correspondingly when a beta is larger than one, say two, an individual's security's returns are twice as responsive to changes in the market, whether the returns are increasing or decreasing. These relationships are shown in the figure 3.1, where the returns are increasing or decreasing where relationship are shown in figure 3.1, where the returns for security A move in direct proportion with the market, that is, the security A has a beta of one.

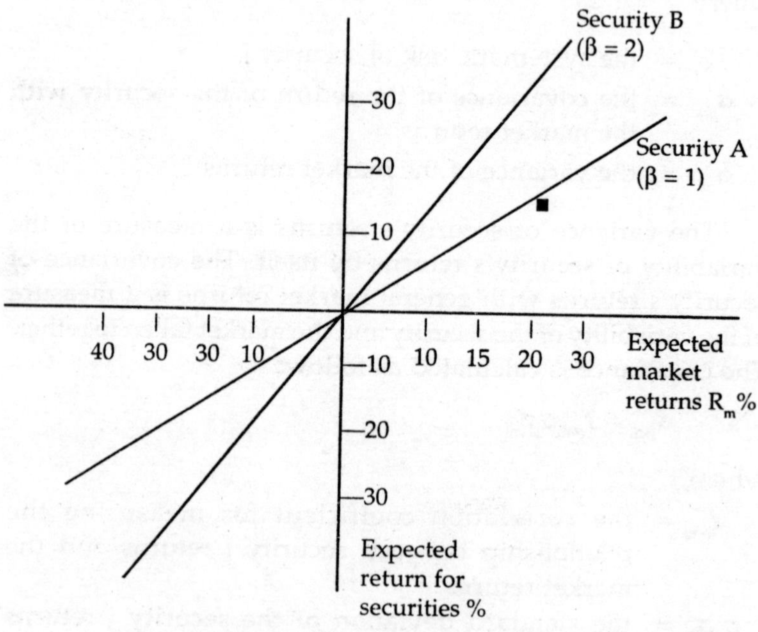

Fig 3.1. Beta 'β' relationships

In comparison, the security β is twice as responsive to market changes (B = 2). For instance, a change in the market returns from 10 to 15% results in increase in security's return from 20% to 30%, or twice the change of the market. Also, the figure clearly shows that decrease in returns are twice as great for security B than for security A as the market returns decline. As a consequence, the security with a beta of two is considered to have twice the risk of a security with a beta of one.

Measuring the required rate of return:

Having recognized systematic risk, as the relevant risk, we now return to the original" equation stating that the required rate of return for a security, R. equals the risk-free rate of return, R_f, plus a risk premium, P:

$$R = R_f + P \quad \text{.......... (2)}$$

Rearranging this equation to solve for the risk premium (P), we have:

$$P = R - R_f \quad \text{.......... (3)}$$

Which simply says that the risk premium R for a security equals the security's expected return, R, less the risk-free rate existing in the market, R_f. For example, if the expected return for a security is 14% and the risk free rate is 8%, the risk premium is 6%. Also, if the expected return for the market, R_m, is 12% and the risk free rate, R_f, is 8%, the risk premium for the general market would be 4%. This 4% risk premium would apply to any security having systematic (non diversifiable) risk equivalent to the general market, or a beta of one. In this same market, a security with a beta of two should provide a risk premium of 8%, or twice the 4% risk premium existing for the market as a whole. Hence, in general, the appropriate required rate of return for the j the security, R_j,

$$R_j R_f + \beta_j (R_m - R_f) \quad \text{.......... (4)}$$

Equation (4) is the Capital Asset Pricing Model (CAPM). This equation designates the risk- return trade off existing in the market, where risk is defined in terms of beta. The following figure graphically illustrates the CAPM as the security market line (SML). As presented in this figure 3.2 securities with betas equal too), 1 and 2 should have required rates of return as follows:

(where R_f = 8% and R_m = 12%)
if $\beta_j = 0$ R_j = 8%+ 0 (12% – 8%) = 8%
if $\beta_j = 1$ R_j = 8%+ 1 (12% – 8%) = 12%
if $\beta_j = 2$ R_j = 8%+ 2 (12% – 8%) = 16%

The SML is drawn under the following assumptions:

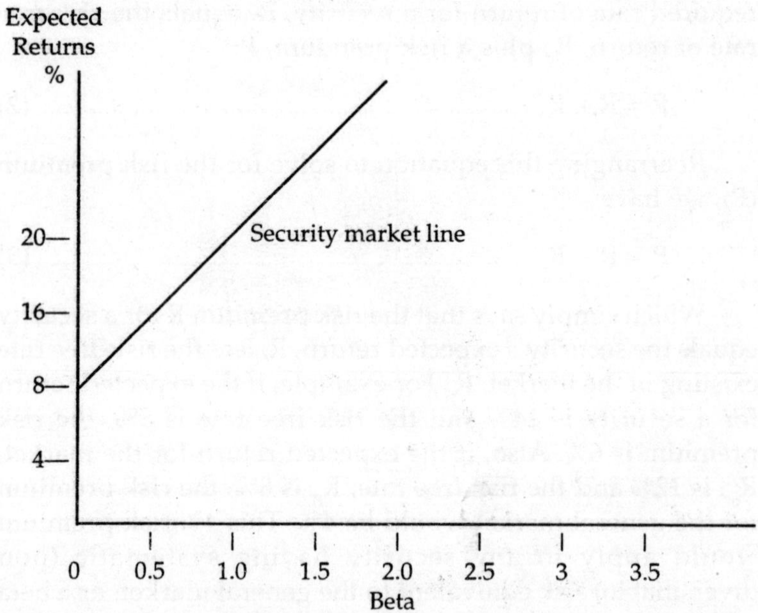

Fig. 3.2. Security Market Line

(1) The market place where the securities are bought and sold is highly efficient.

(2) The model assumes that a perfect market exists.

In summary, we cannot formulate a complete concept of valuation without understanding the nature of the investor's required rate of return. This rate, which serves as the discount rate in the valuation process, represents the minimal acceptable return to induce investor to purchase or hold a security

SECURITY PRICING MODELS

1. Present Value Models

There are a variety of different present value models. However given a company's current dividend and stock price, the basic concept underlying all of their models is that a stock's price change if: (i) the projected dividend growth increases (ii) the investor's required rate of return from the stock decreases, or (iii) some combination of a change in the dividend growth rate and the investor's required return improves the stock's risk-reward relationship.

The simplest definition of the investor's required rate of return that is common to a variety of more complex definitions used in these models is the required rate of return for a stock is the sum of the rate of return available from risk-free investments plus a risk premium necessary to compensate the investor for assuming the added risk of owning the stock. The risk free rate is defined usually in practice as the AAA corporate bond interest rate. The size of the risk premium depends on the level of certainty associated with the projected future dividend stream. As the level of certainty declines, the risk premium increases.

Present value models are used most commonly by those who believe that a theoretical price for an individual stock can be computed. In practice, this theoretical price is compared to the stock's actual price, if the theoretical price is materially different from the actual price, the stock is considered to be either potentially overvalued (theoretical price is less than actual price) or undervalued (theoretical price greater than the actual price).

The next largest category of present value model users are those who begin with the actual price and using their version of present value model, computed, the investor's implied or projected rate of return. This figure is then compared to what the analyst believes to be the appropriate rate of return for the stock. If the implied rate of return seems generous, given the analyst's estimate of risk associated with the future dividend stream, the stock is considered to undervalued.

Other uses of present value models include the computation of the number of years that it takes for a given stock's dividend to grow to the point where the investor's yield on the purchase price equals the current AAA bond rate; and the estimation of the stock's when the expected return from a stock when the expected rate of return for the stock market as a whole is zero.

The formulation and application of present value models by the institutional investment community incorporate much of the theory of equity valuation developed by academics during the last 20 years.

a) Single Holding Period Valuation Model

The price today of a share of common stock (P_o), depends upon (1) the cash flows investors expect to receive if they buy the stock and (2) the riskiness of these expected cash flows. The expected cash flow consists of two element: the dividend expected in each year, t, defined as d_i; and the price investors expect to receive when they sell the stock at the end of year n, defined as P_n, which includes the return of the original investment plus a capital gain (or minus a capital loss). If investors expect to hold the stock for one year, and if the stock price is expected to be P_1 at the end of the year, the value of the common stock is:

$$P_0 = \frac{D_1}{1+R} + \frac{P_1}{1+R}$$

Where,

P_0 = Selling price today (present value of dividend and market price).

P_1 = Selling price at the end of the year 1.

D_1 = Dividend to the received at the end of the year 1

R = Investor's required rate of return or discount rate.

Where the price of the share is expected to grow at a rate of G% annually, the current price for single period holding will be:

$$P_0 = \frac{D_1}{1+R} + \frac{P_0(1+G)}{1+R} = \frac{D_1}{R-G}$$

Since:

P_0 (1+ R) =D_1+ P_0 (1+ G)

P_0 (1+ R)–P_0 (1+ G) = D_1

P_0 (1+ R–1–G) =D_1

P_0 (R–G) =D_1

$$P_0 = \frac{D_1}{(R-G)}$$

Suppose that we buy one share of the ABC company at the beginning of the year for Rs. 25. We hold the stock for one year. One rupee in dividend is collected at year end, and the share is sold for Rs. 26.50, now if we were to determine the rate of return achieved, the purchase price if the required rate of return is 15% (P_1 =Rs. 26.50), and the setting price of the rate of return is 15%? (P_o = Rs. 25). we can proceed as follows:

$$\text{Rate of Return (R)} P_0 = \frac{D_1}{1+R} + \frac{P_1}{1+R}$$

$$\text{Rs. } 25 = \frac{\text{Re } 1}{1+R} + \frac{\text{Rs.} 26.5}{1+R} = \text{Rs.} 25$$

Both sides balance with R =10.

Therefore R= 10%

Purchase price (P_o)

$$P_0 = \frac{\text{Rs. } 1}{1.15} + \frac{\text{Rs. } 26.5}{1.15} = \text{Rs. } 0.87 + \text{Rs. } 23.04 = \text{Rs. } 23.91$$

$$\text{Selling price } (P_1) \text{ Rs. } 25 = \frac{\text{Rs. } 1}{1.15} + \frac{P_1}{1.15}$$

$= \text{Rs. } 0.87 + \text{Rs. } 0.87\ P_1$

Or Rs. 24.13 = Rs. 0.87 P or P = Rs. 27.74

b) Multiple Year Holding Period

Since common stock has no maturity and it is frequently held for many years, a more general multiple holding period valuation model is needed. The general common stock valuation model can be defined as follows:

i) Perpetual Common Stock:

Where the equity share may be expected to bring a dividend stream of infinite duration, the current value of the share is:

$$P_0 = \frac{D_1}{(1+R)} + \frac{D_2}{(1+R)^2} + \ldots\ldots + \frac{D_n}{(1+R)^n} + \frac{P_n}{(1+R)^\alpha}$$

$$\text{or } P_o = \sum_{t=1}^{n} \frac{D_t}{(1+R)^t}$$

(ii) Finite horizon common stock:

Now, we can consider how an equity share would be valued by an investor who plans no hold it for n years, and sell it there after for a price of P_n. The value of the equity share to him is:

$$P_0 = \frac{D_1}{(1+r)} + \frac{D_2}{(1+r)^2} + \ldots\ldots \frac{D_n}{(1+r)^n} + \frac{P_n}{(1+r)^\alpha}$$

$$\text{or } p_o = \sum_{t=1}^{n} \frac{D_t}{(1+r)^t} + \frac{P_n}{(1+r)^n} \ldots\ldots\ldots\ldots\ldots\ldots\ldots\ldots (2)$$

The value of P_n in the equation (2) is the present value of the dividend stream beyond the nth period, this means:

$$P_0 = \frac{D_{n+1}}{(1+r)} + \frac{D_{n+2}}{(1+r)^2} + \ldots\ldots \frac{D\propto}{(1+R)\propto-n}$$

Substituting this value in Eq. 2, we get

$$P_0 = \frac{D_1}{(1+r)} + \frac{D_2}{(1+r)^2} + \ldots\ldots \frac{D_n}{(1+r)^N} + \frac{1}{(1+r)^v}$$

$$P_0 = \frac{D_{n+1}}{(1+r)} + \frac{D_{n+2}}{(1+r)^2} + \ldots\ldots \frac{D\propto}{(1+R)\propto-n}$$

$$\frac{D_1}{(1+r)} + \frac{D_2}{(1+r)^2} + \ldots\ldots \frac{D_{n+1}}{(1+r)^N} + \frac{1}{(1+r)^v} + \frac{D\propto}{(1+r)\propto}$$

$$= \sum_{t=1}^{\alpha} \frac{D_t}{(1+r)^t}$$

Since Eq.1 = Eq.3, we can say that the share valuation model

$$P_0 = \sum_{t=1}^{\alpha} \frac{D_t}{(1+r)^t}$$

is general enough to permit any dividend pattern-rising, declining, constant, or randomly fluctuating.

Consider holding a share of ABC company for 5 years. In most cases the dividend will grow from year to year. To look at some results, let us stipulate the following:

g = annual expected growth in earnings, dividends and price = 6%

e = most recent earnings per share = Rs. 1.89

d/e = dividend payout (%) = 50%

r = required rate of return = 10%

p = price (per share)

p/e = price-earnings ratio = 12.5%

n = holding period in years = 5

Given these assumptions, the present value of a share of stock can be determined by solving the following equation:

$$P = \frac{[\sum^{N} [(eo)\ (\alpha/e)]\ (1+g)^n]}{(1+r)^n} + \frac{[(P/E).(eo)\ (1+g)]^{[N+1]}}{(1+r)^n}$$

This imposing formula says, "Sum the present value of all dividends to be received over the holding period, and add this to the present value of the selling price of the stock at the end of the holding period to arrive at the present value of the stock".

$$\#P=\sum_{n=1}^{5} \frac{.943\ (1.06)^n}{(1.10)^n} = \frac{1}{1.10} + \frac{1.06}{(1.10)^2} + \frac{1.12}{(1.10)^3} + \frac{1.19}{(1.10)^4} + \frac{1.26}{(1.10)^5}$$

$$= .909+ .876+ .844+ .813+ .783 = \text{Rs. } 4.225$$

$$\frac{(12.5)\ [(1.89)\ (1.06)^6]}{(1.10)^5} = \frac{33.45}{(1.10)^5} = \text{Rs. } 20.78$$

$$.P = \text{Rs. } 4.225+ \text{Rs. } 20.78 = \text{Rs. } 25.00$$

Let us estimate the return on McDonald's stock as an investment to be held for five years. McDonald's operates the largest fast food restaurant system in the country Assume that' its common stock can be purchased at the beginning of 1991 for $52. A thorough analysis of expected future earnings, dividends, and price earnings ratio (P/E) has provided the following predictions:

Year	Earnings per share (Rs.)	Dividends per share (Rs.)
1991	5.05	0.82
1992	5.80	0.95
1993	6.65	1.10
1994	7.85	1.25
1995	8.80	1.45

It is estimated that at the end of 1995, the stock will sell for twelve times 1995 earnings (Rs. 105). What rate of return would equate the flow of dividend and the terminal price shown above back to the current price of Rs. 52. In effect, we want the rate of return that will solve the following:

$$\text{Rs. } 52 = \frac{\text{Rs. } 82}{(1+r)} + \frac{\text{Rs. } 0.95}{(1+r)^2} + \frac{\text{Rs.} 1.10}{(1+r)^3} + \frac{\text{Rs.} 1.25}{(1+r)^4} + \frac{\text{Rs. } 1.45}{(1+r)^5} + \frac{\text{Rs } 105}{(1+r)^6}$$

Where r is the rate of return, calculating the rate that will solve the equation is some what tedious task, requiring trail and error computation. Lets turn the equation into columnar form and try a discount rate:

Year	*Receipt-Rs.*	*pV Discount factor at 17%*	*Present value Rs.*
1	.82	.854	.70
2	.95	.730	.69
3	1.10	.624	.69

4	1.25	.533	.67
5	1.45	.456	.66
6	105	.456	47.89
			Rs. 51.30

At 17%, this stream of receipts has present value of Rs. 51.30, which is close to the market price of $ 52. This suggests that the discount rate is just slightly less than 17%.

(c) Multiperiod Valuation with Zero Growth

Suppose the rate of growth is measured by the rate at which dividends are expected to increase. If future growth is expected to be zero, the value of the stock reduces to the same formula as was developed for a perpetual bond:

$$\text{Price} = \frac{\text{Dividend}}{\text{Capitalization rate}}$$

i.e. $P_0 = D/r$

Solving for r, we obtain

$r = D/p_o$

Which states that the required rate of return on a share of stock that has no growth prospects is simply the dividend yield.

Proof:

$$P_0 = \frac{D}{(1+R)} + \frac{D}{(1+R)^2} \quad \frac{D}{(1+R)^3} + \ldots\ldots \times \frac{D}{(1+R)^\alpha}$$

This being an infinite G.P., its sum is given by

$$\underset{n=\propto}{Sn} = \frac{A}{1-R}$$

where

A = 1st term

R = multiplication factor

$$A = \frac{D}{(1+R)}, \quad R = \frac{1}{1+R}$$

$$P_0 = \frac{D/(1+R)}{\left(1-\dfrac{1}{(1+R)}\right)} = \frac{D/(1+R)}{R/(1+R)} = \frac{D}{R}$$

d) Valuation with Constant Growth

The simplest extension of what we have been doing assumes that dividends will grow at the same rate (G) into the indefinite future. Under this assumption, the value of share of stock is:

$$P_0 = \frac{D(1+G)}{1+R} + \frac{D(1+G)^2}{(1+R)^2} + \frac{D(1+G)^3}{(1+R)^3} + \frac{D(1+G)^n}{(1+R)^n} + \ldots\ldots\ldots + \ldots\ldots.$$

where 'n' approaches infinity this equation collapses simply to

$$P_0 = \frac{D_1}{R-G}$$

where

D_1 = Dividend to be received at the end of the year

This model states that the price of a share of stock should be equal to next year's expected dividend by the difference between the appropriate discount rate for the stock and its expected long term growth rate. Alternatively, this model can be stated in term of the rate of return on a stock as

$$R = \frac{D_n}{P_0} + G$$

The constant growth model is often defended as the model that arises from the assumption that the firm will maintain a stable dividend policy (keep its retention rate constant) and earn a stable return on new equity investment overtime.

$$\text{Proof: } P_0 = \frac{D_1}{(1+R)} + \frac{D_2}{(1+R)^2} + \frac{D_3}{(1+R)^3} + \ldots\ldots\ldots\ldots\ldots$$

$$= \frac{D_0(1+G)}{(1+R)} + \frac{D_0(1+G)^2}{(1+R)^2} + \frac{D_0(1+G)^3}{(1+R)^3} + \ldots\ldots\ldots\ldots\ldots$$

$$= \frac{(1+G)}{(1+R)} + \frac{(1+G)^2}{(1+R)^2} + \frac{(1+G)^n}{(1+R)^n} + \ldots\ldots\ldots\ldots\ldots] \quad .(1)$$

Multiply both sides of the equation (1) by (1+ R) / (1+ G)

$$P_0 \frac{(1+R)}{(!+G)} = D_0 \left[1 + \frac{[(1+G)]}{[1+R)]} + \frac{[(1+G)}{[(1+R)} + \frac{(1+G)^2}{(1+R)^2} + \frac{(1+G)^{N-1}]}{(1+R)^{N-1}]}\right] \ldots(2)$$

Substract equation (1) from equation (2)

$$\frac{1+R}{1+G} P_0 - P_0 = D_0\, 1 - \left[\frac{(1+G)^n}{(1+R)^n}\right]$$

$$P_0 \; \frac{1+R}{1+G} - 1 = D_0\, 1 - \left[\frac{(1+G)^n}{(1+R)^n}\right]$$

Assuming R > G, as N – ∝ the term in brackets on the right hand side of the equation – D_0, leaving

$$P_0 \left(\frac{(1+R)-(1-g)}{1+G}\right) = D_0$$

$$P_0 \left[\frac{(R-G)}{1+G} \right] = D_0$$

$$P_0 (R-G) = D_0 (1+G)$$

$$\text{Or } P_0 (R-G) = D1 \ (\# D_0 (1+G) = D_1]$$

$$\# P_0 = \frac{D.}{(R-G)}$$

How might the sing's period model be used to select stocks? One way is to predict next year's dividends, the firm's long term growth rate and the rate of return stock holders require for holding the stock. The equation could then be solved for the theoretical price of the stock that could be compared with its present price. Stocks that have theoretical prices above their actual price are candidates for purchase; those with theoretical prices below their actual price are candidates for sale. Another way to use the approach is to find the rate of return implicit in the price at which the stock is now selling. This can be done by substituting the current price, estimated dividend and estimated growth rate into the equation and solving for the discount rate that equates the present price with the expected flow of future dividends. If this rate is higher than the rate of return considered appropriate for the stock, given its risk, it is a candidate for purchase.

e) Valuation with Two-stage Growth (or Supernormal Growth)

It seems logical to assume that firms which have grown at a very high rate will not continue to do so infinitely. Similarly, firms with very poor growth might improve in the future. While a single growth rate can be found that will yield the same value as a more complex pattern, it is so hard to estimate this single number and the resultant valuation is so sensitive to this number that many analysts have been reluctant to use the constant growth model without modification.

The most logical further extension of the constant growth, model is to assume that a period of extraordinary growth (good or bad) will continue for a certain number of years, after which growth will change to a level at which it is expected to continue indefinitely Firms typically go through life cycles, during part of these cycles their growth is much faster than that of the economy as a whole. Automobile manufacturers in the 1920s, manufacturers of hard calculators in 1970s, and computer manufacturers in the mid 1980s are examples.

The figure 3.3 drawn below illustrates such supernormal growth and compares it with normal growth, zero growth, and negative growth. A negative growth rate represents a declining company A mining company whose profits are falling because of a declining ore body is an example.

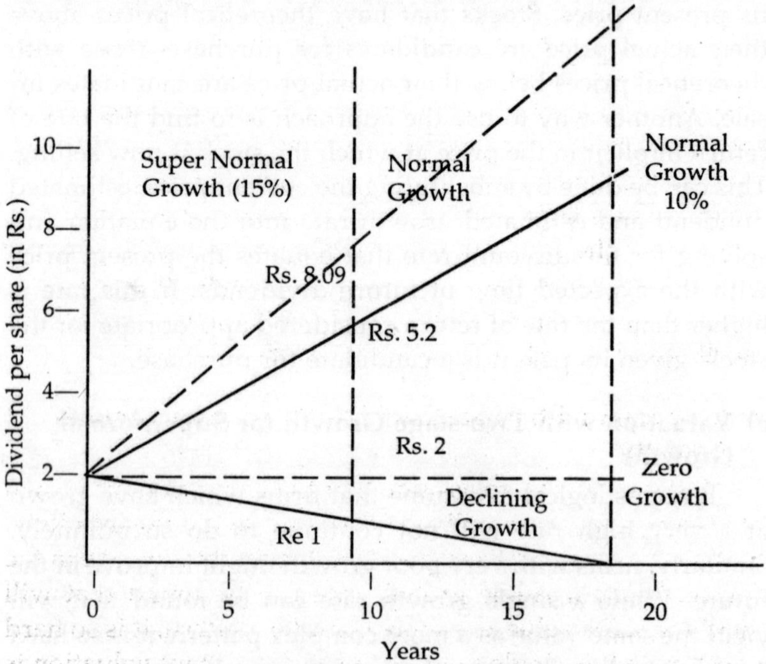

Fig. 3.3. Illustrative Dividend Growth Rates

A hypothetical firm is expected to grow at a rate of 20%

rate for 10 years, then to have its growth rate fall to 4%, the norm for the economy The value of the firm with this growth pattern is determined by the following equation:

Present Price = PV of dividends during above normal growth period+ value of stock at the end of above normal growth period discounted back to present.

$$P_0 = \sum_{t=1}^{n} \frac{D_0 (1+G_s)_t}{(1+R_s)^T} + \frac{D_{n+1}}{R_s - G_n} \cdot \frac{1}{(1+R_s)^n}$$

where

G_s = above normal growth rate
G_n = normal growth rate
n = period of above normal growth rate

Consider, McDonald's whose previous dividend was $ .71 (D_0=$.71), with the dividend expected to increase by 15% a year for 10 years and thereafter at 10% a year indefinitely If a stock holder's required rate of return is 16%, lets find the value of the stock.

We may assume the following:

a) Required rate of return is equal to 16%
b) Growth rate is 15% for 10 years and 10% thereafter (G_s =15%, G_n=10%, n = 10)
c) Last year's dividend was $. 71 (Dp = $ .71)

Step 1: Find the PV of dividends during the rapid growth period i.e., PV of first ten year's dividend

$$P_0 = \sum_{T=1}^{10} \frac{D_0 (1+G_s)_t}{(1+R_s)^t}$$

End of year	*Dividend $.71 (1.15)^t^*	*PVIF=1/ (1-16)^t^*	*Present value*
1	$.82	.862	$.71
2	.95	.743	.71

3	1.10	.640	.70
4	1.25	.552	.69
5	1.45	.476	.69
6	1.66	.410	.68
7	1.90	.354	.67
8	2.18	.305	.66
9	2.51	.263	.66
10	2.88	.226	.65

PV of first ten years dividends

$$= \sum_{t=1}^{10} \frac{D_0 (1+g_s)^t}{(1+ r_s)^T}$$

Step 2: Find the PV of the year 10 stock price (). Find the value of the stock at the end of the year 10:

$$P_{10} = \frac{D_{11}}{r_s - g_n}$$

$$= \frac{\$2.88(1.10)}{.16\ .\ .10} = \$52.80$$

(b) Discount P_{10} back to the present

$$PV = P_{10} \frac{(1)}{(1+ r_s)} \quad 10$$

= \$ 52.80 (.226)

=\$11.93

Step 3: Sum to find the total value of the stock today

P_{10} =\$ 6.82+ \$11.93

=\$ 18.75

Relative Value Model

The relative value model proponents reject the idea that a stock's theoretical price can be computed. Rather, they maintain that individual stocks have value only relative to other stocks and that this relative value is a function of the relationship between certain key company characteristics that are representative of the relative risk reward relationship of a given stock. A potentially overvalued stock under this theory would be one with a price earnings multiple that is greater than say, the S & P 400 index's price earnings multiple, but with a rate of return on equity below the average rate of return on equity for the S&P 400 index.

Market Model

The return generation process has been an area of interest to researchers for over 30 years. Harry Markowitz (1952) first put forward the basic elements of a theory in this direction. He proposed that investors do not maximise the returns in absolute terms but, this return maximisation is seen in the context of risk associated with the return. In other words an investors tries to maximise the return given a certain level of risk or minimises the risk given a certain return. This proposition draws upon a basic premise about human behaviour namely risk aversion. It is assumed in this proposition that investors are risk averse and therefore, they derive more utility by risk-reduction. Risk, for the purpose of this proposition is measured by certain measures of variability in returns. An important advacement was made by sharpe (1963) who suggested that the return on any security can be considered to be related to the performance of some index of business activity as follows:

$$R_{it} = a_i + b_i R_{mt} + e_{it} \qquad (1)$$

Where a_i and b_i are constants for firm i, R_{mt} is the return on some underlying factor (hereafter called market index) in period t, R_{it} is the return on the stock of firm in period t, and

e_{it} is the random-error term for firm i in period t. This is the market model and is based on the assumption that the joint probability distribution between R_{it} and R_{mt} is stationary and bivariate normal. As a result of this assumption, the error term has the following properties

(1) The average value of eit is zero, that is, E $(e_{it}) = 0$

(2) The variance of e_{it}, denoted by s_{ei}^2, is constant, that is, error terms are homoscedastic.

(3) The error terms are uncorrelated with R_{mt}, that is,

$$\text{Cov}(e_{it}, R_{mt}) = 0$$

Although not attributed to the bivariate normality assumption, it is also assumed that the firm's error term in period t, that is uncorrelated with any other firm's error terms in period t, i.e.

$$\text{Cov}(e_{it}, e_{jt}) = 0.$$

Though the market model is not a theoretical model, in the sense of explaining what causes returns, it hypothesizes that there is a systematic linear association between the returns of an individual security (or portfolio) and market index. The market model expresses the relationship between the returns of security i and market index.

. The regression or characteristic line of the market model describes what the return of a given asset will be on an average given a return on the market index. The slope coefficient "B", is referred to as the measure of "systematic risk" or "volatility". The error term e_{it} measures the inaccuracy of the market model. The intercept ai indicates that the return of the underlying security should average a_i when the return of the market is zero.

Assuming that the historical date have been generated by a stationary distribution, the statistical technique of simple regression [that is, ordinary leastsguares (OLS)] can be used to estimate the security-specific parameters a_i, b_i and s^2_{ej}. This statistical technique takes the set of paired sample values of (R_{mt}, R_{it}) and attempts to find the values of a_i and b_i that create a line of "best fit". Here "best fit" means that the sum of the squared vertical distances of the actual values of R_{it} from the line is minimised.

The implication of accepting market model as the model explaining market as the model explaining return generation are as *follows:*

a) The mean return for security i

$R = a_i b_i + R_m$ .... (2)

b) The variance of security i's return

$s_i^2 = b_i^2 . s_m^2 + s_{ei}^2$ .... (3)

(s_m^2 being variance of return on market index)

c) The covariance of returns between securities i and j:

$s_{ij} = b_i . b_j \, s_m^2$ .... (4)

Thus, the expected return has a unique part a and a market related part $b_i . R_m$. Similarly, the variance of a security has a unique (or unsystematic) part s_{ej}^2 and a market related (systematic) part $b_i^2 . s_m^2$. The covariance depends only on market risk.

In the foregoing paragraphs of this section the relationship between the returns of a particular security and the market index as prescribed by the market model was outlined. Any portfolio of securities is also itself a security with returns equal to weighted average returns of individual securities constituting the portfolio. The variance and betas can also be computed on this weighted average of returns. Therefore, whatever has been said in the foregoing or the following paragraphs about a security also holds good about a portfolio of securities which can be taken as a security for the purpose of all the models of return generation process without any loss of applicability of these models. The additional advantage in the taking porfolios for applying these models in that the error term becomes less significant through the process of mutual cancellation in a given portfolio and therefore, the statistical problems are easier to handle than those in a single security.

The Capital Assets Pricing Model (CAPM)

The model primarily tries to relate the returns of a particular security to the associated risk of the security and the returns on market portfolio for the same period. The CAPM is an investigation of the implications of the normative Markowitz model for the equalibrium structure of asset prices. As a result of exploration into the effects of the proposition that all the investors follow the model developed by Markowitz. CAPM was developed due to independent works of Treynor (1961), Sharpe (1964), Lintner (1965) and Mossin (1966). *The assumptions behind CAPM are as follows:*

i) Investors are risk-averse, one-period expected-utility-of-terminal-wealth maximisers which implies that they maximise their utility for one-period returns.

ii) Investors make their investments solely based on the mean and standard deviation of rate of returns associated with an investment proposition.

iii) All capital assets are infinitely divisible, transaction costs and taxes do not exist, the condition of perfect competition exists in the capital market (no individual investor can affect the market prices) and all information is freely and instantly available to every one. These assumptions are collectively called the assumption of perfect capital market.

iv) There is a risk-free borrowing rate and a risk-free lending rate which are equal and at which any investor can borrow or lend unlimited amounts.

v) All assets including human capital are marketable.

vi) Investors have homogeneous expectations about expected returns, variances, co-variances etc.

The standard CAPM describes the process of return generation as follows:

$$\overline{R}_i = \overline{R}_f + b_i(\overline{R}_m - R_f)$$

where, $\overline{R}_i$ is the expected return on asset "i".

R_f is the return on risk free asset.

$\overline{R}_m$ is the expected return on market portfolio.

b_i is the regression coefficient of returns of asset "i" on the returns of market portfolio.

This relationship has a number of implications for returns generation process which may be of Interest to an individual investor or a portfolio manager. First, the expected returns on any two assets differ due to the difference between their betas. The higher the beta the higher is the variation in expected return of the asset. Secondly, the expected return is linearly dependent on the beta of an asset. Thirdly, the returns do not depend on any risk other than that captured by beta. In other words, it is the riskiness of asset's returns with respect to market portfolio (beta) which is relevant to return generation process, any other risk (called unsystematic risk) does not affect the returns.

Two Factor Model

Out of all the assumptions on which the standard form of CAPM is based, two assumptions namely absence of taxation and equal risk free lending and borrowing rates are more stringent. Other assumptions are either true directly or tend towards truth due to presence of intermediaries who make these assumptions a reality through the process of aribitraging (e.g. divisibility of assets). These two assumption has been discussed in this section in greater detail due to the difficulty they pose when juxtaposed to reality

If one assumes that neither risk free borrowing nor lending is allowed the standard CAPM is modified to two factor (or zero beta), CAPM which describes the return generation process as follows:

$$\overline{R}_i = \overline{R}_z + (\overline{R}_m - \overline{R}_z)\beta_i \qquad (3.1)$$

where $\overline{R}_z$ is the expected return on a portfolio uncorrelated with market portfolio (or having its b-value as zero). This model prescribes that in equilibrium all security returns are a linear function of two factors $\overline{R}_z$ and $\overline{R}_m$. Implications of this model are the same as those for standard CAPM with the only difference that R_f has been replaced by R_z. R_z can be shown to have a value less than R_m but, more than R_f even if it does exist for lending only.

The assumption regarding personal income tax (its non-existence) is another important assumption to be explored as this assumption appears to be unreasonable. It is more reasonable to assume that both the taxes on dividend income and those on capital gains exist and are different. Brennan (1970) assumed that there are different tax rates and investors have homogeneous expectations regarding before tax returns with known dividend yields. Based on these assumptions it can be shown that before tax expected return R_i on security "i" in standard CAPM gets modified to

$$\overline{R} = R_f + [(\overline{R}_m - R_f) - T(D_m - R_f)].b_i + T(D_i - R_0) \qquad (3.2)$$

where,

D_i = dividend yield on equity i

D_m = dividend yield on market portfolio

T = a function of rate of taxation on dividend income and rate of taxation on capital gains (T takes the value o when both these rates are equal).

In this model, the investors will choose their optimal portfolio on the basis of after tax return which due to different tax rates differs from- investor to investor. Equation (2) can be rearranged as follows:

$$\overline{R}_i = R_f(1-T)+ [\overline{R}_m-R_f\ (1-T)].\beta_i+ T\ (D_i-\beta_i\ D_m) \ldots\ldots\ (3.3)$$

In the Indian Capital market D, and D_m which range between 3-5% p.a. are too small as compared to R_m and R_i which for the last 16 years have been about 26%' p.a. and for the last 11 years have amounted to 30% p.a. (using geometric means taken over these period for sensex and BSENI respectively). Thus capital gains have been the significant portion of the return with negligible part constituted by dividend yields. Thus the last term $T\ (D_i-\beta_i\ D_m)$ will be negligible compared to the other two terms in equation (3). This contention is further strengthened by the following arguments which contend that the value of T should be zero and D_i and D_m should not appear in CAPM equation (3).

First, for mutual funds which are a major player in the Indian Stock Market tax rate for dividend income and tax rate for capital gains is both equal to zero. Therefore, if some rich individual investors whose tax rate for capital gains is lower than that for dividend income (which has been the case in India in the recent past) value low dividend yield equities more, it presents an arbitrage opportunity to mutual funds. And they, being more rational, more powerful and knowledgeable players in the field will certainly use it till this opportunity exists. Same will be the tendency of less rich investors for whom rate of taxation of dividend income (nil under section 80 L of Income Tax Act upto Rs. 10000) is lower than the tax on capital gains (20%). Further, the rich individuals can purchase units of suitable close ended mutual fund schemes in such a way that the dividend income accuring to mutual funds accrues to them as capital gains at the end of the scheme at the time of redemption of units. This brings to them the opportunity of brining tax rate on their complete returns down to the tax rate on capital gains. Thus in the long run the returns would not differ due to tax differentials and T will be zero after all the aforementioned arbitrage avenues are exhausted by the relevant market players. Secondly, Black and Scholes (1974) argue that firms would adjust their dividend policies to supply the levels of dividend yields that are most in demand. Through this mechanism the firms could increase their current prices and fill the demand for higher or lower payout securities. Thus supply of securities at each level of dividend yield will correspond to the demand at that level and no firm will able to influence its stock prices favourably by changing its dividend payout ratio (or dividend yield). Thus dividend yield is "not a factor in CAPM.

These three arguments together imply that equation (3.3) will take the form.

$$\overline{R}_i = R_f + (\overline{R}_m - R_f).\beta_i \qquad (3.4)$$

which is the standard CAPM form. Thus taxation does not affect the basic return generation process as prescribed in CAPM and one can expect zero beta 'CAPM to hold in a situation where risk free borrowing and lending is not allowed.

Applying CAPM to Equity Prices

A number of researchers have applied CAPM for studying return generation process of equity prices in the stock markets but such studies have not been conducted to any significant extent on Indian Stock market. The two factor CAPM expressed as [refer to equation (1)]

$$\overline{R}_i = \overline{R}_z + (\overline{R}_m - \overline{R}_z).\beta_i$$

In this equation all variables are expressed as expected future values and the relevant beta is also future beta on security "i". As the data on expected return is not available most of the researchers have used ex-post or realised returns for the variables for period t as a proxy to the future expected (ex-ante) returns for period "t+ 1". This has been defended on the grounds that, in the long run, expectations are, on an average, correct. Mathematically, the same defence can be expressed as follows: Market model says (assuming time variation in constant term).

$$R_{it} = \alpha_{it} + \beta R_{mt} + e_{if} \quad \text{.......... (3.5)}$$

Therefore, taking expected values (over a number of observation) for each period.

$$E(R_{it}) = \alpha_{it} + \beta_j E(R_{mt}) \quad \text{.......... (3.6)}$$

because $E(e_{it}) = 0$

substituting the value of it α_{it}, from equation (6) into equation (3.5), we get

$$R_{it} = E(R_{it}) + \beta_i [R_{mt} - E(R_{mt}) + e_{it}, \quad \text{.......... (3.7)}$$

Zero beta CAPM with time varying zero-beta returns is

$$E(R_{it}) = R_{zt} + [E(R_{mt}) - R_{zt}] \beta_i \quad \text{.......... (3.8)}$$

Substituting value of $E(R_{it})$ from (3.8) into (3.7) we get

$$R_{it} = R_{zt} + [R_{mt} - R_{zt}] \beta_i$$

Testing this model with ex-post data is a test of the following hypothesis simultaneously

a) The market model holds in every period.
b) The Zero beta CAPM holds in every period.
c) The beta is stable over time.

Such a test involves computation of realised returns on various securities and the market portfolio (represented by suitable equity price index) for various time periods.

Tests of CAPM Applicability

The capital asset pricing model (CAPM) is popular model

explaining phenomena observed in capital markets for risky assets. The CAPM is widely accepted because of the evident appeal of the equilibrium linear relation between expected return $E(R_j)$ and risk established by the model. It is this pricing relationship which empirical researches have attempted to test. Most of the tests conducted for applicability of CAPM to capital market have been in U.S.A. Consequently, it is the data on equities quoted on New York Stock Exchange (NYSE), American Stock Exchange (AMEX) and over the Counter Stock Exchange of U.S.A. (NASDAQ) that has been used. Most of the studies use the data base of Centre for research in Security Prices (CRSP) at University of Chicago for this purpose. Some efforts have also been made in this direction in other countries like Japan, Germany, U.K., Spain, South Korea, Luxembourg and Canada.

One of the early attempts to test applicability of CAPM to the equity prices of U.S. Capital markets was made by Black, Jensons & Scholes (1972) (hereafter BJS) who conducted time series and cross sectional tests of CAPM using NYSE listed stocks. They used standard CAPM model of the form

$$R_{it} = R_{ft} + \alpha_i + \beta_i (R_{mt} - R_{ft}) + e_{it} \quad \text{......} (3.9)$$

They used thirty five overlapping five year time periods from 1926 to 1964 and ran cross sectional regressions for one year period each. Both the time series regressions and cross sectional regressions were run on portfolios of securities rather than individual securities to take care of the statistical problems arising in individual security regressions due to large error terms. These error terms decreased significantly by formation of portfolios to which CAPM still applied without any dilution of conceptual requirements. These portfolios were formed by arranging all individual securities in ascending order of their estimated betas and then making portfolios based on fractiles. This procedure ensured a good spread of betas of each of the portfolios fairly closely reflected by their estimated betas). There was a possibility of introduction of bias due to grouping of high (estimated) beta securities together and vice-versa but, it was taken care of by forming portfolios from previous year's regression data and computing betas for cross sectional regressions for the years following the prior estimation period. The security "i" was represented by portfolio "i" in equation (3.9). BJS used 10 portfolios and found that a_j's were significantly more than zero or less than zero and the coefficient of b_i's in cross-sectional regressions were significantly less or more than $(R_{mt}-R_{ft})$ respectively for each period. They concluded that this is an evidence for applicability of zero beta model which would rectify this model mis specification.

Fama & Mabeth (1973) (hereafter FM) estimated the following equation 3.10

$$R_{it} = g_{ot} + g_{1t} .\beta(t-1) + g_{2t}.\hat{\beta}_i (t-1)^2 + g_{3t}.\hat{s}e_i (t-1) + s_{it} \text{ .... } (3.10)$$

where Rit denotes the return on portfolio i in month t, $\hat{\beta}$, (t–1) is the estimated beta for portfolio i in month t–1, $\hat{S}$e, (t–1) is the estimated residual standard deviation for portfolio i in month t-1 using the market model, and δit is the unexplained residual return for month t, upon obtaining 402 estimates for g_{0t}, g_{1t}, and g_{3t} FM used monthly returns of all common stocks traded on NYSE during the period 1926 to 1968 extracted from CRSP database on returns. Twenty equally weighted portfolios were made out of those stocks. The procedure followed for portfolio creation was similar to that used by BJS. Test of equation (3.10) by FM amounts to the test of two-factor (or zero beta) CAPM. FM tested this equation for three conditions namely (C1) linearity of relationship between R_{it} and $\beta_i(t-1)$ (C2) non-significance of g_{2t} and g_{3t} to support that no other measure of risk is relevant in return generation process and (C3). Risk aversion of investors i.e. $g_{11} > 0$ [corresponding to $(R_{mt}-R_{zt}) > 0$]. FM found evidence in favour of two factor CAPM for which all the three conditions C1-C3 were found to be statistically true.

Blume and Friend (1973) conducted tests similar to those of FM on post World War II data using 5 year periods and NYSE listed common stock covering 1955-1968 making 12 portfolios of securities. They concluded that standard CAPM assumption about risk free rate did not hold but, two factor CAPM was applicable for their test period. However, the aspect of risk aversion (condetion (3 of FM) was not supported by their results. Gibbons (1982) tested applicability of CAPM, using the argument that CAPM, if it holds true, constrains the market model to

$$R_{it} = R_{zt}\ (1-\beta_t) + R_{mt}\ \beta_1 + e_{it}$$

which means that the constant term is constrained to be R_{zt} $(1+\ \beta_i)$ [or, R_{ft} $(1+\beta_i)$ for standard CAPM]. If CAPM holds then, Gibbsons argued, both the estimates of L_i and B_i without the contraint should be close to the estimates of α_i and β_i with constraint. Gibbson used seemingly unrelated regression model (SURM) for constrained estimation and then used likelihood ratio test to compare these with ordinary least square estimated of α_i and β_i. He used 10 different five years periods from January 1926 to December 1975 using monthly returns on NYSE listed stocks. 40 portfolios were made based on estimated betas for each of the 5 year periods and then the same 5 year period was used for estimate ai, bi and applying likelihood ratio test for each portfolio. Based on those tests Gibbons ruled out applicability of both standard form and two-factor form of CAPM to NYSE.

Stambaugh (1982) tested applicability of CAPM using similar procedure as Gibbsons but broader market proxies. He used Lagrangian multiplier (LM) tests instead of likelihood ratio test used by Gibbson. He found that likelihood ratio test tends to reject the null hypothesis too often and and particularly when the number of securities (or portfolios) is too large. He concluded that standard version of CAPM is applicable to NYSE for a wide range of market proxy

Jobson and Korkie (1982) confirmed the findings of Stambaugh regarding likelihood ratio test and concluded that two factor CAPM, is applicable to NYSE.

In a recent test of applicability of CAPM, Fama and French (1992) using CRSP data on NYSE, AMEX and NASDAQ listed equities for 1962-1989 concluded that beta has no power to explain average returns of individual equities. They used CRSP value-weighted portfolio return as the market proxy They used 100 portfolios construced on the basis of beta values and size of firm to remove the effect of size and beta in their analysis. They also conclude that size of the firm and book-to-market value of equity have a stronger role in explaining average returns and when the variation due to these factors is removed from the returns of equities, beta does not explain the remaining variation. But, their statistical interpretation of average coefficient of beta in regression runs which is the basis of aforementioned conclusions leaves some doubts about their conclusions. The findings of Fama and French are contrary to that of Chen, Roll and Ross (1986) who found a non -zero cross -sectional mean return - beta relation in a univariate test. They also used both value - weighted and equally - weighted NYSE listed indices. Lakonishok and Shapiro (1986) also find that the coefficient of beta generally has the correct sign across various sub-periods though it is not statistically significant.

On the other hand, the more recent papers that reject the applicability of CAPM using various indices in the U.S. Capital market include Shanken (1985) who used NYSE equally weighted index as market proxy and zero beta model, Kandel and Stambaugh (1987 and 1989), Gibbsons, Ross, and Shanken (1989), Zhou (1991) and Mackinalay and Richardson (1991).

It is a possibility that the relationship between beta and average return (as predicted by CAPM) disappears in the more recent periods at U.S. Capital markets as suggested by

Fama and French (1992). Another possibility is that the indices used were not mean-variance efficient in these tests and therefore, inappropriate for being used as CAPM market proxies. This is the possibility which Roll and Ross (1994) have explored. They argue that "there should be some non-zero cross-sectional relation if the index is not too far inside the ex-ante efficient frontier even if it is statistically reliably inside". They conclude that cross-sectional ordinary least Square (OLS) relation is very sensitive to choice of an index and even the indices quite close to efficient frontier can produce different cross-sectional slopes. A generalised Least square (GLS) cross-sectional fit between expected return and beta renders the relation less subject to these 'Knife-edged properties'.

Roll (1977) had raised some doubts about various tests of CAPM as a theory using U.S. stock exchange data alone. His objections pertain to non-observability of true market portfolio on the return of which the CAPM is based. These objections are relevant if one is testing the validity of CAPM as a theory On the other hand if the purpose is only to study the utility of the model in return generation process in limited sense, one can use a reasonably representative market proxy which, if mean variance efficient can still be helpful in understanding return generation process even though market portfolio of CAPM cannot be observed. All the tests of CAPM using different market proxies in various capital markets can be viewed in this light. If one can identify a mean-variance efficient market proxy that explains return generation process in line with CAPM this serves the purpose (whether it is the market portfolio or not) and therefore, can be useful to the portfolio managers and investors.

Arbitrage Pricing Theory (APT)

APT was formulated by Ross (1976) as an alternative to the mean-variance CAPM. It is a plausible alternative to the simple one-factor CAPM because it agrees perfectly with what appears to be the intuition behind the CAPM. The differences between the CAPM and the APT are summarized below.

(i) While the CAPM has only one risk premium to compensate the bearing risks, the APT has several risk premia.

(ii) Under the CAPM, investors are assumed to be risk-averse individuals who maximize the expected utility of their end-of-period wealth, the APT requires no utility assumptions beyond monotonicity and concavity

(iii) The CAPM is confined to a single period, the APT is applicable to both multi -period and single-period cases.

(iv) Unlike the CAPM, the APT does not require either that the market portfolio' must play an important role in the return-generating model or that the market portfolio must be mean-variance efficient.

The basic assumptions behind the APT are as follows:

(i) There exists a perfectly competitive and friction less capital market.

(ii) Individuals have homogeneous beliefs that the random returns for the sets of assets being considered are governed by the linear K-factor model of the form:

$$R_i = E(R_i) + \beta_i 1F1 + \beta_i 2F2 + \text{———} + \beta_{ik} F_k + e_i \text{..........} (3.1)$$

Where,

asset i = 1, 2, ..., n

factor j = 1, 2, ..., k

R_i = random return on i-th asset. E (Ri) = expected return on j-th asset.

β_{ij} = sensitivity of j-th asset's return to movements in j-th common factor, i.e., factor loading.

F_j = mean zero j-th common factor to returns of all assets under consideration.

e_i = random mean zero noise term, reflecting any unsystematic risk for i-th asset.

(iii) The number of assets under consideration, i, must be greater than the number of Factors, j.

(iv) The noise term e_i, must be independent of all factors and of all error terms for other assets.

The important feature of the APT is that in equilibrium, all portfolios that contain no wealth and bear no risk will earn no return on average. Asset pricing theory states that the expected return vector, must be a linear combination of the constant vector and the coefficient vectors, i.e. for all i:

$$E(R_i)=(H)o+(H)1\,\beta_i 1+(H)2\,\beta_i 2+ \text{——} +(H)k\,\beta_i k \quad (3.2)$$

Where (H) j (for all j = 1 to k) represents the risk premium (more specifically, the price of risk) for the j-th factor in equilibrium.

The pricing relationship in equation (3.2) is the central conclusion of the APT The term 'arbitrage' in the APT comes from the simple proof that equation (3.1) implies equation (3.2) using absence of arbitrage alone, for the case in which all the e_i are identically mean zero. If all the e_i were identically mean zero and the linear condition in equation (3.2) did not hold, there would be two portfolios with the same factor loadings but different expected returns. Consequently one could go long on a portfolio that had a higher expected return while financing it by shorting another portfolio with a lower expected return, thus taking advantage of an arbitrage opportunity

A major problem with APT has been that it does not identify theoretically the factors that determine the return generation process. In majority of the empirical tests of APT these factors have been identified as groups (or portfolios) of equities using statistical technique of Factor analysis. But, such definition of factors do not help in predicting the future behaviour of these factors because the economic meaning of these statistical entities still remains ambiguous. In a few studies efforts have been made to identity these factors as economic entities but in the absence of a theoretical basis for the same the efforts have not met with a significant level of success.

Pherwani Committee Recommendations on Valuation of Shares

The Pherwani Committee set up by the Central Government have summarised the principal objectives of valuation guidelines as under:

(1) The principal objective of stipulating guidelines in relation to valuation of shares is necessarily investor protection. Thus, CCI interface need not extend to areas where public interest is not germane to the issue.

(2) The valuation Guidelines would also need to be fair to the issuer in terms of the issue price.

(3) An ancillary objective is the inhibition of malpractices attendant to the issue of securities, especially in terms of unfair advantage taken by either management or the principal shareholders.

The recommendation of the Committee are given as under

(i) *Conceptual limitations of exiting guidelines*:- The guidelines do not wholly take into account the intrinsic characteristic of each company/industry and/or market conditions prevailing at the time of issue. Thus, the fair value determined has little relation to the market price of the share.

As the premia historically permitted have been substantially below market price, the new shareholders have benefitted at the expense of existing shareholders.

The formula adopted differs in relation to equity issues and convertible debenture issues, resulting in a higher premium being permitted in the case of convertible debenture issues.

(ii) *Practical limitations of existing valuation norms:-* The major components of the existing valuation procedure are:

(a) Book Value

(b) Profit earning capacity value (PECV).

Statistically there appears to be a weak relationship between the book value and the market price of a share. For instance, while the market places a premium on companies with an active bonus policy, the net asset value method works against the interest of such companies.

Presently, the PECV is determined by normally applying a capitalisation rate of 15%. Where the issue price varies significantly from average market price, a graded capitalisation up to 8% is used. However, the valuation norms ignore the considerable variations that exist in the P/E (price earning) ratio across corporates and industries.

The average *P/E* ratio of the market has shown a considerable uptrend in the last few years. At present, the P/E ratio ranges between 15 and 25 across a wide spectrum of industries. The capitalisation rate adopted by the existing guidelines is therefore at variance with market valuation.

(iii) *International practice:-* The international practice is for the regulators to approve the disclosure of information made by companies in their prospectus. Pricing of issues is left to market forces, with the scrip being valued by underwriters/ merchant bankers. The principal bench-mark used for pricing is the market price of the scrip in the case of listed companies. In such issues, the underwriters price new issues at a discount of 10% to 20% to prevailing market price, in order to render the issue attractive to prospective investors.

Until recently, India, Pakistan and Bangladesh were the sole countries where the valuation and pricing of new share issues was under taken by regulators. Pakistan had recently abolished statutorily controlled pricing. In, India controlled pricing of share issues has been done away with under the new guidelines envisaging free pricing of securities.

(iv) Available policy alternatives:-

The study Group having received the feed-back opined that there is clearly a need for effecting changes in existing policy and guidelines relating to the valuation of shares, by adopting a market oriented approach. The study Group recommended that ultimately market forces be allowed to determine premia on primary market issues.

The study Group recommended unanimously that besides having SEBI function as the apex monitoring agency, the principles of self-regulation would need to be developed amongst merchant bankers, underwriters, bankers and other participants in the primary market.

The study group also felt it necessary to evolve a system of disclosure of financial information including associated risks where by prospective investors are able to analyse the investment opportunity effectively False statements would be subject to civil and criminal prosecutions.

In view of the above, the study Group had expressed the following two policy alternatives:

(a) Government may immediately opt for total deregulation, and leave the pricing mechanism to the market. Under such a scenario, companies and / or merchant bankers would have complete freedom to price issues based on their perception of the market conditions, etc.

(b) The liberalization process may be carried out in stages, total deregulation may be immediately considered in respect of ail issues of securities where the interest of the eternal public is not involved. In other cases, the pricing process may be made market-oriented in the first stage. Once the set of conditions like appropriate statutory and self-regulatory mechanisms, liquidity of markets both in terms of depth and breadth, rating agencies, etc. are put in place, total deregulation may be effected by allowing the market forces to determine premia on all primary market issues.

Pricing

Based on *the recommendation of Pherwani Committee, the valuation should be based on the following norms:*

(i) The average market price of the preceding six months: The average market price would be calculated using the monthly high / low over the relevant period, and

(ii) The price earning value, based on the actual profit after tax calculated as per existing CCI guidelines (but including actual tax rate), capitalised at the range of rates detailed below. The P/E range relates to the actual based on the last audited annual accounts:

P/E Range	Capitalisaion Rate
Below 4	15%
For a one point increase in P/E	Reduction in capitalisation rate on a pro-rata basis by a factor of 0.7
Above 20	4%

For the purpose of calculating, the actual P/E should be

rounded off to nearest whole number. An illustrative calculation of the issue price cap is given below. A detailed calculation of the issue price cap using the proposed formula is given below:

Valuation Procedure

1. Six months average price has been calculated on the basis of high and low price for each month from April to September, 1991.

Period: April 1991 to September 1991

Month	*High*	*Low*	*Average*
April	156.25	138.00	137.13
May	142.50	126.25	134.38
June	138.75	123.75	131.25
July	161.25	125.00	143.13
August	198.75	155.00	176.88
September	182.50	160.00	171.25

Half yearly average 151.38

2. Based on the price averages for the last six months, the average of 6 months is calculated. EPS for the year 1990 -91 is taken as the basis for calculating the rate at which the EPS is to be capitalised. Issue price is calculated by taking the average of the capitalised earnings and of the simple average of the yearly price averages.

1990-91

	E.P.S.	Avg.Mkt. price Rs.	P/E	Cap. Rate (1)	P.E. price	Issue price
Scrip	A	B	C = (B/A)	D	E= (A/Dx100)	F= (B+ E)/2
Century Textiles	193.43	3878.65	20.05	4	4835.75	4357..20

3. In case of the companies making issues in a ratio greater than 1: 1 the following discount should be applied on the issue price arrived at by the above formula in order to arrive at an appropriate issue price.

Issue Size	Discount rate
1 : 1 > x < = 2 : 1	20%
2 : 1 > x < = 3 : 1	30%
3 : 1 > x < = 4 : 1	40%
4 : 01 : 1 and above	50%

Large Issues

(iii) In the case of companies which have issued bonus or rights in the preceding two years the average market price would need to be suitably adjusted retrospectively in the same ratio. An illustrative calculation of the issue price cap in the case of bonus / rights is given below. A detailed calculation of the issue the proposed formula in the case of bonus or rights is given as under:

Valuation procedure in the Case of Bonus Issue

1. Six months average price has been calculated on the basis of high and low price for each month from April to September, 1991. Period: April 1991 to September 1991

Month	*High*	*Low*	*Average*
April	4950.00	4475.00	4712.50
May	5340.00	4900.00	5120.00
June	5425.00	5090.00	5257.00
July	6950.00	5300.00	6125.00
August	7450.00	6500.00	6975.00
September	9050.00	5650.00	7350.00

Six monthly average 5923.33

2. Century textiles issued bonus in ratio of 3: 5. Century textiles, monthly high-low market prices adjusted in the ratio of the bonus issues.

Period: April 1991 to September, 1991

Month	*High*	*Low*	*Average*
April	3093.75	2796.88	2945.31
May	3337.50	3062.50	3200.00
June	3390.63	3181.25	3285.94
July	4343.75	3312.50	3828.13
August	4656.25	4062.50	4359.38
Sept.	5656.25	5650.00	5653.13

Six monthly Average 3878.65

N.B. Prices are ex-bonus.

3. Based on the price average for six months and the EPS for the year 1990-91 the issue price is calculated. Issue price is calculated by taking the average of the capitalised earnings and of the simple average of the six monthly price average of the six monthly price average.

The following table illustrates how the issue price of Century Textiles is calculated.

1990-91

	E.P.S.	Avg.Mkt. price Rs.	P/E	Cap. Rate	P.E. price	Issue price
Scrip	A	B	C= (B/A)	D	E= (A/Dx100)	F= (B+ E) /2
Century Textiles	193.43	3878.65	20.05	4.00	4835.75	4357..20

4. In case of companies making issues in a ratio greater than 1: 1, the following discount rates, should be applied on the issue price arrived at the above formula in order to arrive at an appropriate issue price.

Issue Size	*Discount Rate*
1 : 1: 1 > x < =2 : 1	20%
2 : 1 > x < = 3 : 1	30%
3 : 1 > x < = 4 : 1	40%
4 : 0 1 : 1 and above	50%

Source: Summary of recommendations-August 31, 1991: Study group for Guidelines relating to valuation and new instruments.

(iv) In the case of companies making issues whether public or rights of equities or convertible debentures in ratio greater than 1: 1, the substantial increase in the floating stock would necessarily have an impact on market price. Consequently, the study Group recommends that the following discount rates be applied on the price as derived by the above formula in order to arrive at an appropriate issue price:

Issue Size	*Discount Rate*
Greater than 1: 1 but less than 2: 1	20%
Greater than 2: 1 but less than 3: 1	30%
Greater than 3: 1 but less than 4: 1	40%
Greater than 4: 1 and above	50%

Illustration 1: Case where the company has not increased its capital base in the preceding 2 years.

The calculation of the fair price cap would be as follows:

(a) Average market price: Monthly average for the previous six months are calculated taking the monthly high / low averages.

For example the yearly averages for Kirloskar Cummins are as follows:

April 1991 to September 1991: Rs. 151.38 Average Market price: Rs. 151.38

(B) The price Earning value:- Based on the price average and the EPS, the P/E for the period is calculated. The capitalistion rate as per the table above is then selected based on the P/E. The price Earning value for the company is then calculated using the applicable capitalisation rate and the EPS. For example, the calculation of the PEV for Kirloskar Cummins as follows:

1990-91

EPS:	Rs. 7.21
Average market price:	Rs. 151.38
P/E:	Rs. 21.00
Capitalisation:	4%
PEV price based on above:	Rs. 180.25
Issue price Cap:	Rs. 165.82

(Average of PEV price and Average market price)

Illustration II: Case where the company has increased capital during preceding 6 months

(a) Century textiles issued a bonus in the ratio 3: 5 in September 1991. For purposes of calculating the average market price, prices in the preceding months were converted to ex-bonus in the same ratio:

Average Market price: Rs. 3878.65

(b) 1990-91

EPS:	Rs. 193.43
Average market price:	Rs. 3878.65
P/E:	Rs. 20.05

Capitalisation:	4%
PEV price based on above:	Rs. 4835.75
Issue price Cap:	Rs. 4357.20

(Average of PEV price and 80% of Average Market Price)

Time was, when a company had to go through a cubersome process before going to the public, and that too at an issue price far below its intrinsic worth.

4

Model for Pricing Issues: Conceptual Framework

After the emergence of free pricing, companies are charging premium invariably on future earnings despite the comprehensive guidelines on Disclosure and Investor protection with reference to free pricing of Issue formulated by SEBI. The idea of formulating the guidelines is to ensure sufficient disclosure to prospective shareholders to evaluate the pricing of issue. To take advantage of the opportunity, a plethora of rights and public issue flooded the market during the period 1992-1993 to 1994-1995. This can be observed from the details given below.

Amount Raised

Period	*Public Issues*		*Right Issues*		*Total*	
	Nos.	*Amount (Rs. in crores)*	*Nos.*	*Amount (Rs. in crores)*	*Nos.*	*Amount (Rs. in crores)*
1990-91	141	1704	209	2250	350	3954
1991-92	196	1711	316	3851	512	5562
1992-93	528	6061	488	12630	1016	18691
1993-94	770	12544	384	9306	1154	21850
1994-95	1343	13312	530	6364	1973	19676

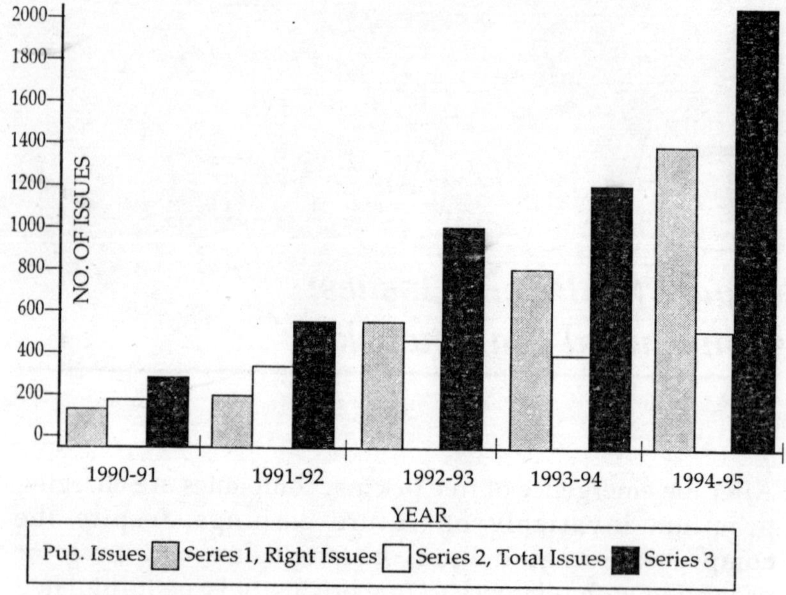

Distribution Analysis by Issue Size: Public

Issue Size (Rs. in crores)	*1994-95*		*1993-94*	
	No. of Issues	*Amount (Rs. in*	*No. of Issues crores)*	*Amount (Rs. in crores)*
a -Below 1	59	45.80	12	8.37
b-1-2	246	377.31	44	72.84
c-2-3	355	806.05	203	494.73
d-3-4	223	757.24	157	532.12
e-4-5	118	517	79	354.79
f-5- 10	197	1352.37	153	1020.59
g-Above 10	165	9455.83	122	10060.60
Total	1343	13311.60	770	12544.04

The role of merchant banker in the entire exercise has increased tremendously in the era of free pricing of issues. The merchant bankers are required to fix the premium on the new issues keeping in view various parameters that determine the share price of a company. The premium assessed by die

1994-95

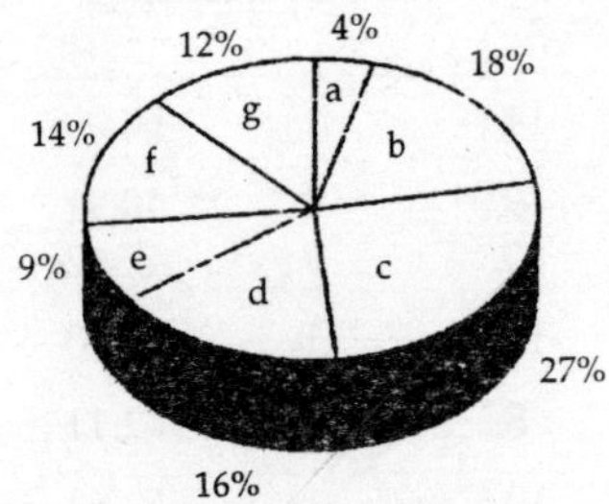

No. of Issues

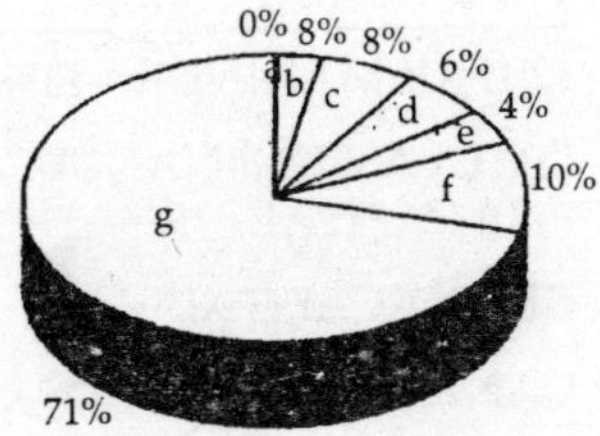

Amount of Issues

1993-94

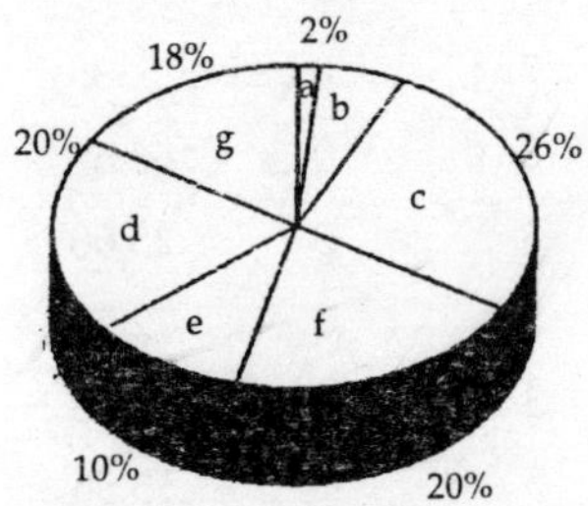

No. of Issues

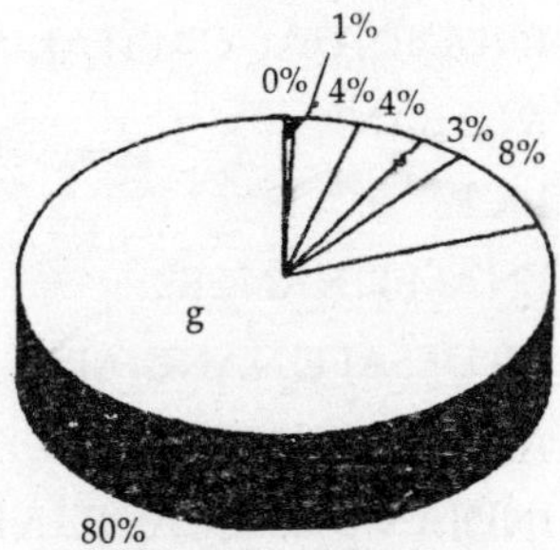

Amount of Issues

Merchant bankers is to be justified to SEBI. Justification of premium is basically based on subjective assessment as there is no specific model to determine the premium on new issues. The data given below indicates that most of merchant bankers have not been able to fairly fix up the premium on issues managed by them.

Merchant Banker	*Total Premium Issues managed*	*No. of Issues Quoted above issue price*	*No. of Issues Quoted below issue price*	*No Gain or Loss Percen- age*	*No. of Issues Quoting below issue price*
1	2	3	4	5	6
SBI CAPITAL	65	21	40	4	61.54
ICICI SECURITIES	40	16	23	1	57.50
IDBI	32	16	15	1	46.88
BANK OF BARODA	31	16	12	3	23.71

1 2	3	4	5	6	
KOTAK MAHINDRA FIN.	28	13	14	1	50.00
ITC CLASSIC FINANCE	22	11	9	2	40.91
PNB CAPITAL	21	11	10	0	47.62
CREDIT CAPITAL	20	5	14	1	70.00
CANARA BANK	19	10	8	1	42.11
DSP FINANCE	19	8	10	1	52.63
BOI FINANCE	14	7	7	0	50.00
PRUDENTIAL CAPITAL	14	9	5	0	35.71
IND BANK	13	6	7	0	5385
IFCI	12	4	8	0	66.67
ENAM FINANCE	12	9	3	0	25.00
VB DESAI FINANCIAL	11	3	8	0	72.73
APPLE INDUSTRIES	9	6	3	0	33.33
INDIAN OVERSEAS BANK	9	3	5	1	55.56
UNION BANK	9	4	5	0	55.56
HB PORTFOLIO LEASING	8	3	5	0	62.50
INDIA-SECURITIES	8	4	4	0	50.00
CENTRAL BANK	7	3	3	1	42.86
IND GLOBAL FINANCE	7	2	5	0	71.43
LLOYD FINANCE	7	2	5	0	71.43
TIMES GUARANTEE	7	4	2	1	28.57
VIDEOCON LEASING	7	0	7	0	100.00
ANAGRAM FINANCE	6	3	3	0	50.00
HMG FINANCIAL	6	4	2	0	33.33
ONIDA FINANCE	6	2	3	1	50.00
PRIME SECURITIES	6	6	0	0	0.00
RELIANCE CAPITAL	6	2	4	0	66.67
CRB CAPITAL	5	2	2	1	40.00
DENA BANK	5	3	2	0	60.00

1 2	3	4	5	6	
EMPIRE FINANCE	4	2	1	1	25.00
SMIFS CAPITAL	4	0	4	0	100.00
21st CENTURY MANAG.	3	1	2	0	66.67
ALLIANZ CAPITAL	3	2	1	0	33.33
ANZ GRINDLAYS BANK	3	2	1	0	33.33
DOOGAR & ASSOCIATES	3	2	1	0	33.33
FEDERAL RANK	3	2	1	0	33.33
IL & FS	3	2	1	1	33.33
LKP MERCHANT FINANCE	3	2	1	0	33.33
VLS FINANCE	3	2	1	0	33.33
20TH CENTURY FINANCE	2	1	1	0	50.00
ALPIC FINANCE	2	2	0	0	0.00
AMERICAN EXPRESS BANK	2	1	1	0	50.00
CEAT FINANCE	2	1	1	0	50.00
KGMC FINANCIAL	2	1	1	0	50.00
MAYAR FINANCE	2	1	1	0	50.00
MEFCOM CAPITAL	2	2	0	0	0.00
NAGARJUNA FINANCE	2	2	0	0	0.00
PN VIJAY FINANCIAL	2	2	0	0	0.00
SRF FINANCE	2	1	1	0	50.00
STATE BANK OF BIKANER	2	2	0	0	0.00
STATE BANK OF HYD.	2	1	1	0	50.00
STATE BANK OF PATIALA	2	0	2	0	100.00
VYSYA BANK	2	1	0	1	0.00
ASHOK LEYLAND INVEST	1	0	1	0	100.00
ANDHRA BANK	1	0	1	0	100.00
BIRLA GLOBAL FINANCE	1	0	1	0	100.00
CITI BANK	1	0	1	0	100.00
CIFCO	1	0	1	0	100.00
DSJ FINANCE	1	0	1	0	100.00
CORPORATION BANK	1	1	0	0	0.00
DCL FINANCE	1	1	0	0	0.00

1	2	3	4	5	6
FORTUNE FINANCIAL	1	1	0	0	0.00
HSIDC	1	1	0	0	0.00
INDUSIN BANK	1	1	0	0	0.00
KARNATAKA BANK	1	0	1	0	100.00
LAKSHMI VILAS BANK	1	1	0	0	0.00
LEBORD FINANCE	1	1	0	0	0.00
MAFAT LAL FINANCE	1	1	0	0	0.00
MEHTA INTEGRATED FIN.	1	1	0	0	0.00
ORIENTAL BANK	1	1	0	0	0.00
VARDHMAN LEASING	1	1	0	0	0.00
SM FINANCE	1	0	1	0	100.00
TATA FINANCIAL	1	0	1	0	100.00
UNITED BANK	1	0	1	0	100.00
SYNDICATE BANK	1	0	1	0	100.00
RAJASHREE FISCAL	1	0	1	0	100.00

Source: The Merchang Banker Update, July 1995

DETAILS REGARDING RIGHT ISSUES

Companies	*Lead Manager*	*Issue Price*	*Date of Opening*	*Post-Issue Price*
NAGARJUNA	JMF	30	9-9-92	25
RATHI ALLOYS	ANZ/HB PORT.	30	11-9-92	26
FINALEX PIPES	ICICI/JMF/SBI/BOB	40	11-9-92	38
ADARSH CHEMICAL	SBI	30	16-9-92	24
PREMIER HOUSING	INDB/BOB	25	16-9-92	25
PATHEJA FINANCE	ICICI/PNB	90	23-9-92	87
VISAKA INDUSTRIES	SBI	35	12-10-92	30
KAKATIYA CEMENT	ICICI	50	16-10-92	47
PARASRAM PURIA SYNTHETICS	ICICI/IFCI/PNB	75	24-10-92	64
GUJARAT LEASE FIN	SCICI/BOB	80	30.10.92	72
KAVERI ENGG. IND.	IND. GL./SAFE	35	4-11-92	27

It appears from the data that merchant bankers preferred to suggest high premium as this would enable them to attract more business. The companies also look for the highest possible premium as it leads to outflow of less equity shares and thereby less dilution of control. In the post free pricing period, the managements have generally opted for a market-related issue price in case of further issues and in most cases indulged in share price rigging prior to the issue to charge unjustifiably high premium on the basis of the ruling market price and optimistic future working projections. The companies in which the promoters have majority of stake in the pre-issue equity capital carries with a public cum right issue so as to maintain their control in the management of the company. For example, in case of Padmini Polymers Ltd., the Company came out with public cum right issue with an offer price of Rs. 200 for the public issue and Rs. 40 for the right issue so that the management could maintain its control in the company without investing large money in the public issue.

Companies are keen on higher premium to get more capital at cheap rates reducing overall cost of capital but SEBI Guidelines require the issuer company to provide justification for the price in the offer document. Now the companies have complete freedom to raise funds to meet their business requirements. There is no restriction on the purposes for which the funds are raised as long as complete disclosures have been made by the companies approaching capital market.

The following facts have been observed after the emergence of free pricing

* Tendency of corporate management to raise funds without any correlation with the credential of the company.
* No restriction on the use of funds raised from the securities market.

* Maturity of decision making at the level of investors in evaluation of investment proposal in new issue markets.

Traditionally, the merchant bankers were willing to ask for as much premium as much desired by the company since CCI used to be the ultimate deciding authority and therefore the merchant bankers were not supposed to observe as much responsibility as required by them nowadays. In the free pricing era the merchant bankers will have to take greater diligence. They would have to critically appraise projects in terms of its profitability and play a decisive role in pricing of issues. Their credibility and reputation would be at a stake and this would keep them alert. The merchant bankers would not be able to escape their responsibilities for long. They will have to excercise their full diligence, prudence and experience while pricing an issue so that their credibility and reputation can be built up and maintained in the capital market. They should base their pricing on financial and technical analysis of the company as well as industries. This will lead to reasonable and fair pricing of issue which will generate confidence of investors on merchant banker. The performance of the top five merchant banker in the terms of number of issues and amount of issues managed by them is displayed below for the period 1994-95 and 1993-94.

Merchant Bankers: Ranking by no. of issues

	1994-95		*1993-94*	
Rank	*Public Issue*	*Right Issue*	*Public Issue*	*Right Issue*
1	SBI Caps	SBI Caps	SBI Caps	I-Sec
2	BOB	I-Sec	I-Sec	SBI Caps
3	Prudential Caps	IDBI	PNB Caps	IDBI
4	Canara Bank	PNB Caps	BOB	JM Fics
5	PNB Cap	JMFics	Ind Bank	DSP

In case of free pricing, supply and demand forces determine the fair price for an issue provided full information is available to investor with complete disclosure by the company about promoters status. Industries Status, Company specific fundamentals, future growth prospects in the changing economic environment and government policy frame work. These factors should be taken into account by the merchant banker while advising the company on fixing premium for the issue. In those cases where proper information desired for interpretation is not available to investors, the merchant banker should not involve themselves in such issues. Investor would excercise their own judgement and accept what is fair and reject the unreasonable part of game.

Merchant Bankers: Ranking by Issue Amount

	1994-95		*1993-94*	
Rank	*Public*	*Right Issue*	*Public Issue*	*Right Issue*
Issue				
1	SBI Caps	SBI Caps	SBI Caps	I-Sec
2	I-Sec	I-Sec	I-Sec	SBI Caps
3	JM Fics	IDBI	IDBI	DSP
4	IDBI	Canara Bank	JM Fics	IDBI
5	DSP	JM Fics	Enam	JM Fics

Thus, the role of merchant banker needs to be modified and more responsibility is required to be laid down on them for consequences relating to unfair valuation of premium.

The interaction with the various primary market intermediaries and their responses to the questionnaire prepared for the research helped in finding out various factors being considered in estimating the premium on new issues of company. *Various primary market intermediaries interacted for making broader estimate of premium calculation are listed below.*

1. ITC Classic Finance Ltd.
2. Master Trust Ltd.
3. Lloyds Finance Ltd.
4. Sunrise Securities Ltd.
5. Onida Finance Ltd.
6. Apple Industries Ltd.
7. First Capital India Ltd.
8. K.M. Capital Ltd.
9. Escorts Finance Ltd.
10. Dabur Finance Ltd.
11. Vijaya Bank Ltd.
12. IFCI
13. Prime Securities Ltd.
14. Western India Securities Ltd.
15. PNB Capital Services Ltd.
16. SBI Capital Markets Ltd.

It was found that almost all the merchant bankers who have been interacted for the research suggested the following parameters for estimating the premium on new issue of company.

1. Promoter's Stake in the Issue
2. Size of the Issue.
3. Past performance of a Company
4. Projected Earning per share
5. Book value per share of a company
6. Performance and growth potential of industry.

The factors which determine the premium of the new issue, could be broadly classified into qualitative and quantitative nature. These are discussed in detail below:

QUALITATIVE FACTORS

These are the factors for which a merchant banker acting a lead manager to the issue has to make subjective assessment or in other words we may say that their effect in estimating the premium cannot be incorporated through quantitative mode. Various qualificative factor mentioned by different merchant bankers are as under:

1. Timing of the Issue
2. Brand name of the product being manufactured by the company
3. Promoter's track record.
4. Time gap between allotment of shares and accrual of profit from the proposed plan in the issue.
5. State of secondary market during the time when the issue would be kept open for public subscription.

The relationship between these factors and the premium on new issue is discussed in detail as under:

TIMING OF THE ISSUE

As it has already been mentioned that the merchant bankers are inclined for the highest possible premium by presenting rosy picture of the company to the Investors. Therefore they advise the companies to plan their issues during the period when investors are having with enough funds or have an ability to spare their funds for investment in primary market i.e. during Diwali period when employees of most of the companies are provided with bonus or some other gratituous payment from their employer. Thus, availability of funds with common investors is ensured.

Secondly they also prefer to keep the subscription of shares open during the period when no other issue which is likely to get better support from investors is due to open."

For example, when IDBI came out with mega public issue, most of the issues in the primary market during the same period could not be properly subscribed. Similarly, when L&T and TISCO simultaneously entered the primary market with their mega bend Issue, none of the two could be subscribed. Thus the merchant bankers consider time of the issue as important parameter to enable company to raise funds from primary market comfortably.

However, the discretion of merchant banker on time of opening of subscription list is limited as the issue must be opened up before the expiry of three months from the date of SEBI acknowledgment card. If a company fails to comply with the necessary formalities required to be done after receiving SEBI Acknowledgement Card and finally is not able to open the issue before the expiry of three months of SEBI Acknowledgement

Card, then it has to again approach SEBI for seeking fresh approval of the issue which is a tedious task for any company.

BRAND NAME OF THE PRODUCT

A company whose products have got well developed market can easily generate huge profits after undertaking any modernisation/diversification programme. However in case of companies which have product not well known to the market has to make additional efforts in developing market for their product and to overcome the competitive force of their competitors. The companies having well known products are in better position to convince the investors regarding the projected profitability made in their prospectus. In certain cases a company may have strong fundamental but if its product is not very well known to the market it may face difficulty on fixing higher premium and may have to satisfiy itself with lower amount of premium. It has been observed that the merchant bankers take into account the popularity of the company and its products. while deciding the premium on the issues. The name or photograph of the product is boldly highlighted on the prospectus of the company to attract the common investors and to display the nexus between company and product. Thus it is concluded that the reputed name of the company and its product helps in inflating the amount of premium.

PROMOTERS' TRACK RECORDS

The track record of promotor has got dose relationship with the amount of premium to be charged. The experience of promoters is highlighted in the prospectus with the view to inform investors about the preciseness and certainities related with the projected profitability of the company. The investors perceive higher risks in case of inexperienced promoters as compared to the ones having large experience. It is felt that the experienced promoters have better idea about the ways to increase profit margin by decreasing expenses per unit and increasing sales price per unit. The promoters track records also encompasses the educational background of the promoters. The promoters having educational background which may facilitate them in executing operation proposed to be undertaken by a company are preferred by investors. The success of the project is linked with track record of promoter. The investors normally avoid to put their funds in the issue of a company which is starting with a project in which promoters have lack of experience.

In view of the aforesaid reasons the merchant banker charges higher premium in case of issues where promoters have vast experience and adequate academic background in relation to the activities to be under taken by a company.

TIME GAP BETWEEN ALLOTMENT OF SHARES AND ACCRUAL OF PROFIT FROM THE PROPOSED PLAN

The time gap between allotment of shares and accrual of

the profit from the proposed project is another important consideration which the merchant banker have to keep in mind while deciding the amount of premium. It has been observed that where the profits from the proposed plan are likely to accrue after considerable period of time, the merchant banker may have to adopt conservative approach while fixing the amount of premium. This is due to the fact that impact of additional profits would not be reflected in the initial period of projected profitability. However the expenses during the same period would be comparatively higher than those which would occur in the later years. Therefore, the companies where the time gap is small, the premium charged would be more compared to those where same time gap is large. Moreover in case of large time gap, the uncertainties relating to timely commencement of production and preciseness of projections also get enhanced. Therefore, the merchant bankers fix higher premium in case of companies where the profits of the proposed plan are likely to accrue within short period after the allotment of shares.

STATE OF SECONDARY MARKET DURING THE TIME WHEN THE ISSUE WOULD BE KEPT OPEN FOR PUBLIC SUBSCRIPTION

The state of secondary market also plays a vital role in subscribing the issues of primary market. The merchant bankers face difficulty in incorporating the impact of this variable on the amount of premium to be charged. They have to make a subjective assessment for it depending upon the prevailing state of the market and the economy. The problems of merchant bankers in this regard are worth considering since the procedure involved in the issue of shares is very lengthy. Only after three months of the ratification of the companies decision of premium by the shareholders at annual general meeting, or extraordinary general meeting, a rights issue can be opened. Similarly, in the case of public issues, the duration is two months. It is very difficult to forecast the lavements of share prices in India's imperfect stock market, three months in advance.

QUANTITATIVE FACTORS

There are certain factors which are expressed in quantitative terms and can be easily projected on the basis of past records available with a company. Some of the quantitative factors which are generally considered while pricing an issue by merchant bankers are listed below.

1. Promoter's stake in the post issued paid up capital.
2. Projected Earning per share.
3. Projected Book value of a share.
4. Size of an Issue.
5. Projected profitability of the Company.

PROMOTER'S STAKE

The promoter's stake refers to the quantity of shares to be held by promoters subsequent to the allotment of share to the public. It has been observed that the investors generally prefer those issue where the promoter's stake is high because the higher stake of promoter's reflects higher confidence of the promoter about the success of project. It also indicates higher responsibility of the promoters in the proposed project because the shares allotted to the promoters are subject to lock in period for a certain period depending upon different situation as required by SEBI guidelines in Disclosure and Investor protection. Hence, the higher promoter stake enables a company to charge higher premium. According to SEBI guidelines, the promoter stake cannot be less than 25% of the paid up equity capital and more than 75% of the total paid up equity capital.

Projected Earning Per Share

The Projected earning per share is also one of the most

important variable from the investors point of view as it enable the common investors to easily assess the profitability of a company. The earning per share is derived by dividing the profit after tax by the total number of shares and it conveys to the shareholder about the earnings, a I; company has made on a share.

Among all the ratios expressing profitability of a company, earning per shares is i widely used by all the common investors in India to assess their expected returns from investment in the shares of any company.

PROJECTED BOOK VALUE OF A SHARE

The book value per share is obtained by dividing the networth of a company from the total numbers of shares of a company, i.e. Book Value per share = Networth/No. of shares. In Indian securities market, most of the Investor use this ratio, to ascertain risk attached with their equity investment. Normally, the prevailing market price is compared against the book value per share and if the prevailing market price is significantly higher than the book value per share of a company, the chances of downfall of price are more and therefore higher amount of risk is perceived by the investors in such cases. It has also been observed that the prices at which the shares are offered in the primary market are very close to the existing the book value per share of a company.

SIZE OF AN ISSUE

Size of an issue is also one of the important factor which is kept under consideration by primary market investor while applying for shares in the public issue. The investors ascertain their chance of getting allotment of shares on the basis of size. The investors perceives higher chances of getting allotment if the size of issue is big i.e. no of share to be allotted are more. The investors gets attracted towards those issues where the number of shares to be allotted are more and the premium asked for is reasonable keeping in new the credentials of a company.

PROJECTED PROFITABILITY OF THE COMPANY

Another qualitative factors which helps considerably all the primary market investors in evaluating the investment proposals in the profitability of a company which is determined by profit after tax of a company. The profit after tax as an absolute figure do not help much to the investors in assessing the profitability prospects and therefore it is advisable to study this parameter is relation to save other parameter such as size of an equity capital, debt, total assets of a company, sales of a company. Thus, the relvance of this parameter arises only when it is studied in relation to some other financial parameters.

Keeping in view the aforesaid variables, the evaluation of premium in case of new issues and further issues has been studied separately. Part A of the present chapter deals with evaluation of premium in case of 'new issues' and Part B of the chapter deals with the case of "further issue'.

PART A

NEW ISSUES

On the basis of Information collected from various primary and secondary sources, the model for pricing the Issue has been developed. An attempt has also been made to explore different variables which determine the amount of premium to be charged and the extent of role they play in determining the amount of premium. It is very difficult to define the adequate amount of premium because underpricing leads to over subscription and vice versa. Thus, the model has been developed to assess the amount of premium which when added to par value should be almost equal to the average price of six months from the date of listing. *The basis for this assumption is given* as *under:*

(1) The moment the scrip gets listed on a stock exchange, significant fluctuations are observed in its price movement. If the primary market investors are bullish about the performance of the company and find opening price of scrip inadequate to offload their holding, they retain and wait for appropriate price and time. On the other hand, if they are bearish about the performance of the company and find the opening price of the scrip as adequate enough to make expected returns, they offload their holdings immediately. Thus, it has been observed in many cases that the price of any scrip takes about four to six months to stabilise in the field having forces from sides other then credentials of the company.

(2) The transaction during the first six month are executed on the basis of information published in the prospectus. Thus, the price of any scrip during first few months of its listing is mainly based on the information communicated to the investors through prospectus.

(3) The price of the scrip during the first few months of listing also displays sentiments of common investor about the company developed on the basis of information generated after the closure of subscription list of the company.

On the basis of above factors, the ideal price of any new issue is assumed to be its average price during the first six months after the date of listing on any stock exchange.

Statistical tools such as multiple regression, correlation etc. have been used to assess the relationship between the premium and several variables and to develop a model for pricing the new issues, the main objectives of multiple regression and correlation analysis are given as under:

(1) Deriving an equation which provides estimate of the dependent variable from value of the two or more independent variables.

(2) To find out a measure of the error involved in using regression equation as a basis for estimation.

(3) To obtain a measure of the proportion of variance in the dependent variable accounted for or explained by the independent variables.

Data of 17 companies operating under textile industry which have come with a premium issue during the period April 1993 to December 95 has been used to derive a methodology to evaluate the amount of premium to be charged on new issues. The details of the companies have been seperately dealt in the next section. The summary position in regard to premium promoter's stake, average PAT issue size average book value and EPS for the sample companies is provided in Table 4.1.

ACKNIT KNITTING LIMITED

Brief History of the Company

The Company was originally incorporated under Companies Act 1956 as a private Limited Company on 12.10.1990. Subsequently the Company and the name was changed to Acknit Knitting Limited. In pursuance of its object, the Company has set up a 100% Export Oriented Unit at Falta Export Processing Zone, West Bengal in the year 1991. Encouraged with the potential of manufacture and export of the product, the Company embarked upon an expansion plan during the second year of production itself with another 40 fully automatic computerised knitting machines of Japanese make. All these machines have been successfully commissioned and commercial production therefrom has already commenced. The Company has been able to successfully export its products to countries like Italy and France. To penetrate other overseas markets as well as for expansion of export sales in their existing markets, the Company had been awarded with grant assistance of US $ 16, 500 by Bank Of Baroda under its World Bank aided Export Development Fund in the year 1993-94.

Main Objects of the Company

To establish, carry on, maintain, operate and run in India or elsewhere business of trading, re-sale, manufacture, production, process, conservation and to do job work oof all kinds and forms cotton. To import, export, buy, sell or deal in hand-gloves, socks, sleeves, underwear-garments, readymade garments and hosiery, curtain and furnishing items.

Details of the Equity Shares Offered Through the Prospectus Dated 24.01.95

No. of Shares	*Category*
14,50,000	Public (Premium of Rs. 20)
5,00,000	Promoters

1,50,000	Kothari Pioneer Mutual Fund
5,00,000	NRI/OCB

Promoters Stake

Date of Allotment promoters	*No. of Shares Allotted to Capital*	*% of post issue*	*Lock-in period*
B 01.10.1990	200	0.01	NIL
B29.08.1991	49, 800	1.66	NIL
B30.09.1991	50,000	1.66	NIL
B25.03.1994	50,000	1.66	NIL
B25.03.1994	50,000	1.66	Upto 24.3.1999
B26.04.1994	2,00,000	6.66	Upto 25.4.1999
D Present	5,00,000	16.66	Five years from date of corn mencement of the date of allotment or 5 years from the commercial production in the expansion project whichever occurs later.
	9,00,000	30.00	

Object of the Present Issue

The present issue is being made with the object to raise funds to part finance the costs of:

i) Capacity expansion of the existing 100% Export Oriented unit manufacturing Seamless knitted hand gloves from the present installed capacity of 3,24,000 dozen pairs to 6,27,000 dozen pairs per annum.

ii) Expenses of the present issue.

Highlight of the Issue

Existing company making profit since 1991-92 and paid maiden dividend in 93-94.

* Existing 100% export oriented unit already engaged in manufacture and export of seamless knitted handgloves, undergoing capacity expansion.
* Knitted handgloves are under Apparel Export Promotion Council purview and Govt of India has declared Apparel as one of the thrust area of export from India.
* Company has been awarded grant assistance of US $ 16.500 (Rs. Equivalent: Rs. 5 lacs approx) under World Bank aided Export Development Programme by Bank of Baroda for export marketing in the year 1993-94.
* Easy liquidity - Listing at Calcutta, Bombay, Delhi and Madras Stock Exchanges.
* Tax Benefits: u/s 10B, 80 (1A), SOL, 80M and Wealth Tax Benefits Under Income Tax Act, 1961.

Means of Financing

The above mentioned project cost of Rs. 412.19 lacs is proposed to be financed as under:

	(Rs in lacs)
Increase in Equity Share Capital	260.00
Share Premium	130.00
Internal Acurals	22.19
Total	412.19

Brief of the Promoters

Name of Promoter	*Educational*	*Expereince Background*
S.K. Saraf	BSc	17 Years
D.K. Saraf	Commerce Graduate	7 Years

Marketing and Selling Arrangements

The product of the Company are used mainly as industrial

safety apparel in developed countries. Being a mandatory item for industrial workers with a very short life (mostly one time use), such products are having good markets in developed countries like Germany, France, U.K., Italy, U.S.A., Japan etc. With good marketing efforts and by maintaining quality, the Company had been able to procure substantial repeat orders from some of the European countries in the past. Starting with a level of export of the export to the tune of only Rs. 17.41 lacs in the year 1991-92, the Company has already achieved export sales of more than 126.00 lacs in 1993-94, the very second full year of operation. In the first four months of the current financial year the Company has already effected export of hand gloves worth Rs. 69.23 lacs.

Justification of Premium

The premium for the equity shares has been fixed in consultation with the Lead Managers who are satisfied with the basis of arriving at the same and which has been found to be reasonable and justified.

(Amount in Rs. lacs)

	30.09.94 (6 mts)	*31.03.94 (12 mts)*	*31.03.93 (12 mts)*	*31.03.92 (7 mis)*
Sales	93.71	126.52	80.81	17.41
Profit after tax	17.36	23.67	10.42	1.90
Capital	40.00 (+)	20.00	10.00	10.00
Reserve/Surplus	36.32	32.61	12.31	1.89
Net Worth	75.17	52.61	22: 21	11.78
Book Value per Share (Rs.)	18.79	26.26	22.21	11.78
Earning per Share (Rs)	9.34*	23.29	10.42	3.25-
Dividend: per cent	-	15.00	-	-
Amount	-	1.53	-	-

(+) Bonus shares issued on 1: 1 basis out of general reserves to the extent of Rs.20/- lacs.

* Annualised on weighted average capital.

The following parameters have been considered white arriving at the premium of

Rs. 5/- per share:

A. Financial Factors

i) The following table shows the key financial indicators of the Company for last 3 years and the 6 months period ending 30.09.94 based on Audited Accounts.

ii) The projected profitability of the Company for the year ended 31.03.95 and the next three years thereafter are:

(Amount in Rs. lacs)

	31.03.95	*31.03.96*	*31.03.97*
Sales	205.72	685.83	800.39
Pprofit after tax	28.26	113.71	164.42
Equity Capital	300.00	300.00	300.00
Reserve/Surplus	161.12	209.83	294.25
Net Worth	461.12	509.83	594.25
Book Value per Share (Rs.)	13.87	15-66	18.64
EPS (Rs.)	4.35-	3.79	5.48
Dividend (%)	15%	20%	25%

*Annualised

iii) The average EPS for the above said 3 years works out to Rs. 4.54 on the expanded capital. Based on the offer price of Rs. 15/- per share, the public issue is being made at a P/E multiple of only 3.30 as against the industry average P/E Ratio of 22.78 for Textile-Hosiery/Knitwear (Source: Capital Market, Vol IX/7 dated 20.11.94.)

B. Qualitative Factors

The Company is having an existing fully operational 100% EOU for manufacture of knitted handgloves with established market for its products. The Company has maintained consistent growth in sales and profitability and is confident of maintaining similar trend in future also, barring unforeseen circumstances.

There had been three fold increase in capacity with a high rate of utilisation within a short span of 3 years since its inception.

Audited Financial Information

	31.03.93	*31.03.94*	*30.04.94*
SOURCES OF FUND			
Share Capital	10.00	20.00	40.00
Share Application	—	—	40.00
Money	—	—	1.35
Reserve & Surplus	12.30	32.60	34.97
Secured Loans	56.98	125.03	138.16
Unsecured Loans	2.65	1.37	—
APPLICATION OF FUNDS			
Fixed Assets	35.64	98.20	158.28
Current Assets	38.37	84.75	104.25
Misc. Expenditure (to the extent not written off)	0.10	0.87	0.87

TUNI TEXTILE MILLS LTD.

Brief History of the Company

Promoted by Shri Prabhu Dayal Sureka and his sons Shri Narendra Kumar

Sureka and Shri Pradeep Kumar Sureka, Tuni Textile Mills Limited was incorporated as a private Limited Company on 6th July, 1987 and was converted into a Public Limited Company by passing a Special Resolution u/s 31 of the Act on 25th March, 1992 and certificate dated 6th August, 1992 was obtained from Registrar of Companies, Maharashtra to that effect. The Company is engaged in the manufacture of synthetic fabric having a plant at MIDC, Murbad, Dist. Thane. The Company commenced commercial production at the said plant in February 1989.

Main Objects of the Company

The main objects of the Company are as set out in the Memorandum of Association and inter alia include:

1. To take over and/or acquire business of M/s. Tuni Silk Mills.
2. To promote, establish and/or carry on the business of manufacturing, bleaching, dyeing, printing, selling, buying, importing and exporting, processing of yarn, cloth, linen and other fabrics made from cotton, silk, wool, fibre including manmade, jute and other suitable materials.

Details of Equity Shares Offered Through the Prospectus Dated 17.10.1995

No. of Shares	*Category*
1454200	Public (Premium of Rs.2.50 per share)
795000	Indian Financial Institutions
771800	NRI/FIIs
495000	Mutual Funds

Promoters Stake

1. The date of allotment of Shares to the promoters and associates and the corresponding Lock-in-period is as under:

Date of Issue	*No. of Shares*	*%age Period*	*Lock-In*
06.07.87	40	—	Nil
29.09.87	5500	0.10	Nil
31.03.88	114460	1.98	Nil
19.09.88	300000	5.18	Nil
25.03.92	704600	12.17	Nil
TOTAL (A)	1124600	19.43	
25.03.92	125400	2.17	5 Years
10.03.95	937500	16.20	5 Years
TO BE ALLOTTED	384000	6.63	5 Years
TOTAL (B)	1446900	25.00	
TOTAL (A+ B)	2571500	44.43	

Objects of the Present Issue

The objects of this issue are as under:

1. To finance texturised Roto yarn project
2. To augment the long term working capital requirements and to meet the needs of expanding business.
3. To enlist the Equity Shares of the Company.

Highlights of the Issue

COMPANY 1. Maiden issue of an existing profit making Company with a track record of consistent profitability engaged in manufacturing of fabrics, now proposing backward integration.

PROMOTERS 2. Experienced promoters having presence

of over three decades in the Textile Industry.

PROJECT 3. Proposed project located at Dadra in Union Territory of Dadra & Nagar Haveli, a Centrally notified Backward Area, eligible for 100% income tax deduction for 5 years, 30% of income in subsequent 5 years and Sales Tax exemption for 15 years.

4. Tax Benefits - Income Tax Benefits u/s 80 IA, 80M, and for NRI investors u/s 115-F, 115-F in additional to Wealth Tax and Gift Tax Benefits.

MARKETING 5. MOU signed with Santogen Silk Mills Ltd. a well known Company of the Santogen Group for buying the surplus production of texturised yarn being produced by the Company.

6. Easy liquidity - Listing proposed at Bombay, Ahmedabad, Indore and Jaipur Stock Exchanges.

Means of Financing

(Rs. in lacs)

Equity Share Capital		
Promoters	36.40	360.00
Public	321.60	
Share Premium		
Promoters	9.60	
Public	80.40	90.00
	450.00	

Brief Details of the Promoters

Sr. No.	*Name of the Promoter*	*Age (Years)*	*Quali-fication*	*Experience*
1.	Mr. Prabhudayal Sureka	65	S.S.C.	a) 20 years experience of Commission agent in Textiles.

			b) Worked in Santogen Silk Mill Ltd. for 10 years.
			c) In business for last 6 years.
2. Mr. Narendrakumar Sureka	42	B.Com.	a) 7 years experience in Santogen Silk Mills Ltd.
			b) Subsequently, in textiles business for last 15 years.
3. Mr. Pradeep Kumar Sureka	35	B.Com.	Started his career in family Business of textile since last 15 years.
4. Mr. Annapurna Devi Sureka	31	B.A.	In Textile business for last 10 years.

Marketing and Selling Arrangements

From the proposed production of texturised yarn almost 75% of the production will be used by the company as captive consumption. Thus, the Company need to market only about 25% of the production. Although, the company has its own agency network for marketing this production, it has signed an MOD with Santogen Silk Mills Limited for buying up the Company will not face any problem in marketing the increased production.

Justification of Premium

A. Qualitative Factors

1) The company is a profit making company with a proven track record.
2) Promoters have over three decades experience in textile industry.
3) Company enjoys locational advantage i.e. in Backward Integrated area, where the company will enjoy tax exemption for 5 years.
4) The company's products are well accepted in the market.

5) Product of Dadra Unit is raw material for existing fabric manufacturing unit at Murbad. 8.

B. Quantitative Factors

1. The company is constantly expanding its manufacturing and marketing network which is reflected in the financial performance of the company during the last 5 years as shown in the table given herein below:

Past Performance

(Rs. in lacs)

	1990/91	*1991/92*	*1992/93*	*1993/94*	*1994/95*	*1995/96*
Sales	513.68	814.21	812.81	1091.81	1569.73	676.81
profit before tax	31.01	31.26	40.71	40.45	65.10	31.65
Profit after tax	31.01	27.76	27.27	27.95	44.10	31.65
Share Capital	42.00	50.30	91.80	109.00	218.75	218.75
Book Value per Share	23.29	26.62	21.45	22.15	14.66	16.05
EPS (Rs)	7.38	5.52	2.97	2.56	3.38*	4.34"

* On weighted average basis

** Annualised

The future projected profitability parameters are shown in the following table.

2. Future Projects

(Rs. in lacs)

Year	*1995-96*	*1996-97*	*1997-98*	*1998-99*
Sales & other Income	2207.44	3516.61	3870.33	4050.33
Profit before tax	153.44	304.66	353.62	380.84
Profit after tax	9595	230.68	264.40	278.15
Dividend	20%	25%	30%	35%
Share Capital	578.75	578.75	578.75	578.75
Book-Value (Rs.)	12.73	14.30	15.94	17.32
EPS (Rs.)	3.11*	3.99	4.57	4.81

* On weighted average basis.

The following table shows the projected Earning Per share (EPS) and the discounting factor with respect to the offer price of Rs. 12.50 per share.

	1996	*1997*	*1998*	*1999*
E.P.S. (Rs.)	3.11*	3.99	4.57	4.81
Book Value (Rs.)	12.73	14.30	15.94	17.32
Offer Price (Rs. 12.50 per share)				
Discounting Factor (EPS)	4.02	3.13	2.74	2.60
——do——(BV)	1.02	114	1.28	1.38

Hence the offer price of Rs. 12.50 per share discounts the 1996 earnings 4.02 times and 1998 earnings (when the project goes on stream) 2.74 times as against the industry average of over 12

(Source: Capital Market March 1995). In view of the above factors, the Company and the Lead Managers, in consultation with whom the premium has been fixed, are of the opinion that the premium is reasonable and justified.

Audited Financial Information

Source of Funds (4 Months)	*31.3.94*	*31.3.95*	*31.7.95*
Share Capital	109.00	218.75	218.75
Reserves and surplus	132.42	104.31	135.90
Secured Loans	341.43	316.79	307.03
Unsecured Loans	0.57	18.87	18.87
Current Liabilities	131.42	229.41	375.48
Aapplication of funds	——	——	——
Fixed Assets	196.04	188.51	196.11
Current Assets	3.02	3.02	3.00
Miscellaneous Expenditure (To the Extent not Written Off)	0.10	2.33	3.55

THE RAI SAHEB REKHCHAND MOHOTA SPG. & WVG. MILLS LIMITED.

Brief History of the Company

The Rai Saheb Rekhchand Mohota Spg & Wvg Mills. Fax No. 022 2081556 was established as early as 1898. as a proprietary concern by Mr. Rekhchand Mohota which was converted into partnership firm over a period of time. It was converted into full fledged Public Company vide Special Resolution passed on 26.09.1994. The Mill started its operations with an installed capacity of 12,000 Spindles and 200 Looms for manufacturing of cotton yarn & fabric and over decades efforts were made to modernise the Mill or Werks in order to gear up the qualitative standards of its output to match with the International Standard. The Company has established its sales through its Agents in various parts of India in order to cater directly to the domestic consumers. The company's proposed modernisation project would result in increasing the product mix capacity and also enlarge the facilities for value addition.

Main Objects of the Company

1. To purchase and otherwise acquire and take over the Spinning and Weaving Mills known as Rai Saheb Rekhchand Mohota Spinning and Weaving Mills of Hinganghat and with a view thereto enter into agreements. 2. To carry on business of ginning, preparing, combing, spinning, weaving, manufacturing, bleaching, dyeing, mercerising, printing, selling, buying and otherwise working or dealing in cotton, silk. 3. To purchase or otherwise acquire, repurchase, sell, resell or otherwise dispose of, or deal in. either for further or ready delivery and either absolutely or conditionally, cotton, yarn, piecegoods, silk, jute, flax, linen, hessian, gunnies, gold silver.

Details of Equity Shares Offered Through the Prospectus Dated 20, Jan, 1995

No. of Share	*Category*
10, 77, 470	Public (Premium of Rs.80 per share)
16,400	PROMOTERS
32, 470	MFS

Promoters Stake

The Equity share pertaining to the Promoters shall be locked in the following manner:

Date of Allotments	*No.of Equity Shares of Rs. 10/- each*	*Percentage of Total Equity-*	*Lock in Period*	*Consideration Price*
23.10 47	1010	00.02	**5 Years	Cash
23.10.47	46490	01.31	**5 Years	Cash
01.08.47	452500	10.83	**5 Years	Cash
08.09.47	45000	01.08	**5 Years	Cash
22.10.50	(109000)	(261)	*N.A.	Cash
05.02.56	(174400)	(4.17)	*N.A.	Cash
25.09.87	258110	06.17	5 Years	Cash
10.11.90	509000	12.18	**5 Years	Cash
20.08.94	2057420	49.22	Nil	Bonus
Present Issue	16400	00.39	**5 Years	Cash
TOTAL	3102530	74.22		

* Denotes reduction in the capital.

** Lock in Period is applicable from the date of commencement of commercial production of the Modernisation Project.

Object of the Present Issue

1. To part finance the capital expenditure on modernisation.
2. To meet the long term working capital requirements.
3. To meet the expenses of the public issue and to

list the Equity Shares of the Company with Stock Exchanges.

Highlights of the Issue

1. Existing Company since 1946 with business presence from the year 1898 & consistently profit making since 1980 onwards.
2. Embarking on a modernisation programme to enhance its sales by improving product mix from cotton yarn to PV yarn for better value addition.
3. The present Promoters have over Six decades of experience in this industry.
4. This modernisation Project being funded by IDBI for Rs. 600 lakhs under Assets Credit Scheme, i.e. 37.78% of the project cost.
5. Promoters holding would be 74.22% of the post issue capital. (This includes 49.22% acquired through capitalisation of Revaluation Reserves).
6. The company had availed earlier Term Loans from All India Financial Institutions viz; IDBI, ICICI, IFCI and IRBI.
7. Project is situated in the cotton growing area.
8. Easy liquidity, listing at Bombay, Bangalore and Ahmedabad stock exchanges.
9. Tax Benefits under section 35 (1) (iv), 35AB, 35D, 80HHC, 80L, 80M and 112 of Income Tax Act, 1956.

Means of Financing

Equity:		
Promoters:		
Face value	1.64	
Premium	13.12	
	———	14.76
Public:		
Face Value	107.75	

Premium	861.97
	969.72
Rupee Loan from IDBI	600.00
Internal Cash Accruals	*3.52
Total	1588.00

Brief Details of the Promoters

Name of Promoter	*Educational Background*	*Expereince*
Mr. Girdhardar Mohota	Not Mentioned	more than 3 decade
Dr. Ranchodas Mohota	-do-	-do-

Marketing and Selling Arrangement

The Company has its own full fledged sales office with a staff strength of 17 in Bombay for the sale of both cloth and yarn. The company has sales depcsits in Bhiwandi. Ichalkaranji and Bumanpur (MP) and dealers network in other parts of the country. Apart from this the company has appointed Commission Agents. The Company has no sole selling agent. At present the company proposes to sell its product in the domestic market. In future it may consider the international market also.

Justification of Premium

The premium for the share was fixed jointly by the lead managers and the company is considered reasonable and justifiable in view of the factors enumerated below:

1. Quantitative Factors

A) Past Performance

The company has been in this business since 1948. The company has been performing consistently well in the past four years which is substantiated by the following highlights:

(Rupees in lakhs) 5 months ended

Year ended March 31	*31.3.91*	*31.3.92*	*31.3.93*	*31.3.94*	*31.8.94*
Sales	3183.31	3684.35	4292.93	5838.72	2646.82
Other Incomes	31.03	13.91	27.85	14.46	2.81
Increase/ (Decrease) in stock	(12.65)	138.60	82.46	4.99	(25.95)
TOTAL	3226.99	3836.86	4403.24	5858.17	2675.58
Profit After Tax	31.41	53.30	58.00	118.17	194.59
Equity Share Capital	102.87	102.87	102.87	102.87	308.61
Earning per Share (Rs.)	3.05	5.18	5.64	11.49	15.13
Book Value (Rs. per share) (Annualised)	38.08	43.90	48.90	60.38	58.14

Notes

1. The face value of the shares was originally Rs.100 per share. The company has vide resolution passed in AGM dated Sept. 26, 1994, subdivided in the shares into Rs. 10/- each. However for the sake of convenience the EPS and Book Value above are calculated on the basis of face value of Rs.10/- per share.
2. The Company has issued 20, 57, 420 Bonus Shares in the ratio of 2 Bonus Shares for every 1 share on Aug. 20, 1994 out of the revaluation reserve of Rs. 1030.28 lakhs created from the revaluation of Plant & Machinery carried out in May 3, 1994 by the Govt. registered valuer.
3. The Earning Per Share and Book Value for the five months period ended Aug 31, 1994 is calculated on the basis of shares including Bonus shares as mentioned in Note 2 above.

b) Growth Rate

The rate of growth since 1991 is 10% p.a.

c) Future Projects

The company's this project has been funded by IDBI to the extent of Rs. 600 lakhs under its Asset Credit Scheme. The future projections as submitted to them are as under:

(Rs. in lakhs)

Year ending March 31	*1995*	*1996*	*1997*	*1998*	*1999*
Sates & other income	3170.80	7224.90	7503.60	7508.44	7513.76
Profit after Tax	247.28	330.00	340.23	313.22	287.14
Dividend (%)	(20%)	(20%)	(25%)	-(25%)	(25%)
Equity Share Capital	418.00	418.00	418.00	418.00	418.00
Earning per Share (Rs.)	11.09	7.89	8.14	7.49	6.67
Book Value (Rs. per share)	48.14	57.04	59.68	64.67	69.04

Note

1. The EPS for the year ending March 31, 1995 is calculated after annualising the increase in share capital due to bonus and ignoring the capital of. the proposed issue.
2. The Book Value as on March, 31, 1995 is calculated on the total capital.
3. The average EPS of the years 1995, 1996, 1997 works out to Rs, 9.04. This would result in PE Multiple of 9.96 for the issue price of Rs. 90/-. This is comparatively favourable with the industry average of 32.4 for the Textile Industry. (Source: Capital Market, September 12-25, 1994)

2. Qualitative Factors

1. The company is an existing profit making company having a track record of more than five years and continuous growth in turn over figures.

2. The company belongs to the well established group and in the business for 96 years.
3. The groups products are sold in the market at a premium. After considering the past performance of the Company & the future projects of profitability, measures of internal risk, competitiveness in the industry and the premium price of the company's shares, the company/lead managers believe that the premium of Rs. 80/- per share is reasonable & justified.

Audited Financial Information

Source of Funds	*31.3.93*	*31.3.94*	*31.8.94 (4 Months)*
Share Capital	102.87	102.87	308.61
Unsecured Loans	317.03	128.44	150.88
Application of Funds			
Fixed Assets	56.11	71.11	15.00
Current Assets	1926.58	2314.29	3540.56
Miscellaneous Expenditure (To the Extent not written Off)			

SUNIL INDUSTRIES LIMITED

Brief History of the Company

The present Sunil Industries Limited was initially incorporated as a private limited company, on 19.11.1976, in the state of Maharashtra, as Raj Ratan Textile Processors Private Limited. The Company's name was subsequently changed to Sunil Industries Limited and a fresh certificate of incorporation was obtained on 30.3.1994. Initially SIL was engaged in the manual processing of cotton textiles. Later it started processing of synthetic fabrics and blended fabrics. In 1984 it also started power processing Currently, the Company is engaged in manual and power processing of all types of fabric for a wide range of thread count.

Main Objects of the Company

1) To acquire and take over as running concern the Business carried on by partners of M/s. Raj Ratan Textiles Processors together with all its assets and liabilities.
2) To run a process house.
3) To undertake Dyeing, Bleaching, Sanforising, mercerising, printing or otherwise processing of man made Fibers, Cotton fibers, Fabrics of Cotton.

Details of Equity Shares Offered Through the Prospectus Dated Nov 9, 1994

No. of Shares	*Category*
15.75,000	Public (Premium of Rs. 20 per share)
2.00,000	Mutual Funds
4,00,000	NRI/OCB
25,000	Employees.

Promoters Stake

The Equity Shares held by the promoters, their friends and relatives after the Public Issue will constitute 47.62% of the Issued capital of the company.

Sl.No.	*Date of allotment*	*No. of Shares*	*Face Value (Rs.)*	*Issue price*	*% of post-issue*
i.	Till 29.11.90	2,40,000	24,00,000	10	5.71
ii.	13.07.91	1,51,100	15,11,000	10	3.61
iii.	31: 03.92	11,08,900	1,10,89,000	10	26.40
iv.	This Issue	5,00,000	50.00,00	3	11.90

The shares were converted from Rs. 100/- paid-up into Rs. 10/- paid-up on 1.4.1991. All the shares were issued for cash consideration.

Object of the Present Issue

The objects of the Issue are;

1) to part finance the cost of the proposed expansion project mentioned elsewhere in the prospectus.
2) to list the shares of the Company on the stock exchanges.
3) to meet the expenses of the present issue.
4) to meet the working capital requirements.

Highlight of the Issue

An existing profit making (since 1989-90), dividend paying (since 1991-92) Company with an established track record, engaged in the processing of cotton and synthetic fabrics for sale on it's own account as also on a job-work basis. Promoted and directed by experienced persons who have been associated with the industry for nearly 3 decades. Promoter's contribution Rs. 150 lakhs brought in on September 2, 1994 at the same premium as the present offer to the public, constituting 11.90% of post issue equity. Promoter's Post Issue stake 47.62%.

Proven track record as reflected by the financials of the company for the last three years:

(Rs. in Lacs)

Year	*1991-92*	*1992-93*	*1993-94*
Tolal Income	1456.94	244.96	3765.60
PAT	30.58	78.00	87.89
Book Value (Rs.)	17.70	21.40	25.66
CEPS (Rs.)	4.53	9.18	10.92
EPS (Rs.)	2.04	5.20	5.86
Dividend	12%	15%	16%

Rs. 65.23 lakhs of excess depredation was written back in 1990-91. The attention of the investors is drawn to the notes under the Auditor's Report in Part II of this prospectus. Expansion and upgradation of processing - dyeing and printing capacity from 600 lakh mts p.a. to 1050 lakh mts p.a. in the existing premises at Dombivil (East), Thane for greater value addition. Expansion project financed by Industrial Development Bank of India (IDBI) to the extent of Rs. 300 lakhs under Equipment Finance Scheme, Extended limits of Rs. 750 lakhs against the currently sanctioned limit of Rs. 500 lakhs (to miit the Working Capital requirements after expansion) already sanctioned by the regular banders of the Company. Very low gestation period as commercial production of expansion project to commence by November, 1994. Low Cash Break Even of 16.79%. Easy liquidity, listing at Ahmedabad, Bombay, Calcutta and Delhi Stock Exchanges.

Means of Financing

The project is proposed to be financed as below:

(Rs. in Lacs)

Share Capital	
- Promoters	150.00
- Public	660.00

Internal Accruals	87.76
Term Loan from IDBI under the EFS scheme	300.00
Total	1200.76

Brief Details of the Promoters

Name of Promoter	*Educational Background*	*Experience*
Vinod Lath	Not Mentioned	Not Mentioned

Marketing and Selling Arrangement

The Company has been processing cloth on a job - work basis for many years and has recently also started selling cloth which it processes on it's own account. The company has established relationship with it's clients and does not expect to face any problems in procuring new business.

Justification of Premium

Future Projections

Year	*1994-95*	*1995-96*	*1996-97*
PAT (Rs. in lakhs)	250.69	227.82	257.11
EPS (Rs./Share)	5.97	5.42	6.12
BOOK VALUE (Rs./Share)	31.77	35.38	39.70

*EPS is calculated on the expanded capital. Annualized EPS is Rs. 8.80

Past Performance

Year	*1991-92*	*1992-93*	*1993-94*
PAT* (Rs. in lakhs)	30.57	78.00	87.89
EPS (Rs./Share)	2.04	5.20	5.86
BOOK VALUE (Rs./Share)	17.70	21.40	25.66

* PAT includes prior period adjustments and excess depn. for earlier years written back but excludes transfer to Investment Allowance Reserve.

Note

The increase in PAT for the years 1992-93 and 1993-94 was the result of the expansion programme undertaken by the company where various machinery were installed at an approximate cost of Rs. 1 crore so as to give greater value addition (such as discharge and disperse printing on multi-colored rotary printing machines) as opposed to the past when mere processing of grey fabrics was done. The company consequently increased the quantity of higher quality processing of fabrics. This involved multiple processing on the stenter, consequently lower capacity utilisation and higher profits on the same quantity of processed fabric.

Qualitative Factors

SIL is an existing profit making, dividend paying company. It has recorded a growth in turnover of 320.20 per cent for the last 5 years, during which period the PAT grew by 1204%. There will be no gestation period since this is an expansion of already existing facilities. The company has an established track record in the textile industry and it's processing quality is perceived to be superior. The company also has established relationship with it's clients and does not foresee any problems in achieving the projections.

Quantitative Factors

The book-value per share Pre-Issue is Rs. 25.66. Post Issue, the book value will go up to Rs. 28.455. The projected EPS for the next 5 years according to the appraisal | of Indband Merchant Banking Services is as follows:

Year	*1994-95*	*1995-96*	*1996-97*	*1997-98*	*1998-99*
	5.97	5.42	6.12	6.96	7.04

The EPS for the year 1994-95 is expected to be higher owing to the 100% depreciation chargeable on some of the proposed machinery, and consequently lower tax liability.

The offer price of Rs. 30/- discounts the 1994-95 earnings only 5 times, whereas the Industry P/E is 12.4. (Source - *Capital Market,* Vol. IX/11 Aug. 28, 1994 Industry Code 183). This therefore leaves lots of scope for appreciation. The company has also consistently been paying higher dividends for the last three years and proposes to continue this in future. The issue price of Rs.30/- (inclusive of premium of Rs. 20/-) has been determined in consultation with the Lead Managers to the Issue. In the opinion of the Company and the Lead Managers to the Issue, the price is fair and reasonable:

Audited Financial Information

Source of Funds	31.3.93	31.3.94	30.6.94
Share Capital	1,50,00,000	1,50,00,000	5,00,00.000
Share Application Money	91,000	91,000	91,000
Reserves and Surplus	1,70,09,065	2,33,98,358	2,74,62,530
Secured Loans	6,91,07,162	9,26,53,557	9,10.29,202
Unsecured Loans	64,80,804	1,07,35.654	1,22,77,336
Application of Funds			
Fixed Assets	5,38,25,158	6,76,77,858	6,59,76,735
Current Assets			

BHILWARA SPINNERS LIMITED

Brief History of the Company

Bhilwara Spinners Ltd, a closely held Company, belonging to the BHILWARA GROUP with controlling interest vested in Rajasthan Spinning & Weaving Mills Ltd. and Bharat Investments Growth Ltd. changed into public limited company under the name of Bhilwara Spinners Ltd. vide fresh Certificate of Incorporation dated 11th Febrauary 1983 issued by the Register of the companies, Delhi and Haryana, New Delhi.

The Company is engaged in the manufacture of cotton yarn, mercerised cotton yarn, synthetic blended yarn, hosiery yarn, and sewing threads in cotton and synthetics with an installed capacity of 29, 536 spindles and 672 Rotors at its plant located at Bhilwara, Rajasthan. *Main Objects of the Company*

1. To carry on the business of manufactures, producers, combers, bleachers, finishers, processors, dyers, spinners, weavers, knitwears, laminators.
2. To carry on the business of manufacturers, producers, processors, importers, buyers, sellers and dealers in and as brokers, agents stockists, distributors, and suppliers of all kinds of readymade garments.
3. To manufacture, buy sell, exchange, barter, ship, import, export make advance upon and otherwise deal in whether as principals agents, stockists, distributors, brokers, wholesale and retail dealers or otherwise either for ready or forward transactions in silk, art silk, artificial and synthetic.

Details of Equity Shares Offered Throught the Prospectus Dated 10 March, 1993

No. of Shares	*Category*
37,50,000	Public (Premium of Rs. 10 per share)

10,00,000	NRI
1,87,500	EMPLOYEES
5,00,000	PROMOTERS

Promoters Stake

The promoters contribution and the lock in period shall be as follows:

No. of Share	*% age*	*Lock in Period*
5,00,000	7.34	5 YEARS
8,55,010	12.55	5 YEARS
2,65,000	3.89	5 YEARS
83,750	1.23	2 YEARS
	25.01	

Objets of the Present Issue

The Issue is being made with the object of:

a) raising part finance for meeting the capital expenditure under the modernisation programme undertaken by the company.

b) augmenting long term resources for the working capital requirements of the company.

c) meeting the expenses of this Public Issue, and

d) getting the equity shares listed on the Stock Exchanges.

Highlight of the Issue

- Existing, Established Profit making Company.
- Member of the "BHILWARA GROUP" having a good track record.
- Promoted by Rajasthan Spinning & Weaving Mills Limited, a flagship company of the "BHILWARA GROUP".
- Modernisation of the entire unit to be completed

by the end of March, 1993, resulting in higher productivity and better quality of the product.
Easy liquidity - listing at Delhi, Ahmedabad, Bombay, Calcutta and Jaipur.

Means of Financing

(Rs. in Lacs)

	Nominal Value	share Premium	Total Amount
A. Equity Capital			
a) Promoters. Directors, their friends and relatives	50.00	50.00	100.00
b) Public Issue	375.00	375.00	750.00
			850.00
B. Term Loan			
I.F.C.I. Rupee Term Loan-under Equipment Finance Scheme.		275.00	
Under Equipment Credit Scheme		178.00	453.00
			40.00
C. Internal Accruals			
TOTAL			1343.00

Brief Details of the Promoters

Name of Promoter	*Educational Background*	*Experience*
L.N. JHUNJHUNWALA	GRADUATION IN MATHS	30 YEARS

Marketing and Selling Arrangements

The company's yarn is well accepted in the domestic and overseas markets due

to consistently good quality of the products and the longstanding business relations 'the company enjoys backed by the reputation of BHILWARA GROUP.

Justification of Premium

The company proposes to issue 42,50,000 equity share of Rs.10/- each for cash at a premium of Rs. 10/- per share.

The issue price of Rs. 20/- per share has been arrived at by the company in consultation with Bank of Baroda, and State Bank of Bikaner and Jaipur, Lead Managers .to the Issue and Doogar & Associated Ltd. Advisors to the issued by the Securities and Exchange Board of India [SEBI]. The Issue price is justified on the following grounds:

1. The company is an existing profit making company well established in its line of business with a good track record.

2. The financial performance of the company since it ceased to be a subsidiary Rajasthan Spinning & Weaving Mills Ltd and became an independent company in the year 1990-91 has been highly satisfactory as stated elsewhere in the prospectus.

3. The company had made a Bonus Issue of 8,55,010 equity shares of Rs. 10/- each in the ratio of 1: 2 in September 1992.

4. The company belongs to the BHILWARA GROUP set up under the stewardship of Shri L.N. Jhunjhunwala a diversified group having varied interests in the fields of Textiles, Graphite Electrodes, Oil drilling, Sponge Iron, Glass Insulators and construction. The Group has & good reputation for the quality and integrity of its management.

5. The BHILWARA GROUP financial highlights for the last three years as stated elsewhere in the prospectus which indicate that the Group has been growing from strength to strength. The estimated Group turnover for the year 1992-93 is likely to be around Rs. 500 crores.

6. A table indicating Equity, Free reserves, Networth,

Profit after tax, Earning Per share [EPS] and Dividend [audited figures for the last 3 years upto 1991-92 and estimated figures for 1992-93 and projections for the next 3 years from 1993-94 to 1995-96 are given below:

(Rs. in Lacs)

Year	*Equity Reserves*	*Free Worth*	*Net After Tax*	*Profit [Rs.]*	*EPS [%]*	*Dividend*	*Book Value [Rs.]*
1989-90	145	132	277	10	0.69	-	19.10
1990-91	171	379	550	246	14.39	-	32.38
1991-92	171	434	605	55	3.22	-	35.38
Upto 31st Dec.							
19 Mons]	256.5	462	718	114	5.91	-	28.00
ESTIMATES							
1992-93	257	518	775	170	6.63	-	30.16
PROJECTIONS							
1993-94	682	1047	1689	256	3.76	15	25.36
1994-95	682	1213	1860	302	4.43	20	27.80
1995-96	682	1449	2101	372	5.45	20	31.26

Note: The Company had made a Bonus issue of 855010 equity shares of Rs.10/ - each in the ratio of 1: 2 in the month of September. 1992 to the Promoters by way of capitalising the existing reserves of the company.

7. The share premium has been calculated taking two elements namely Net Asset Value [NAV] and Profit Earning Capacity Value [PECV] as given below:

A. Net Asset Value

(a) Average book value per share of the preceding three years namely 1989-90. 1990-91 and 1991-92 [based on audited actual figures]. Rs. 28.00

(b) Estimated book value per share for the current years ending 31/3/1993. Rs. 30.16

(c) Average book value per share of the next three

years namely 1993-94, 1994-95 and 1995-96. RS.28.14

(d) Average Net Asset Value per share of (a+ b+ c] RS.29.06

B. Profit Earning Capacity Value

(a) Average earnings per share of the precading three years namely 1990-91 and 1991-92 [Based on Audited actual figures] RS.6.10

(b) Estimated Earnings per share of the current year ending 31/3/1993.Rs.6-63

(c) Average Earnings per share of next three years namely 1993- 94, 1994-95 and 1995-96. RS. 4.55

(d) Average Earning per share [a+ b+ c] Rs. 5.76

(e) By capitalising the average EPS at the rate of 12% [P.E. Ratio of 8.33 times] keeping in view the characteristics stated above.

Profit Earnings Capacity Value [PECV] Rs. 48.00

Average pf A [a] and B [a] Rs. 39.85

Audited Financial Information

Source of Funds	*31.12.92*	*31.3.92*	*31.3.91*
SHARE APPLICATION MONEY	256.50	171.00	171.00
RESERVES AND SURPLUS	461.82	433.04	378.80
SECURED LOANS	1141.84	1673.04	1675.48
UNSECURED LOANS	989.82	372.04	123.00
APPLICATION OF FUNDS			
FIXED ASSETS	1184.99	1147.86	1196.28
CURRENT ASSETS			

SRI NACHAMMAI COTTON MILLS LTD.

Brief History of the Company

Sri Nachammai Cotton Mills Limited (SNCM) was incorporated in March 1980 as a wholly owned subsidiary of the The Jawahar Mills Ltd. The assets of the Chettainad unit of The Jawahar Mills Ltd. with an installed capacity of 16120 spindles were transferred to SNCM in May 1980.

The Company offered 46000 equity shares of Rs.10/- each to the Public, after it was converted into a Public Limited Company in June 1982. It ceased to be a subsidiary of The Jawahar Mills Limited with the allotment of the said 46000 shares of 9.8.1982.

Over the years the company has been expanding and modernising its Plant. Modernisation and ungradation has enabled the Company to improve the quality of its products and enter the export market.

The Company manufactures combed and carded cotton hosiery yarn of counts ranging from 20s to 40s which are used by the manufacturers to convert the same into fabric or garments for export.

Main Objects of the Company

1. To carry on the business of ginners of kapas; spinners, doublers, twisters, combers, weavers, knitters, finishers, bleachers, dyers, artificial silk mercers, hoisers and carpet makers.
2. To comb, prepare, spin. dye and deal in cotton, waste cotton, staple fibre, silk, artificial silk, rayon, nylon, polyester, linen, flax, hemp. jute, worsted, wool, and other natural and/or synthetic fibrous substances; to weave or otherwise manufacture doth, silk, linen ready made dress articles and other textile goods; and sell any such goods whether in wholesale or in a retail.

3. To carry on the business of spinning, twisting, weaving and/or knitting mills in cotton, waste cotton, staple fibre, silk, artificial silk, either on own account or on commission.
4. To carry on the business of cotton, waste cotton, staple fibre, silk, artificial silk, rayon, nylon, polyester, linen, flax, hemp, jute, worsted, wool and other natural and/or synthetic fiberous substances.
5. To cultivate cotton and other natural fibers, to prepare gin. clean, press and pack the same, to buy, sell and deal in raw or finished cotton, waste cotton, wool, jute, silk, artificial silk, staple fibre, nylon, in wholesale or in retail, either on own account or on commission basis.

Details of Equity Shares Offered Through the Prospectus Dated 7.12.94

No. of Shares	*Category*
1110000	Public (Premium of Rs.60 per share)
35000	IDBI (Premium of Rs. 70 per share)

Promoters Stake

No. of Shares	*% to Post Issue Capital*	*Date of Allotment*	*Lock in Period (in Years)*
586968	13.65	Allotment prior to 26.4.1993	Nil
405146	9.42	26.4.1993	Nil
687044	20.63	26.4.1993	4 years
187956	4.37	6.12.1994	5 years
2067114	48.07		

Objects of the Present Issue

The objects of the issue are to

1. part finance the capital expenditure on modernisation and diversification projects

2. augment long term resources for working capital and
3. list the equity shares of the Company.

Project Details

Modernisation scheme

It now proposes to further modernise its unit by replacing/ adding major equipments like 3 Nos. of draw frames, 3 Nos. of LR combers, 3 Nos. of Crosrol Cards etc in the preparatory sections and 1 No. Murato Auto coner in the post spinning section.

To reduce cost of power and to ensure uninterrupted supply, the company proposes to install 4 Nos. of Wind Turbine generators of 250 KW each diversify its activity into wind energy generation.

Highlights of the Issue

Well established company with consistent performance records.

* Five bonus issues in 8 Years (1: 1 in 1987, 1: 1 in 1991, 21: 8 in 1993 and 1: 10 in 1994)
* Uninterrupted dividends from 1983.
* Belongs to Nachammai Group of Companies with aggregate spindleage exceeding 95,000 spindles.
* Promoters are well experienced in textile industry and have a successful track record.
* Present projects are for modernisation and diversification into Wind Energy generation.
* Project appraised and assisted by IDBI. Finn allotment to IDBI in the Public Issue.
* Easy liquidity - Listing at Coimbatore, Bombay and Madras Stock Exchanges.

Means of Financing

The proposed Means of Finance were as given below:

IDBI - Rupee Term Loan	328	
Equity participation		
Public Issue - Net offer	752	
Internal accruals	100	
Total	100	1,180

Profitability Projections

(Appraised by IDBI)

	1994-95	*1995-96*	*1996-97*
Capacity Utilisation (%)	95	95	95
Sales	4800	5700	5800
Equity Capital	319	430	430
Pat	371	588	457
Dividend	64	86	.86
Book Value	33.75	54.85	63.50
EPS	12.45	13.65	10.60

(Rs. in Lakhs)

Past Financial Record

Year	1993	1994	6 Months (30.9.94)
Capacity Utilisation (%)	95	95	95
Sales	2947.46	3618.80	2169.57
Equity Capital	80	290	290
Pat	105.84	277.42	150.64
Dividend (%)25	20	—	
Book-Value	69.70	26.50	—
EPS	13.25	9.60	—

Brief Detials of Promoters

Name of Promoter	*Educational*	*Expereince Background*
SHRI R.M. RAMANATHAN	INTER. COMMERCE	More than 50 years Textile Industries
SHRI R.M. PALANIAPPAN	B.E. (Mechenical)	More than 20 years

Marketing and Selling Arrangement

It markets bulk of its production to units at Tirupur, internationally known for its exports of knitted garments and active business centre hosieries.

Export obligation

The Company has purchased 2 Autoconers under the Export Promotion Capital Goods (EPCG) scheme at a concessional custom duty of 40% instead of the normal applicable levels. With the present level of export activities, the Company does not foresee and difficulty in fulfilling the above obligation.

Justification of Premium

The Company and the Lead Managers to the issue, in consultation with whom the premium has been decided, are of the opinion that the issue price is justified in view of the following reasons:

1. The financial indicators for the past 5 years and for the future 3 years (as appraised by IDBI) are as follows:

Year ended March 31	*1990*	*1991*	*1992*	*1993*	*1994*	*6 Mts 30.9.94*	*1995*	*1996*	*1997*
Actuals (Audited) Projections									
Total Income	1706.12	1774.72	2296.72	2976.00	3626.92	217289	4800	5744	5844
PRIDT	404.14	269.45	310.05	463.91	624.35	355.43	869	1052	1118
PBT	275.41	139.98	101.54	142.84	289.42	150.64	467	650	737
PAT	105.41	89.98	100.54	105.84	277.42	150.64	371	588	457
Equity Capital	40.00	80.00	80.00	80.00	290.00	290.00	391	430	430

Net Worth	347.91	403.04	481.32	557.49	769.20	921.59	1076	2359	2730
EPS (Rs.)	26.35	20.80#	12.60	13.25	9.60	12.45#	13.65	10.60	
Cash EPS (Rs.)	92.05	37.60#	22.85	31.15	14.05	17.20#	18.00	15.75	
Book value (Rs.)	87.00	50.40	60.20	69.70	26.50	33.75	54.85	63.50	

On pro-rata capital.

2. Thus, the offer price of Rs. 70/- is

	1993-94	*1994-95* (*projections*)	*1994-95 to 96-97* (*projections average*)
Book value (times)	2.65	2.10	1.40
P/E multiple	7.30	5.60	5.70
P/C multiple	5.00	4.10	4.10

For textile - Spinning - Cotton/Blended', the average P/E is 19.6 and P/C is 12.4 (Source: Capital Market Vol. IX/17 dated November 20, 1994)

3. The company is well established, professionally managed and has registered consistent growth.

4. The company has been rewarding its shareholders through consistent dividend payments and liberal bonus issues. It made give bonus issues in the last eight years.

5. The company has been regularly modernising and expanding the unit as ongoing measures.

Audited Financial Information

Source of Funds	*As at 31.3.94*	*As at 30.9.94*
Share Capital	290.00	290.00
Reserves and Surplus	479.20	631.59
Secured Loans	865.41	993.84
Unsecured Loans	661.89	766.93
Current Liabilities	699.13	348.27
Application of Funds		
Fixed Assets,	1309.05	1454.44
Current Assets	1661.20	1535.81

SAMBANDAM SPINNING MILLS LTD.

Brief History of the Company

Sambandam Spinning Mills Limited was incorporated as a private limited company on 7th Nov. 1973 under The Companies Act, 1956. The company became full fledged Public Company with effect from 17.June 1994.

The company has two units situated at Salem and Ayeepatayam. At present the Company has a combined aggregate installed capacity of 37.700 Spindles.

The company has a sound track record of productivity and profitability, and has been producing high quality yarn for the domestic market. The company's products are well received in the local and international markets.

Main Objects of thc Company

1. To carry on the business of cotton, staple fibré, silk, artificial silk, rayon, flax, hemp, jute, worsted and woollen spinners; cotton ginners and doublers.
2. To comb, prepare, spin, dye and deal in cotton, waste cotton, wool, silk, artificial silk, staple-fibre, rayon, flax, hemp, jute and other fibrous substances.
3. To carry on the business of spinning and weaving mills in cotton, waste cotton, silk; artificial silk, staple -fibre, rayon, wool, flax, hemp, jute and any other fibrous substances.
4. To carry on the business of cotton, waste cotton, silk artificial silk, staple fibre, rayon, flax.
5. To cultivate, buy, sell and deal in raw or finished cotton, waste cotton, wool, jute, silk, staple - fibre, mercerised.

Details of Equity Shares Offered Through the Prospectus Dated 25.11.94

No. of Shares	*Category*
10,80,000	Public (Premium of Rs.40 per share)
1,20,000	PROMOTERS.

Promoters Stake

Out of the promoters' holdings, 10, 71.600 Equity shares of Rs.10/- each constituting 25% of the post-issue capital will be locked-in as per details given below:

Date of Allotment	*No.of Equity Shares*	*percentage of post-issue capital (%)*
05.08.1994	2,10,000	19.60
04.05.1994	7,71,600	72.00
04.01.1993	90,000	8.40
Total	10,71,600	25.00

The above shares shall not be sold/hypothecated/transferred for a period of 5 years from the date of allotment in the present issue or commencement of commercial production whichever is Safer.

Objects of the Present Issue

The Present Issue of equity Shares is being made -

1. To part - finance the Company's Project for expansion of capacity of Unit II from the present spindleage of 12, 480 to 24, 960 Spindles, and modernisation of Unit I.
2. To have the shares of the company listed in the Stock Exchanges, and
3. To meet the expenses of the present issue.

Highlights of the Issue

1. Existing, profit-making, dividend-paying Company.

2. Flagship Company of the Rs. 70 Crore Sambandam Group.
3. Promoters with proven track record in the industry for the past two decades.
4. Post - Issue holding by Promoters works out to 69.90%:
5. Project for addition of 12, 480 Spindles in Unit II, and modernisation of Unit I, leading to increase in spindleage from 37, 700 to 50, 460.
6. Project Appraised by IFCI and part financed by SBI.
7. Firm Allotment to ICICI to the extent of Rs. 60 lac at the same premium.
8. Tax Benefits under Section 80L and 80M. 141
9. Easy Liquidity - Listing at Coimbatore, Madras and Bombay Stock Exchanges.

Means of Finance

(Rs. in Lakhs.)

Rupee Term Loans- IFCI	650
SBI	300
Rights issue of Equity Shares	150
Public issue of Equity Shares	600
Unsecured Loans from promoters	50
Internal accruals	450
Total	2200

Brief Details of Promoters

Name of the Promoter	*Educational Background*	*Expereince*
S. R SAMBAUDAM	INTERMEDIATE	50 Years
S. P RAJENDRAN	——DO——	50 Years
	COMMERCE GRADUATE	20 Years

Marketing and Selling Arrangement

The product range proposed to be manufactured will include Carded and Combed Yarn in the Counts ranging from 10s to 100s. The end use of the product will be in fabrics manufactured through weaving, knitting and handloom process in both domestic and international markets.

The Company proposes to market its products in South East Asia, Hong Kong, Italy, and Germany.

The Company has already got an established market network of brokers and agents in Salem, Erode, Karur, Tirupur, Madras, Ichalkaranji and Bombay. As such the Company envisages no difficulty in marketing the additional output.

Justification of Premium

The premium of Rs.40 per share has been justified on the following grounds:

1. SSML is an existing profit-making, dividend-paying Company.
2. The past track record of the Company as summarised below:

(Rs.in lacs)

	1989-90	*1990-91*	*1991-92*	*1992-93*	*1993-94*
Net sales	1160	1285	1849	2445	2937
Pat	15.70	55.31	115.99	59.24	183.54
Equity Capital	46.44	46.44	46.44	185.76	185.76
Net Worth	260.55	311.22	422.57	465.89	612.28
EPS (Rs)	3.38	11.90	24.97	3.18	9.88
Book Value	56.10	67.01	90.99	25.97	32.96
Dividend (%)	10	10	10	20	20

3. The future projection (as per Company's estimates) as summarised below:

(Rs.in Lakhs)

	1994-95	*1995-96*	*1996-97*
Net Sales	2, 847	3, 903	4, 417
PAT	246	442	409
Net Worth	1016	1, 378	1, 708
Book Value (Rs)	23.68	32.12	39.81
Dividend (%)	20	20	20

4. The offer price of Rs. 50/- discounts the average (discounted at the rate of 20%) EPS Tor the next 3 years i.e., Rs. 6.98, by a mere 7.17 times as against an industry P/E ratio of 19.9, leaving considerable scope for capital appreciation.

5. The Promoters have been in this line of business for nearly 2 decades.

6. Apart from the reasons mentioned above, the Company and the lead managers to the Issue, in consultation with whom the premium was determined, are of the opinion that the premium is reasonable and justified.

Audited Financial Information

Source of Funds	*31.3.94*	*31.7.94*
Share Capital	185.76	278.64
Share Application Money	—	—
Reserves and Surplus	426.53	441.01
Secured Loans	822.55	806.95
Unsecured Loans	569.40	535.96
Current Liabilities		
Application of Funds		
Fixed Assets	1088.68	1277.66
Current Assets	1429.55	1336.79
Miscellaneous Expenditure		
(To the Extent not Written Off)		

SPICE ISLANDS APPARELS LTD.

Brief History of the Company

Spice Island Apparels Ltd. was incorporated on December 28, 1988 as a Private Limited company. Subsequently, the company was converted into a Public Limited Company on October 6, 1994.

The product range includes ladies and children's wear.

The company is presently engaged in exporting readymade garments mainly to the United Kingdom, Japan and other countries of EES as a merchant exporter.

Main Objects of the Company

To carry on the business of makers, manufacturers, producers, processors, purchasers, in all types of knitted textiles, hosiery, belting, cords, nets, carpets, blankets, and to transact all manufacturing or curing and preparing processes.

Details of Equity Shares Offered Through the Prospectus dated January 3, 1995

No. of Shares	*Category*
10,75,000	Public (Premium of Rs. 25 per share)
1,00,000	Promoters.
10,000	Employees.
2,15,000	Mutual Funds.

Promoters Stake

Date of Allotment	*Total No. of equity shares*	*Equity shares locked*	*Period of lock-in in*
On incorporation	20		
30.3.90	1.980		
11.3.91	8.000		
25.3.94	17,40,000		
29.8.94	11.50.000	10, 75.000	5 years from the

			date allotment in this issue or from the date of commercial production as stated in the prospect us whichever is later
To be alloted alongwith the public the issue to promoters, friends & Associates	1,00,000	1,00,000	As above.

Promoter shareholding	BEFORE THE ISSUE	AFTER THE ISSUE
	100%	60.70%

Objects of the Present Issue

The object of the present issue of Equity shares is

1. To set up manufacturing facilities for readymade garments at the existing location i.e Bhandup (west) in Bombay.
2. To acquire new office-cum-showroom premises at Bombay.
3. To setup a knitting unit for manufacturing knitted Fabrics.
4. To meet the expenses of the Public Issue.

Highlights of the Issue

1. Existing profit making and dividend paying Company.
2. Export profits exempted from income tax. The Exports are 92% of the total turnover in the years 1992 and 1993 and 100% for the year 1994.
3. Company is in the business of export of readymade garments which has been declared as a thrust area by the Government of India.
4. Low gestation period - Commercial production from expansion project to commence in May, 1995.
5. Easy liquidity. The company's Equity Shares are. to be listed on Bombay, Pune, and Ahemdabad Stock Exchanges.

Means of Financing

(Rs. in lakhs)

Public Issue of Equity Shares	140
premium Account	350
Internal Accruals	90
Total	580

Brief Details of the Promoters

Name of Promoter	*Educational*	*Expereince Background*
UMESH KATRE	MBA	15 Years

The main products manufactured by the Company fall into two categories:

1. Readymade garments
2. Knitted fabrics/garments

In view of the present exports, satisfied clientele, increase in production capacity coupled with enhanced infrastructure, and substantial export potential, the management does not foresee any difficulty in achieving in the projected export targets.

Jurisdication of Premium

Past Performance of the Company
(Based on Audited Account)

(Rs. in lacs)

Particulars	*31.3.1991*	*31.2.1992*	*31.3.1993*	*31.3.94 (7 mths)*
Profit After Tax	116.17	81.72	99.71	51.22
Book Value per Share (Rs)	1769.30	2571.80	19.38	13.45
Earnings per Share (Rs)	161.70	817.20	302.50**	3.62**

**Annualised and weighted average

At present, the Company is only an exporter of garments and other merchant export items. Hence capacity utilisation has not been mentioned here.

The Company issued 17,40,000 Bonus Shares of the face value of Rs. 174 lacs in March 1994. Thereafter, it issued further Bonus Shares of the face value of Rs. 115 tecs in August, 1994 bringing up the paid - up capital to Rs. 290 lacs.

The financial projection of the Company for the next three years as given by the Company are as follows:

(Rs. in lacs)

For the year ending March 31	*1995*	*1996*	*1997*	*1998*
Profit after Tax	116.77	221.23	256.45	302.82
Book Value per share (Rs)	31.50	24.94	28.90	33.45
Earnings per share (Rs)	4.02	5.14	5.96	7.04

No developments after the appraisal have taken place which will have bearing on the Industry / Company / Promoters. No warrants / Debentures have been issued by the Company. Hence, there will be no effect on the projected EPS and Book Value.

The fair value of the share computed as per CCI guidelines works out to Rs. 37 per share at a capitalisation rate of 10%.

The Company and the Lead Managers, in consultation with whom the premium has been decided, are of the opinion that the Issue price is reasonable and justified.

Audited Financial Information

(Rs. in lacs)

Source of Funds	*31.393*	*31.3.94*	*31.10.94*
Share Capital	1.00	175.00	290.00
Reserves and Surplus	256.19	164.32	100.54
Secured Loans	—	—	20.00

Unsecured Loans	—	—	—
Current Liabilities	6.73	2.08	7.20
Application of Funds			
Fixed Assets	48.29	48.50	48.69
Current Assets	169.78	227.85	312.08
Miscellaneous Expenditure (To the Extent not Written Off)	0.05	0.04	5.69

VALSON SYNTHETICS LTD.

Brief History of the Company

Valson Synthetics Ltd. (hereinafter referred to as VSL) - was incorporated on 2nd June, 1983 as a Private Limited Company and was converted into Public Limited Company on 27th September, 1994.

VSL is an existing, profit making, dividend paying, eleven year old Company involved in texturing, twisting, dyeing and combing of yarns.

The Company is presently planning to expand its capacity for texturising and twisting from 40 tons to 100 tons per month and dyeing and conning capacity from 60 tons to 100 tons per month. This will also balance the in house capacity of the Company for all the four processes. The Company has already set up the texturising plant which went on stream in November, 1994.

Main Objects of the Company

1. To carry on the business of exporters, importers, manufacturs, spinners, knitters, weavers, ginners, processors, packers and balers of cotton, jute, hemp, silk, artificial silk, rayon, nylon, strechlon, polyester yarn, man-made synthetics fibres, staple fibres.

2. To carry on the business of spinners, knitters, weavers, processors, dyers, sizers, finishers, manufacturers and/or dealers in cotton, linen flax, hemp, jute.

3. To purchase, sell import, export and/or otherwise deal in raw materials and manufacture articles.

Details of Equity Shares Offered Through the Prospectus Dated 10.03.95

No. of Shares	*Category*
7,70,000	Public (PREMIUM OF Rs. 20)
4,00,000	Promoters

Promoters Stake

Particulars regarding Promoters contribution and Lock in period

Ref	*No. of Shares*	*% to Total Equity*	*Date of Allotment*	*Lock in Period*
B	50,000	1.63	30.09.94	
B	1,50,000	4.89	23.11.92	
B	3,00,000	9.77	22.11.93	
B	3,82,000	12.44	01.11.94	**
B	3,68,000	11.99	01.11.94	**
B	6,50,000	21.18	19.12.94	**
D	4,00,000	13.02	same as public	*

* 5 years from the date of allotment of the present issue or commencement of commercial production whichever is later.

** 3 years from the date of allotment of the present issue or commencement of commercial production whichever is later.

Promoters contribution in post issue equity is 74.92%.

Objects of the Present Issue

1. To part finance the cost of the expansion project as described in the prospectus.
2. To obtain enlistment of the Company's Equity Shares on one or more Stock Exchange/s.
3. To meet the expenses of this issue and other incidental expenses.

Flights of the Issue

1. An existing profit making Company in operations for the last eleven years.
2. Project part funded by ICICI to the extent of Rs. 200 Lacs under its Asset Credit Scheme.
3. Promoters well experienced in the synthetic yarn field with more than a decade's experience.

4. Company to commence operations for expanded capacity in trenches with complete project to go on stream by October, 1995.
5. Easy Liquidity - Listing at Ahmedabad and Bombay Stock Exchanges.
6. Silvassa unit of the Company is eligible for 15 years Sales Tax holiday and Income Tax holiday for initial 5 years and concession of 30% for the next 5 years.
7. Tax benefits available under Section 80 L & 80 M of the Income Tax Act, 1961.

Means of Financing

Equity				
—	Promoters	40		
—	Public	77	—	117
Premium				
—	Promoters	80		
—	Public	154	—	
Term Loan ICICI		200		
Internal accruals		75	—	234
Total		626	—	

Profitability Projects	1994-95	1995-96	1996-97
Capacity Utilisation	46	85	94
Sales	1166.00	216541	2408.66
Equity Capital	190	307	307
PAT	118.04	143.57	166.74
Dividend	20%	20%	20%
Book Value	15.90	23.95	27.38
EPS	6.21	4.68	5.43
Past Financial Record	31/12/94	31/03/94	31/03/93
Capacity Utilisation	82	81	61

Sales	670.53	391.16	ı11.92
Equity Capital	190	50	20
PAT	111.08	25.52	4.07
Book Value	16.87	28.82	33.38
EPS	7.80	5.10	2.04

Brief Details of the Promoters

Name of Promoters	*Educational Background*	*Experience*
Shamlal V. Mehta Graduate	Arts & Eduction	30 years
Suresh N. Mutreja	Commerce Graduate	20 years

Marketing and Selling Arrangements

The Company is already marketing grey and dyed yarn of about 60 tons per month. The existing client list of the Company includes reputed textile Companies such as Siyaram Silk Mills, Adhunik Synthetic Ltd., Seasons Textile Ltd., L.S. Synthetics, D.C. Polyesters, D.C. Textile Mills with whom VSL has established long term business relationship and goodwill. In view of the above the Company is confident of marketing its entire production.

Justification of Premium

The Company in consultation with the Lead Manager is of the opinion that the premium is reasonable and justified in view of the factors given below:

Financial

* Past EPS and BV in Rs.

Year end	*31.12.94*	*1994*	*1993*	*1992*	*1991*
BV	16.87	28.82	33.38	95.36	86.72
EPS	7.80 #	5.10	2.04	8.64	10.76

annualised

* The average industry P/E is 21 (As of 14th August,

1994 Capital Market) denoting the investor confidence in the industry.

* Considering EPS of Rs. 5.10 for the last accounting year (1993-94), the price of I Rs. 30 works out to a P/E multiple of 5.88. An annualised EPS of Rs. 7.80 for 31.12.94 gives P/E ratio of only 3.85.
* The offer price of Rs. 30/- is only 1.04 times the Book Value of Rs. 28.82 for 1993-94.
* The average EPS of last 4 years work out to Rs. 6,635 at which the *P/E* work out to only 4.52.
* Future EPS and BV in Rs.

Year ending	*31.03.95*	*31.03.96*	*31.03.97*
EPS	6.21	4.68	5.43
BV	15.90	23.95	27.38

* The EPS for 1994-95 is estimated at Rs. 6.21 at which the P/E works out to only 4.83.
* The average EPS estimated for next 3 years is Rs. 5.44, at which the P/E works out to only 5.51.
* Emerging Book Value after the issue and after considering projected profits as on 31.03.95 would be Rs. 15.90 at which the price of Rs. 30 works out to a multiple of 1, 89.

Company Strength

* An existing 11 years old profit making company.
* Promoters contribution of 74.92% of the post Equity Capital, denotes their strong commitment and confidence.
* Promoters well experienced in the field.

In view of the above factors, the premium is considered reasonable and justified.

Audited Financial Information

	31.12.94	*31.03.94*	*31.03.93*
SOURCES OF FUND			
Share Capital	226.35	78.80	20.00
Reserve & Surplus	30.66	94.12	46.76
Secured Loans	123.67	56.94	1.46
Unsecured Loans	64.61	47.28	3.37
Current Liabilities	151.11	60.57	33.94
APPLICATION OF FUNDS			
Fixed Assets	365.80	218.47	11.01
Current Assets	198.76	117.47	57.08
Misc. Expenditure (to the extent not written off)	0	0	0

AKAI IMPEX LTD.

Brief History of the Company

Akai Impex Limited, an existing profit making companis a Government recognised Trading House' engaged in the export of textiles, garments, dyes and chemicals, pharmaceuticals and engineering goods. The Company is also a bulk indentor of Partially Oriented Yarn (POY) and Polyester Filament Yarn (PFY) in the domestic market.

The Company was incorporated in 1977 as a private limited company and became a deemed Public Company w.e.f. 1-7-89 and subsequenlty converted into full fledged Public Limited Company on 5-2-93 and Certificate obtained on 4-8-94.

The company was initially set up to promote sale of engineering items including bicycles, diesel engines, agricultural implements and spare parts. The Company has subsequently diversified into the trading of textiles, garments, dyes and chemicals, pharmaceuticals, etc.

Main Objects of the Company

To carry on business in India and elsewhere, of exporters, importers, commission agents, consigners, selling agents, distributors, stockists, fabricators, transporters, warehouse man muccadams, brokers, clearing agents, manufactures and processors on small scale mainly for export purposes and otherwise dealers in textiles.

Details of Equity Shares Offered Through the Prospectus Dated October 27,1994

No. of Share	*Category*
3,06,8800	PUBLIC (PREMIUM OF Rs. 50/- SHARE)
3,96,200	PROMOTERS
5,85,000	UTI
7,50,000	NRI/OCB
2,00,000	LIC MUTUAL FUND

Promoters Stake

* SHAREHOLDING PATTERN: EXISTING			AFTER THE PROPOSED ISSUE (Rs. in Lacs)	
	Amt.	%	Amt.	%
Promoters & Associates	610.00	100.00	649.62	58.52
public	—	—	460.36	41.48

Objects of the Present Issue

The objects of the issue are as follows:

1. To part finance the project for setting up facilities for the manufacture of 12,000 tpa of Polyster Oriented Yarn (POY), 6,000 tpa of Texurised Yarn and 1,750 tpa of Knitted Fabrics.
2. To list the Equity Shares of the Company on the Stock Exchanges-
3. To meet the expenses of the Issue.

Highlights of the Issue

Established well diversified Government recognised Export Trading House with proven track record of performance and profitability.

Backward integration for the installation of manufacturing facility to produce 18,000 tpa of Polyester Filament Yam (PFY) and 1,750 tpa of Knitted Fabrics.

Company is entering the high growth field of Polyester Filament Yarn Industry. Production of PFY has registered compound growth of 14.5% per annum over the last decade.

Project is located at Silvassa which enjoys a Sales Tax Holiday for 15 Years and Income Tax Holiday for 5 Years.

Project has been appraised by Industrial Credit and Investment Corporation of India (ICICI) and financial participation in the Project from ICICI, SCICI Ltd., State Bank of India and Unit Trust of India.

Firm allotment of Equity Share at the same premium to Unit Trust of India aggregating Rs. 351 lakhs, to LIC Mutual Fund aggregating 120 lakh and to Non-resident Indians (NRIs) and Overseas Corporate Bodies (OCBs) aggregating Rs. 450 lakhs.

Equity Shares to be listed in Bombay, Ahmedabad and Delhi Stock Exchanges.

Means of Financing

Financing plan has been formulated as follows:. PA

(Rs. in lacs)

	As per the ICICI apprisal note	*Revised*
Means of Finance		
Foreign Currency Loan	—	1964
Buyers Line of Credit	2564	600
Non Convertible Debentures	349	350
Issue of Equity Shares at Premium		
- Public	3000	3000
- Rights	660	660
Cash Accruals	1310	1309
Total	7883	7883

Brief Details of the Promoters

Name *Promoters*	*Educational Back Ground*	Experience
Mr. S.N. Baheti	Electrical Engineer	20 years
Mr. V.K. Taparia	Commerce Graduate	15 years

Marketing and Selling Arrangements

The Company has an established marketing network for POY in domestic markets and Texturised Yarns in foreign markets. Its products will be sold under its own brand name in the domestic market of Surat, Bombay, Bhivandi, Silvassa etc. through authorised agents and brokers. For exports the Company has already established market for texturised yams and knitted fabrics in various countries like U.K., Columbo, Egypt, Singapore, Bangladesh, Kenya etc.

Justification of Premium

The premium of Rs. 50 per Equity Share has been fixed taking into consideration the following parameters:

1. The Company has a proven record of performance and profitability. The

Financial Highlights for the past three years are as follows:

(Rs. in lacs)

Year ended March	1992	1993	1994
Total Income	2909	4407	5207
Net Profit	338	451	463
Earning Per Share (Rs.)	676	8.94	9.26
Book Value (Rs.)	3458	43.10	50.58

2. The Company has allotted 11,00,000 Equity Shares to the existing Shareholders on a rights basis on September 5, 1994 at a premium of Rs. 50 per share resulting in the increase of paid up capital to Rs. 610 lacs. The corresponding Book Value after the increase in the capital is Rs. 52.28 and the Earning per share based on the profit of 1993-94 is Rs. 7.59.

3. The projections of the management are as follows:

(Rs. in lacs)

Year ended March	*1995*	*1996*	*1997*	*1998*
Total Income	5500	12276	13815	14854
Net Profit	547	1228	1475	1900
Earning Per Share (Rs.)	4.93	11.06	13.29	17.12
Book Value (Rs.)	59.75	69.01	80.50	95.81

4. The Book Value of the Equity Share of the Company as on March, 1994 works to Rs. 50.58. As against this, the Company proposes to offer the Equity Shares at a price of Rs. 60 which works out 1.19 times the present Book Value.

5. As per the projections of the management, Earning per Share in 1997-98, the year of normal operation would be Rs. 17.12. Assuming a PE multiple of 15, the expected market price in April 1998 works out to Rs. 257 per share.

The offer price of Rs. 60 discounts the Earning Per Share of 1993-94 by only 6.48 times (The average of Price Earnings of Trading Companies is 19.2 and of Polyester Filament yarn manufacturing Companies is 15.5).

Audited Financial Information

Source of Funds	*31/07/94*	*31/03/94*
Share Capital		
Share Application Money	500	500
Reserve & Surplus	750	—
Secured Loans	2192.93	2028.62
Unsecured Loans	1192.75	1069.44
Current Liabilities	50	
Application of Funds		
Fixed Assets	117.97	53.41
Current Assets	4129.19	3171.11
Miscellaneous Expenditure	7.18	3.20
(To the extent not written off)		

YORK EXPORT LIMITED

Brief History of the Company

York Export Limited (YEL) was incorporated as a Private Limited Company on March 21, 1983 as York Exports Pvt. Ltd. under Companies Act, 1956. On September 26, the company became full fledged public limited company.

YEL is presently engaged in manufacture of woollen knitwear/hosiery goods for exports with capacity of 2 lacs pcs. per annum at its factory at Civil Lines, Ludhiana. The new project unit is proposed to be set up at village Nandpur, Sahnewal, 10 kms from Ludhiana on the Ludhiana-Delhi Highway.

Majority of YEL's production is being exported to Russia and now it proposes to expanded and diversify its exports to European markets, and sell in Indian Markets.

Main Objects of the Company

1. To carry on in India or elsewhere all or any of the business or businesses of Manufacturers, Merchants, Processors, Dealers, Indenting Agents of all types and description of Hosiery goods, Knitwears, Blankets, Clothes, Fabrics.
2. To acquire, develop and render technical know-how and consultancy services in all or any of the matters including in the field of textile designing.

Details of Equality Shares Offered through the Prospectus Dated 08.03.1995

No. of Shares	Category
1550000	PUBLIC (PREMIUM OF Rs. 15/-)
100000	PNB
50000	NRI
200000	PROMOTERS

Promoters Stake

1. The post issue shareholding of the Promoters, Directors their friends relatives and associates will be 53.91% of the expanded equity capital of the company which shall be locked in as follows:

Date of Allotment	*No. of Shares*	*% of the Expanded Equity Capital*	*Locked in upto*	*Nature of Allotment*
Subscriber to Memorandum	200	0.10		for cash at par
17.08.84	3500	0.10		for cash at par
31.03.86	10000	0.30		for cash at par
10.05.88	125000.37			for cash at par
20.02.89	500	0.02		for cash at par
25.03.89	11700	0.35		for cash at par
25.01.92*	38400*	1.14		Bonus shares
15.10.94*	895300*	26.62	3 years*	Bonus shares
15.10.94*	640700	19.0	5 years*	Bonus shares
Present Issue	200000 premium of Rs. 15	5.95	5 years*	Bonus shares

* All these shares have been allotted as Bonus shares out of free reserves.

** Lock in period would commence from the date of allotment or date of commercial production whichever is later.

Highlight of the Issue

1. Existing profit making company.
2. Post Issue holding of promoter: 53.91%
3. Promoter having over three decades of experience in knitwear export.
4. Income Tax Benefits under Section 80 HHC, 80 L, 80 M, and 80IA of the Income Tax Act. 1961 and Wealth Tax Benefit.

5. Easy Liquidity - Listing proposed at Delhi, Bombay. Ludhiana and Jaipur Stock Exchange.

Means of Financing

PARTICULARS	AMOUNT (Rs. In lacs)
Equity Capital	
—Promoters	20.00
—Public	155.00 Share Premium
—Promoters	30.00
—Public (including firm allotments)	242.00
Internal Accruals	12.50
TOTAL	460.00

Brief Details of the Promoters

Name of Promoters	Education Background	Experience
Mr. Gian Chnd Dhawan		More than Founder Secretary of Hoisery Manufacture, Exports Organisation Science graduate

Marketing and Selling Arrangements

Presently, YEL's exports have been only to Russia. In addition to this, Company also has office arrangements through its marketing associates in Russia to enable it directly confront global competition. In order to expand and diversify its exports into European markets, and sell in the Indian Markets, it proposes to draw upon the resources and expertise of its Group firms.

For international marketing. Group Firm, York Exports which also exports woollen/ cotton goods to Russia as well as to other countries like Germany, France, USA and Switzerland has an established agent network in New Delhi and in Switzerland.

Justification of Premium

YEL has fixed the premium at Rs. 15 per share for the issue in consultation with Lead Managers. The premium has been considered as reasonable and justifiable on the following grounds.

Qualitative

1. YEL's Promoters has extensive experience of three decades in the woollen knitwear/hosiery goods industry.
2. YEL has a well established market in Russia for its products, detailed as follows:

(Year ended March 31)

Rs. in lacs	1990	1991	1992	1993	1994	Apr-Oct 1994
Turnover	579.61	615.16	289.70	282.63	489.13	170.02

Quantitative

1. YEL has a consistent profit making record of over 5 years and for the seven months ended Oct. '94 as proven by its financial results given below

(Year ended March 31)

(Rs. in lacs)

	1990	*1991*	*1992*	*1993*	*1994*	*Apr-Oct 1994*
Turnover	598.81	630.78	338.68	355.38	513.70	225.15
Profit before tax	42.33	33.76	21.64	68.58	120.95	62.95
Profit after tax	42.08	33.48	21.42	63.93	120.40	56.20
Equity capital	3.84	3.84	7.68	7.68	7.68	161.28
Reserve & Surplus	163.79	193.11	206.34	270.27	386.02	289.22

Dividend						
-Equity	—	0.96	1.15	—	0.92	—
-Preference	3.20	3.20	3.20	—	3.13	—
EPS (Rs)*	109.58	87.19	47.61"	83.24	156.77	13.02"
Book Value (Rs per share)	436.54	512.89	278.67	361.71	504.41	27.93

* Assuming the face value of each share to be Rs 10/-

** Annualised

2. YEL has a high book value, evidence profit generation and steady accumulation of such profits for growth and development.
3. YEL's post-expansion projections have been appraised at an average EPS of Rs. 7.53 for the three years 1995-96 to 1997-98 as shown below:. PA

(Rs. in lacs)

	1994-95	*1995-96*	*1996-97*	*1997-98*
Turnover	510.00	886.00	1044.00	1134.00
Profit before tax	148.18	222-40	264.59	291.17
Profit after tax	141.78	222.40	264.59	291.17
Equity capital	161.28	336.28	336.28	336.28
Reserve & Surplus	370.30	803.75	997.88	1218.59
EPS (Rs)*	18.08*	6.07	7.87	8.66
Book Value (Rs per share)	32.96	33.90	39.67	46.24
Dividend Equity Capital (%)	436.54	512.89	278.67	361.91

*annualised

The average P/E Ratio for the industry is 22.7 (Source: *Capital Market;* Vol IX/17. November 20, 1994), equivalent to a projected reference share price for this scrip, when listed, at Rs. 170.90. Since the Issue is being made at a price of only Rs

25, there is enough scope for capital appreciation in the hands of the primary investors.

Audited Financial Information

	31.10.94	*1993-1994*	*1992-1993 (7 months)*
Sources of Fund			
Share Capital	161.28	7,68	7.68
Reserve & Surplus	289.22	386.62	270.62
Secured Loans			
Unsecured Loans			
Current Liabilities			
Application of Funds			
Fixed Assets	41.52	46,07	57.39
Current Assets	527.61	461.68	345.55
Misc. Expenditure (to the extent not written off)	490.34	429.59	302.02

ARIHANT THREADS LIMITED

Brief History of the Company

ARIHANT THREADS LIMITED was promoted in Joint Sector by Arihant Industries Limited and Arihant Costyn Limited in collaboration with The Punjab State Industrial Development Corporation Limited (PSIDC). It was incorporated as a Public Limited company on 14th February, 1992 and received Certificate of Commencement of Business on 24th February, 1992.

The company is in the process of setting up a Ring Unit of 25200 spindles for the manufacture of cotton/cotton blended yarns at Goindwal Sahib in Amritsar Distt. in the State of Punjab.

Main Objects of the Company

1. To carry on the business of spinners, weavers, knitters, combers, manufacturers, producers, processors, importers, exporters, buyers, sellers of and dealers in all kinds of yams and fibers.
2. To undertake ginning, spinning, weaving, knitting, bleachin, dyeing, combing and pressing of varieties of synthetic fiber and yarns such as rayon.
3. To carry on the business of manufactures, producers, processors, importers, exporters, buyers, sellers of and dealers in all kinds of fabrics and textiles.

Details of Equity Shares Offered Through the Prospectus Dated 20, September, 1984

NO. OF SHARES	CATEGORY
1,75,60,000	PUBLIC (PREMIUM OF Rs. 2.50 EACH)
30,00,000	INDIAN MFS
8,00,000	————
28,00,000	FII/OCB/NRI

1,00,000	PROMOTERS
4,60,000	EMPLOYEES

Promotors Stake

Equity shares already allotted and to be allotted to Promoters as stated in B (ii) & D above shall not be sold / hypothecated / transferred as under:

Sl. No.	*Name Allotment Issue (Rs.)*	*Date of Price to commence Capital*	*Issue Shares from*	*No, of Post*	*% of "in-period*	*Lock to*
1.	Subscribers to MOA	12.2.92	10.00	700	Negligible	Nil-
2.	Arihant Industries Ltd.	27.3.93				
3.	Arihant Industries Ltd.	22.11.93				
4.	Arihant Industries Ltd.	To be allotted				
5.	Arihant Costyn Lid.					
6.	Arihant Costyn Ltd.					
7.	Arihant Costyn Ltd.					
8.	PSIDC					
9.	PSIDC					
10.	PSIDC					
11.	PSIDC					

Object of the Present Issue

1. This issue is being made to part finance the cost of Ring Spinning Unit with an installed capacity of 25,200 spindles for the manufacture of cotton / cotton blended yarns.
2. To meet expenses of issue.
3. To get shares listed on various recognised Stock Exchanges.

Highlights of the Issue

Project promoted in joint sector with The Punjab State

Industrial Development Corporation Limited. Promoters having an established track record. Export Oriented Unit to manufacture Combed Cotton Yarn. Locational advantage due to proximity to the source of major Raw Materials i.e. cotton growing areas of Punjab. Project appraised and assisted by industrial Development Bank Of India (IDBI). A part of Plant & Machinery being imported from Reiter of Switzerland and Schlafhorst of Germany.

Export Profits exempt from Income Tax, Tax benefits U/S 80 IA to the Company, SOL & 80M of the Income Tax Act, 1961 to the Investors. Project eligible for backward area benefits/incentives. Other concession include concessional duty on import of capital goods. Easy liquidity: Listing at Ludhiana, Delhi, Bombay, Calcutta, Madras and Ahmedabad Stock Exchange.

Means of Financing

Means of finance as per IDBI letter No. PFD.22.B (1953) /8066 dated March 28, 1994 is as under:

Particulars			
A) Equity: (Rs. in lacs)			
i)	Promoters		
—	PSIDC	1572.00	
—	Arihant Group	718.00	2290.00
ii)	Public Issue	2195.00	4485.00
B) Foreign Currency Loan (IDBI)		931.00	
C) DPG tor land (GIICP)		94.00	
D) Subsidy from State Government		30.00	
	Total	5540.00	

Brief Details of the Promoters

The Company has been promoted in joint sector by

Arihant Industries Ltd.

Arihant Costyn Ltd.

Punjab State Industrial Development Corporation Ltd.

Justification of Premium

Particulars	*1995-96*	*1996-97*	*1997-98*
Capacity utilisation	75%	85%	95%
PAT	444	566	714
Book Value (Rs.)	12.82	13.29	13.79
Share Capital	3588	3588	3588
Net worth	4600	4737	4949
Dividend (%)	10%	12%	14%
EPS (Rs.)	1.24	1.58	1.99

Audited Financial Information

Sources of Funds	*30.6.94*	*31.3.94*	*31.3.93*
SHARE CAPITAL	9,09,49,600	9,09,49,600	5,00,00,000
SHARE APPLICATION MONEY	8,51,24,550	8,51,24,550	4,81,57,000
APPLICATION OF FUNDS			
FIXED ASSETS	1,42,64,427	1,41,96,830	1,28,61,750

PRANAVADITYA SPINNING MILLS LIMITED

Brief History of the Company

The company was incorporated as a Public Limited Company on 12th September 1990. and obtained the certificate for commencement of Business on 16th October 1990. The Company started commercial production of cotton yarn on 1st July, 1992, with an installed capacity of 12,768 spindles.

For further upgradation of the technology and to modernise the plant the Company had planned to installed State of the art machineries, and accordingly the company had raised the necessary funds by way of placement of equity shares with Kotak Mahindra Finance Limited, and its associates.

Main Objects of the Company

To carry on business as manufacturers, processors, cultivators, fabricators, assemblers, ginners, balers, pressers, carders, sizers, spinners woolcombers, worsted spinners, all kinds of yarns and thread, including sewing thread and type cord yarn, natural and man-made fibers including cotton, staple fiber, synthetic.

Details of Equity Shares Offered Through the Prospectus Dated 20.06.1995

NO. OF SHARES	CATEGORY
3000000	Public (PREMIUM OF Rs. 5/-)

No reservation/Firm allotment

Promoters Stake

Type of Issue	*Date of Allotment*	*No. of Shares*	*Period*
Promoters	03.09.90	700	
Equity	27.11.90	650000	
-do-	01.02.92	849300	
-do-	31.03.92	102031	

-do-	31.03.92	897969	5 Yrs.
-do-	26.06.93	1285000	5 Yrs. 25%
-do-	20.09.93	724100	5 Yrs.
- do-	19.08.94	92931	5 Yrs.
Rights	17.01.95	1000000	3 Yrs.

@ NOTE: The lock-in period applicable to the promoters holdings as per the guidelines issued by the Securities and Exchange Board of India (SEBI) would be apply to 25% of the post offer for sale share capital of (he Company. Therefore 3000000 Equity Shares would be locked in for 5 years commencing from the date of allotment or commercial production whichever is later.

Object of the Present Issue

With an object to enable to Company to comply with the listing requirements of the Stock Exchanges, Kotak Mahindra Finance Limited, as a Shareholder of the Company (referred to in this offer for Sale Document as "the Offerer") has agreed to offer for sale 30.00,000 Equity Shares of Rs.10/- each for cash at a price of Rs. 15/- per share..PA

Highlight of the Issue

1. Existing Profit making Company, engaged in the production of cotton yams.
2. The Company is promoted by the Partners and Directors of Keshavlal Talakchand (KT) group of companies, exporters and manufacturers of Yarn, Textiles and Garments, having an experience of five decades.
3. The promoters are having established track record in the field of Textile Industry and the group companies/firms are winners of Fifty Five Export Award for outstanding Export performance.
4. Installation of expanded capacity to be completed by October, 1995.
5. Backward Area Benefits alongwith Sales Tax exemption for 7 years upto 1999.
6. Easy liquidity - listing proposed on Bombay & Ahmedabad Stock Exchanges.

Means of Financing

The total funds deployed for the expansion of the project is Rs. 1034.54 lacs as on 28th February, 1995. The detail of the sources of funds are as follows:

Source	*Amount (Rs. Lacs)*
Foreign Currency Loan	300.00
Share Capital/Premium	
Promoters	400.00
Bought Out	300.00
Internal accruals	34.54

Brief Details of the Promoters Name of Educational Experience

Name of Promoters	*Educational Background*	*Experience*	
Mr. Kantilal Keshavlal	Not mentioned	The group	
Mr Hari Kishore	—	do	-has
Mr. Madusudan D. Vora	do	—	experience
Mr. Bharat P Shah 50 years.	do	—	of more than

Marketing and Selling Arrangements

In addition to selling cotton yarn to local units, the group exports cotton yarn to Australia, USA, Canada, U.K., Germany, Switzerland, Belgium, Netherlands, Luxembourg, Portugal, Italy, Hungry, Poland, Czechoslovakia, Turnkey, Indonesia, Taiwan, Korea, Hongkong, Singapore, Mauritius etc. The group has already several selling agents and also extensive network in the countries of operation. The company proposes to utilise the service and expertise of export houses of the group to market its products aboard. For sale within the domestic market, the company has development a sales network throughout the company.

Justification of Premium

1. The Company has maintained consistent track record of profitability.

2. The Company is promoted by K.T. group, who has a established track record in Textile Industry of over five decades.
3. The Company is already in commercial production with no gestation period for expanded capacity.
4. The important financial indicators are as follows:

	FY93	*FY94*	*FY95*	*FY96*	*FY97*
Income	588.17	1635.67	2809.12	3432.54	3492.77
PAT	12.71	92.98	172.13	240.11	261.18
Equity	250.00	600.00	1200.00	1200.00	1200.00
EPS (Rs.)	0.51	1.55	1 44	2.00	2.18
Book Value (Rs.)	10.50	11.76	13.14	15.14	17.32

The present offer price of Rs. 15/- per share is at a Price Earnings (P/E) multiple of 10.41 based on the Earnings per share for 1994-95, as against industry P/E of 13.2 (Source *Capital Market* Vol. X/6 June 18, 1995). The offer price based on average projected earnings (1995-97) is at a P/E of 8.02, which is very conservative.

Audited Financial Information

	31.01.95	*31.03.94*	*31.03.93*
SOURCES OF FUND			
Share Capital	1200.00	600,00	250.00
Reserve & Surplus	—	—	487.00
Secured Loans	364.00	105.00	12.00
Unsecured Loans	94.00	4.36	26.00
Current Liabilities	375.00	216.00	77.00
APPLICATION OF FUNDS			
Fixed Assets	2249.00	76.72	99.52
Current Assets	1031.00	1073.00	26.26
Misc. Expenditure (to the extent not written off)	0	0	0

PRAKASH WOOLEN MILLS LIMITED

Brief History of the Company

The company was incorporated on the 23rd August 1979 as a Private Limited Company.

The company was converted into a Public Limited Company by passing a Special Resolution in the Extra-Ordinary General Meeting held on the 1st April 1993 and obtained a fresh certificate for change of the name on conversion on the 14th May 1993 from the Reigstrar of Companies, Uttar Pradesh, Kanpur.

With a view to diversify its activities, the company has entered into a technical collaboration with B.S. Corporation, South Korea, for manufacture of Acrylic Mink Blankets with an installed capacity of 4.32 lac pieces per annum.

Main Objects of the Company

To undertake dying, bleaching, or printing of woolen cloth, wool in process raw wool, synthetic & Terrywool, nylon, silk or other fibre for any person.

To carry on the business of ginning, processing, carding, spinning, weaving, bleaching, doubling or manufacturing and dealing in wool.

To carry on the business of wool and wool mix as spinner & doublers, cloth manufacturers, wool combers, worsted spinners, woollen spinners, wool and woollen product merchant, worsted stuff manufacturers.

To carry on the business of manufacture of and dealer in yarn, printed and embroided knitted cloth, fabrics, and other kind of woollen cloth nets.

Details of Equity Shares Offered Through the Prospectus Dated 14.09.95

No. of Share	*Category*
22,73,400	Public (PREMIUM OF Rs. 20) 50,000 Promoters
2,50,000	Mutual Funds
2,60,000	Indian Financial Institutions
1,00,000	NRI
1,00,000	Indian Mutual Fund
1,50,000	FIIs/NRIs/OCBs

Promoters Stake

The shares held by the Promoters representing 55.08% of the total Paid-up Equity Capital, after the Public Issue, will be locked-in as under:

	No. of Shares	*Date of Allotment*	*% of G above*	*Issue Price*	*Mode of Payment*	*Lock-in Period*
Contribution from Core Promoters						
	479078	Before 30.9.82	9.43	10	Cash/purchase consideration	Nil
	11222	30.9.92	0.22	10	Cash	5 Yrs.
	140100	15.2.93	2.76	10	-do-	-do-
	249301	18.11.93	4.90	10	-do-	-do-
	700000	6.10.94	13.77	—	Bonus out of Free Reserves	-do-
	120299	15.3.94	2.36	10	cash	-do-
	911700	5.1.95	17.93	10	-do-	3 Yrs.
	50000	To be alloted in the present Issue	0.99	30	-do-	5 Yrs.
	2661700	52.36				

Contribution from Indian and relatives of the Promoters

138300	5.1.95	2.72	10	Cash	3 Yrs.*
2800000	55.08				

Total No. of Shareholders - 203

* The lock-in period would commence from the date of allotment or from the last date of month in which commercial production commences, whichever is later.

Object of the Present Issue

The Objects of the present issue are:

1. To. part finance diversification of the company's existing facilities for manufacture of Acrylic Mink Blankets.
2. To meet the working capital requirements for the diversification project.
3. To meet the Issue expenses and
4. To get the Equity Shares of the company listed on Stock Exchanges.

Hightlights of the Issue

1. Existing profit-making Company, engaged in manufacturing of woollen blankets and woollen yarn.
2. Experience promoters with about 15 years experience in woolen blankets business.
3. Promoters, friends & relatives would hold 55.08% of the post-issue capital.
4. The company would produce acyclic mink blankets using Korean Know-how.
5. Participation by the State bank of India, Lucknow Local Head Office, in the Project by way of sanction of Rupee Term Loan to the tune of Rs. 370 lacs and Letter of Credit Rs. 342 lacs.
6. Listing on Bombay, Delhi, Kanpur, Jaipur and Ahmedabad Stock Exchanges.

Means of Financing

The total cost of the project amounting to Rs. 1175.02 lacs would be financed as under:

Equity Share Capital Rs. in lacs	
— Promoters	110.00
— Public/FIs, Mutuals Funds, NRIs	228.34
Share Premium	
— Promoters 10.00	
— Public/FIs. Mutuals Funds, NRIs	456.68
Term Loans	370.00
Total Means of Finance	1175.02

Brief Details of Promoters

Name of Promoters	*Educational Back Ground*	*Experience*
J.K. Gupta	Graduate	8 years
O.K. Gupta	Graduate Over	20 years
Vijay Gupta	Not Mentioned	16 years
R.K. Gupta	Graduate	35 years

Marketing and Selling Arrangements

The Company had envisaged to export 75% of its production through ready established network of trade in the Middle East. The Export turnover is estimated at Rs. 686.82 lacs in 1995-96 and Rs. 1664.38 lacs in 1996-97. The Company has received several offers from reputed Middle East dealers, who are agreeable to market Acrylic Mink Blankets manufactured by the Company.

In the domestic market, blanket industry is in an unorganised sector and therefore, it is difficult to estimate the real demand for blankets. However, the Company through its established network of dealers is already selling around 4 lacs pieces of blankets per annum, it should therefore, not be difficult for the Company to sell 25% of production which is being targeted for in the domestic market, through its established dealer network.

Justification of Premium

The Premium of Rs. 20 per Equity Share for this Public Issue has been determined by the Company, in consultation with the Lead Manager to the issue, on the basis of the following:

Qualitative Factors

1. Promoters have long experience in the field of Blanket industry.
2. The Company's proposed project is synergic to existing line of activity.
3. The Company had established a wide network of dealers/selling agents across the country.
4. Acrylic Mink Blankets have export potential, mainly to Middle East Countries.

Quantitive Factors

1. This is a well-established, profit-making and dividend paying Company. The past profitability records of the Company for the last 5 years and for the Five months ended 31st July, 1995 (audited) are as follows:

(Rs. in lacs)

Year ended	*31.3.91*	*31.3.92*	*31.3.93*	*31.3.94*	*31.3.95*	*31.3.96*
Total Income	273.36	395.43	588.53	757.80	933.38	365.79
PAT	0.25	21.54	15.33***	38.81	60.26	27.32
Share Capital	24.20	35.02	63.04	100.00	275.00	275.00
Reserve	14.07	30.60	45.93	442.46	* 395.41	* 418.41

EPS (RS) @	1.10	6.15	2.43	3.88	3.89	2.98
Book Value (Rs)	**15.81	18.74	18.02	17.91	11.70	12.69
Dividend (%)	NIL	20.00	NIL	20.00	15.00	—

* Including Revaluation Reserve of Rs. 362.27 lacs in 1993-94, Rs. 348.69 lacs in 1994-95 and Rs. 344.10 as on 31.7.95.

** Excluding Revaluation Reserve.

*** Includes prior period adjustment of Rs. 7.18 lacs. Annaulised value.

2. The projected key indicators for the next *A* years are as follows:

(Rs. in lacs)

For the year ended March 31	*1996*	*1997*	*1998*	*1999*
Total Income	2170.22	3551.95	3861.46	3867.47
PBDIT	398.38	670.79	722.11	736.78
Profit After Tax	175.38	401.64	484.33	538.13
Share Capital	508.34	508.34	508.34	508.34
Reserve	628.05	902.61	1259.86	1665.83
Dividend	20%	25%	25%	50%
Earning Per Share	3.45	7.90	9.52	10.51
Book value per share	22.35	27.76	34.72	42.77

*Annualised

3. The effective P/E ratio for the issue price of Rs.30 per share works to 8.70 in the first year of commercial production, after implementation of the diversification project i.e. 1995-96, as compared to the industry P/E of 14.3 for woollen industry (Capital/Market Vol. IX/24 dated 26.2.1995)
4. The company and the Lead Manager to the issue of the view that the premium is reasonable and justified.

Audited Financial Information

	31.04.94	*31.03.95*	*31.07.95*
SOURCES OF FUND			
Share Capital	100.00	275.00	275.00
Share Application Money	—	—	—
Reserve & Surplus	442.46	395.41	418.14
Secured Loans	329.50	376.44	446.93
Unsecured Loans	43.88	48.47	74.99
APPLICATION OF FUNDS			
Fixed Assets	687.01	722.05	743.51
Current Assets	360.40	729.08	667.73
Misc. Expenditure (to the extent not written off)	0	0	0

ANJANI SYNTHETICS LIMITED

Brief History of the Company

Anjani Synthetics Limited was incorporated by the Registrar of Companies, Gujarat, Ahmedabad as a Private Limited Company on 28th June 1984 in the name of Anjani Synthetics Private Limited and subsequently the company was converted into a Public Limited Company on 15th Júne, 1994.

Anjani Group is one of the leading groups in Textiles Industries in Ahmedabad engaged in printing, dyeing and processing of cotton cloth and man made synthetic fabrics.

Main Objects of the Company

The main objects to be pursued by the company on its incorporation are:

1. To carry on the business of spinners, weavers, manufacturers, ginners, prossers, packers, balers, liners and any other fiberous materials and the cultivation thereof.
2. To carry on the business of manufacturing weaving, bleaching, dyeing, processing, mercerising, designing, printing, sizing, weaving, and processing mill proprietors in all other branches

Details of Equity Shares Offered Through the Prospectus Dated 01.08.1995

NO. OF SHARES	CATEGORY
1689200	Public
700000	NRI/OCB/FIIs.
600000	Mutual Funds,
10800	Preferential Allotment to employees.

Promoters Stake

Date of Allotment	*No. of Share allotted*	*Face Value*	*% to D*	*Period upto which locked in*
15.10.64	9030	100	1.67%	Nil
15.12.84	10	100	—	Nil
29.09.95	970	100	0.18%	Nil
06.01.85	20	100	—	Nil
20.06.86	40	100	—	Nil
24.11.86	1930	100	0.36%	Nil
08.06.89	8000	100	1.48%	Nil
05.03.90	3734	100	0.69%	
*	23734			
08.10.93	175000	10	3.24%	5 years
08.10.93	87560	10	1.61%	Nil
10.03.94	250000	10	4.63%	5 years
05.04.94	725000	10	13.43%	Nil
05.04.94	400000	10	7.41%	5 years
31.12.94	525000	10	9.42%	5 years
	2400000	10	44.44%	

Objects of the Present Issue

The objects of the issue are as under:

1. To part finance the capital cost of the project.
2. To meet the margin money requirements for working capital.
3. To meet the expenses of this issue.
4. To list the Company's shares on the Stock Exchanges at Ahmedabad, Bombay & Madras.

Highlights of the Issue

1. Profit Making Flagship Company of the Anjani

Group of Ahmedabad, engaged in Processing and Printing of wide varieties of fabrics.

2. Promoted by experienced Promoters in the Textile Industry.
3. The projects is Appraised by Bank of Baroda, who have also sanctioned fresh term loan of Rs. 48 Lacs.
4. Proposed listing at Ahmedabad, Bombay and Madras Stock Exchanges.

Means of Financing

Particulars	*Present as on 31.03.94*	*Proposed after 31.3.94*	*Total*
Share Capital			
- Promoters	75.00	165.00	240.00
- Public	0.00	300.00	300.00
Reserve & Surplus	465.89	(-) 112.50	353.39
Share Premium	000	176.25	176.25
Term Loans	33.92	48.00	81.92
Unsecured Loans	135.06	(-) 86.69	48.37
TOTAL	709.87	490.06	1199.93

Profitability Projections

	1995-96	*1996-97*	*1997-98*
CAPACITY UTILISATION	77.50%	80.00%	84.00%
SALES	3712.74	3869.52	4129.13
EQUITY CAPITAL	540	540	540
PAT	277.19	288.05	310.03
DIVIDEND	15%	18%	21%
BOOK VALUE	17.28	20.81	24.45
EPS	5.13	5.33	5.74

PAST FINANCIAL RECORD

CAPACITY UTILISATION	76.36%	75.25%	87.69%
SALES	3855.17	3274.40	2328.22
EQUITY CAPITAL	240	75	23.73
PAT	107.05	48.56	23.78
BOOK VALUE	15.25	24.03	33.88
EPS	4.25	6.49	10.02

Brief Details of Promoters

Name of Promoters	*Educational Back Ground*	*Experience*
Mr Radheshyam Aggarwal	Matriculate	30 years
Mr Subh Karan Aggarwal	- do -	30 years
Mr Ram Bhagat Saraogi	Commerce Graduate	25 years

Marketing and Selling Arrangements

The company is already marketing its products through local dealers/brokers. The company has its sales outlet in the famous New Cloth Market, Ahmedabad. The company is also planning for direct export of bed sheets and other products in the near future.

After this modernisation, the capacity of the company would increase from 400 lacs mtrs. to 440 lacs mtrs. per annum. Due to high capacity of the unit. the different varieties of fabrics of better quality is possible to cater at a time. So the company is in the position to capture big indirect export orders from the merchant exporters.

Justification of Premium

Anjani Synthetics Limited is an existing profit making company with satisfactory track record.

The last 3 years performance and future 2 years performance (estimated) have been summarised as under:

	92-93 *(Acutal)*	93-94 *(Prov.)*	94-95 *(Projection).*	95-96	96-97
Net Profit After Tax	23.76	48.56	107.05	277.19	288.05
Share Capital	23.73	75.00	240.00	540.00	540.00
EPS (Rs.)	10.01	6.47	4.25	5.13	5.33

The average EPS of the three years ending March, 1995, 1996 & 1997 is 5.09 and the shares is offered at P/E ratio of 2.95

The Price Earning ratio of textile processing industry as per the latest Capital Market (Vol. IX/24 Feb. 26, 1995) issue is stated to be 14.6

Apart from the reasons mentioned above, the Company and the Leads Managers to the issue in consultation with whom the premium has been decided are of the opinion that the premium is reasonable and justified.

Audited Financial Information

	31.03.93	*31-03.94*	*28.02.95*
SOURCES OF FUND			
Share Capital	80.39	539.24	689.27
Reserve & Surplus	56.65	465.89	450.92
Secured Loans	278.05	360.41	365.91
Unsecured Loans	250.52	135.05	254.55
Current Liabilities	372.87	447.72	389.88
APPLICATION OF FUNDS			
Fixed Assets	220.39	599.96	631.54
Current Assets	761.43	882.67	1068.08
Misc. Expenditure (to the extent not written off)	0.017	1.65	1.65

COIMBATORE SPINNING MILLS LTD.

The company was formed with an objective to manufacture cotton yams. The promoter had 52.50 percent stake in the post issue paid up capital. The average profit after tax was projected to be Rs. 434 lacs for the next three years from the year in which the company come out the public issues. The company offered 33440000 equity shares at premium of Rs. 20 per share by way of public issues. The average earning per share was projected to be Rs. 10.85. The commercial project was stated to be started within 6 months from the date of issue.

TOWELS INDIA EXPORTS LTD.

Brief History of the Company

Towels India Exports Limited was incorporated under the Companies Act, 1956 on 7th August, 1985 as a Private Limited Company and was converted into Public Limited Company on 18th October, 1993. The Company set up its existing plant for manufacture of Cotton Terry Towels at Lote Purshuram, Dist. Ratangiri Maharashtra during 1988-89 and commercial production was started on 6th January, 1989.

Towels India Exports Limited promoted by Shri. Kulin H. Kothari belongs to Padamshi -Meghji 'group, which is in business since 1931. The company has been incorporated to carry on the business of manufacture and export of Cotton Terry Towels.

The company has been engaged in 100% exports of Cotton Terry Towels since inception.

Main Objects of the Company

To carry on, in any part of India the business of weaving or otherswise manufacturing, bleaching, dyeing, printing and selling yam, towels and napkins and of buying, selling and dealing as merchants exporters, exports house, importers, brokers, agents, indenters of yam, cloth, linen and other goods or merchandise made thereof whether textile, frebled. netted or looped including towels and napkins.

Details of Equity Shares Offered Through the Prospectus Dated 03.10.1994

No. of Shares	*Category*
1210000	PUBLIC (PREMIUM OF Rs. 25/-) 210000 NRI/OCB/FIIS
100000	Kothari Prioner Prima Funds
100000	Tauras Mutual Fund
50000	Industrial Reconstruction Bank of India

Promoters Stake

'Promoters' Holding	*Before Public Issue*	*After Public Issue*
No. of Equity Shares	2507200	2507200
Nominal Value (Rs.)	25072000	25072000
Percentage Holding	82.67%	51.68%

On 07.09.94 there are 379 Shareholders in the Company. Apart from promoters the existing share are being held by their friends, relatives and associates.

Objects of the Present Issue

1. To part finance the Company's project of expansion of Cotton Terry Towels manufacturing capacity and diversification in Processing and Printing of Bed Sheets at Solapur, Maharashtra.
2. To enlist the equity shares of the company on the Bombay, Delhi and Ahmedabad Stock Exchange.
3. To meet the issue expenses.

Highlights of the Issue

The Company belongs to Padamshi Meghji Group. Padamsni Meghji was established in 1931 and enjoyed a status of Government Recognised Export House for more than a decade ending 1992-93.

- Exiting, profit making and dividend paying Company.
- Winner of the Bronze Trophy, for excellent export performance (Exports 95.41% of total production) for the year 1991-92 and winner of Silver Trophy for being highest exporter (Exports 99% of total production) for the year 1992-93, as a Manufacturer -Exporter in Made-ups category for Cotton Terry Towels awarded by TEXPRECIL.
- The largest quota holder based on past performance for exports of Cotton Terry Towels to U.S.A., the

Company's share being the largest in export of Cotton Terry Towels from India to U.S.A. for 1992-93.

- Average annual growth rate in terms of sales is more than 70% over a period of last four years.
- Project appraised by SICOM and financed to the extent of Rs. 150 Lacs by way of Foreign Currency Loan from EXIM BANK and Rs. 30 lacs by way of Rupee Term Loan from SICOM.
- Latest State-of-the-art Machineries being imported from Nuovo Pignone, Italy.
- Low Gestation Period - Commercial Production for expanded capacity to commence from December, 1994.
- Sales tax exemption and other benefits for backward area.
- Tax benefit available u/s. 80 HHC and 801A to the Company and u/s 80L and 80M of the Income Tax Act, to the investors.
- Easy liquidity - Proposed to be listed on the Bombay, Ahmadabad and Delhi Stock Exchanges.

Means of Financing

The cost of project is proposed to be financed as under:- (Rs. in lacs)

Equity Share Capital - Public	180.00
Share Premium	450.00
	630.00
Foreign Currency Loan from Exim Bank	150.00
Rupee Term Loan from SICOM	30.00
180.00 Internal Cash Accurals	20.00
Total (Rs.)	830.00

PROFITABILITY PROJECTIONS

	1995	*1996*	*1997*
CAPACITY UTILISATION			
SALES	1416.00	3444.00	4757.00
EQUITY CAPITAL	483	483	483
PAT	241.50	543.00	806.90
BOOK VALUE	24.88	34.11	48.81
EPS	7.30	11.23	16.70

Brief Details of Promoters

Names of Promoters	Educational Back Ground	Experience
Sh. Kulin Hiralal Kothari	Not mentioned	25 years

Marketing and Selling Arrangements

The company started its commercial production in January 1989 and has been very successful in exporting terry towels. Cotton Textile Export Promotion Council distributes exports quotas based on numerous parameters. One of these parameters being "Export Performance in two years proceeding to the previous year" (PPQ). The company is the largest quota holder based on past performance for Export of Cotton Terry Towels to the U.S.A., the company's share being the largest in Export of Cotton Terry Towels form India to U.S.A. for 1992-93.

Justification of Premium

The premium has been calculated on the basis of various factors including past and present performance, future projections, hidden strength of the Company, Unique Position of the Company in the market etc. The following Points have been considered track record.

Qualitative Aspects

1. The company is promoted by Padamshi Meghji Group with rich experience in the field of manufacturing and export of Cotton Terry Towels and has established track record.
2. The company is an existing, Profit Making, dividend paying Company with high export potentials. Over the years, the company has gained good experience, contacts and goodwill in the international market.
3. The company is the winner of the Bronze Trophy, for excellent export performance (Export 95.41% of total production) for the year 1991-92 and winner of Silver Trophy for being highest exporter (Export 99% of total production) for the year 1992-93 awarded by TEXPROCIL as a Manufacturer-Exporter in Madeups category, for Cotton Terry Towels awarded by TEXPROCIL.
4. The Company's Products are well established in the international market and whole of its Production is created for export.
5. The company possesses quota for Terry Towels exports for 23,28,360 pieces for the year 1994 based on past performance.

Financial Aspects

1. The E.P.S. and Book Value of the Company are as under:

a) Past Performance:

Year ended 31.03.	*1992*	*1993*	*1994*
EPS (Rs.)	9.80	4.39	*7.47
Book Value (Rs.)	15.97	19.17	**17.86
Average Past E.P.S.*	Rs.	7.22	
Average Book Value**	Rs.	17.67	

b) Past Performance:

Year ended 31.03.	*1995*	*1996*	*1997*
EPS (Rs.)	7.30	11.23	16.70
Book Value (Rs.)	24.68	34.11	48.81
Average Past E.P.S. *Rs			11.74
Average Book Value **Rs.			35.93

* On Weighted Average Capital

** Excluding Revaluation Reserve

c) Price/Earning Ratio (P/E) Ratio

The offer price of Rs. 35/- is being discounted as follows, at various EPS

EPS	*P/E RATIO*
Average EPS of Rs. 7.22 for last 3 years	4.85 Times
Average Projected EPS of Rs. 11.74 for next 3 years	2.98 Times
EPS of Rs.* 7.47 for year 1993-94	4.69 Times
Projected EPS of Rs.* 7.30 for the year 1994-95	4.79 Times

*On Weighted Average Capital

Hence looking to the figure and based on the past performance, Book Value, future outlook and on the qualitative aspects of the Company, a premium of Rs. 25/- is considered reasonable and justified.

Audited Financial Information

	30.06.94	*31.03.94*	*31.03.93 (3 months)*
SOURCES OF FUND			
Share Capital	107.88	81.00	54.00
Share Application Money	138.41	136.79	—
Reserve & Surplus	372.54	363.82	49.67
Secured Loans	704.32	452.39	359.05
Unsecured Loans	6.26	7.75	52.33
Current Liabilities	103.32	62.91	63.98

TABLE 4.1

S. No.	Name of Company Stake (%)	Premium PAT Sue	Promoter's B.V	Avg. E.RS.	Issue	Avg.	Avg.
		Y	X_1	X_2	X_3	X_4	X_5
1.	Sambandam Spinning Mills Ltd.	40.000	69.90	206.33	1200000	36.54	5.12
2.	Sri Nachammai Cotton Mills Ltd.	60.00	48.07	508.33	1110000	6367	11.80
3.	The Rai Saheb Rekhchand Mohota Spinning & Weaving Mills Ltd.	80.00	74.22	30353	1077470	64.4.47	7.59
4.	Acknit Knitting Ltd.	5.00	30.00	151.97	2100000	18.62	5.07
5.	Spice Island Apparels Ltd.	25.00	60.70	260.16	1400000	29.10	6.05
6.	Valson Synthetics Ltd.	20.00	74.92	142.79	770000	22.41	544
7.	Prakash Woollen Mills Ltd.	20.00	55.08	474.70	2283400	3509	9.31
8.	Tuni Textile Mills Ltd.	2.50	44.44	257.75	3216000	15.66	446
9.	Pranavaditya Spinning Mills Ltd.	5.00	46.68	224.48	300000	15.20	1.88
10.	Anjani Synthetics Ltd.	5.00	44.44	291.76	3000000	20.85	5.40
11.	York Exports Ltd.	15.00	53.91	259.39	1550000	39.94	7.54
12.	Sunil Industries Ltd.	20.00	47.62	245.21	2200000	3562	5.84
13.	Akai Impex Ltd.	50.00	58.52	1534.67	3068800	80.00	12.66
14.	Arihant Threads Ltd.	2.50	26.05	575.67	17560000	13.30	1 31
15.	Bhilwara Spinners Ltd	10.00	25.01	310	75000000	28.14	4.54
16.	Towels India Exports Ltd.	25.00	58.27	530.40	18000000	41.46	13.96
17.	Coimbatore Spinning Milts Ltd.	20.00	52.50	434	33440000	47.55	10.85

AVG: Average PAT: Profit after Tax B.V: Book Value E.PS.: Earning per share

APPLICATION OF FUNDS			
Fixed Assets	436.72	158.22	3.37
Current Assets	14 96	12.78	9.70
Misc. Expenditure (to the extent not written off)	0.14	0.14	0.18

The correlation coefficient between premium and other variable considered in study are:

Premium	Variable	Coefficient of Correlation
-do-	Book Value	0.3074
-do-	Earning per share	0.8564
-do-	Profit After Tax	0.3356
-do-	Issue size	- 0.2392
-do-	Promoter stake	+ 0.24384

As can be seen from the table drawn above, the premium has positive correlation with book value, earning for share, profit after tax, promoter stake and negative correlation with issue size. Thus, it signifies if the the amount of book value, earning per share, profit after tax, and promoter stake are higher, the higher amount of premium can be charged. Similarly, the larger the issue size the smaller the amount of premium that can be charged. Practically also it has been observed that in the case of large issues, the merchant bankers try to adopt conservative approach and prefer to fix slightly lower premium than what they could have charged in case small issues for the same company.

The other important conclusion which is drawn from various coefficients of correlation is that the amount of premium is highly correlated with the projected earning per share, which undoubtedly is one of the most important parameter widely used by investors in India to asses their investment proposals in securities market. Another point which needs to be highlighted is that PAT and EPS are closely related but premium shows high correlation with EPS and low correlation with PAT. This is due to the fact that the investors are more inclined towards high EPS rather than high PAT. A company having certain PAT with low equity would be preferred over the company having equal amount of PAT with large equity as it would lead to distribution of larger profit among several shareholder.

The promoter stake has also shown positive correlation with the amount of premium charged. This indicates higher the percentage of shares held by promoters, larger the amount of premium that can be charged. When the promoter stake is higher, the investors are more assured of higher returns and they do not mind in paying higher premium. It strengthens the confidence of investors in the success of the project and towers the perception of investor about the riskiness associated with cash inflows on the commissioning up of project. The relationship between the amount of premium and the aforementioned variable is also displayed through the figures drawn on pages 194, 195& 196.

After assessing the relationship between the premium and variables considered important in determining the premium, a multiple regression was run on the premium charged (dependent variable) and all other variables as Independent variables. The statistical result so obtained is given as under:

1. Intercept: - 22.019
2.

	Coefficient	Standard Error	t-ratio
Avg Book value (X_1)	1.38	0.187	7.38
Issue Size (X_2)	.0.00000001	0.00000139	0.0072
Average PAT (X_3)	- 0.032	0.0107	2.98
Promoter Stake (X_4)	0.157	0.149	1.05
Average EPS (X_5)	0.021	0.011	1.31

3. Coefficient of Determination (R^2) = 0.87

Diagram Displaying Relationship Between Premium and Promoter's Stake

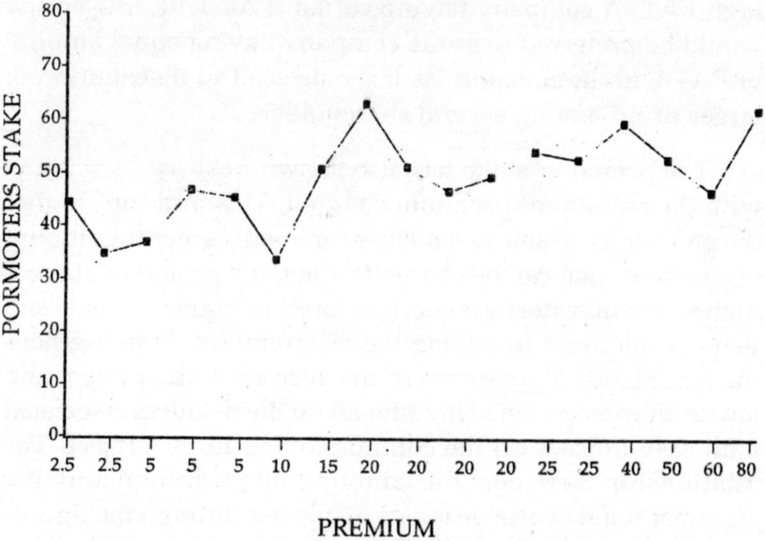

Diagram Displaying Relationship Between Premium and Average PAT

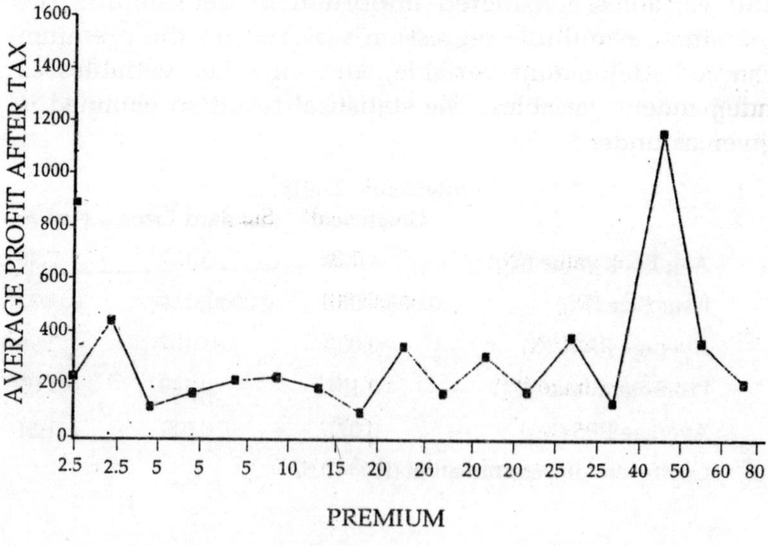

Diagram Displaying Relationship Between Premium and Average EPS

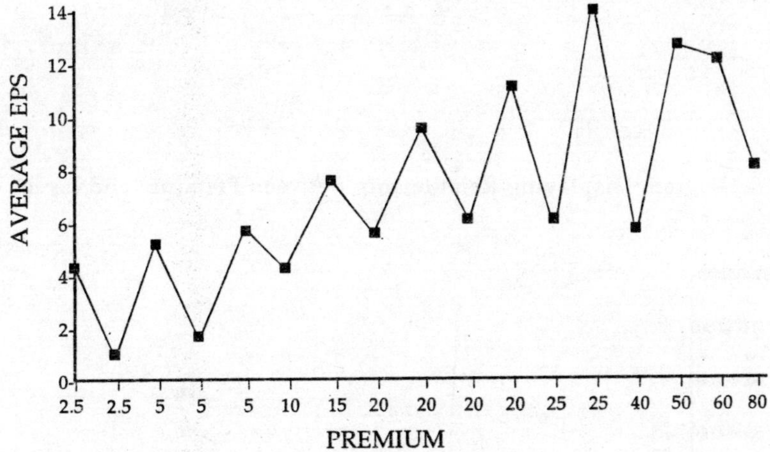

Diagram Displaying Relationship Between Premium and Average Book Value

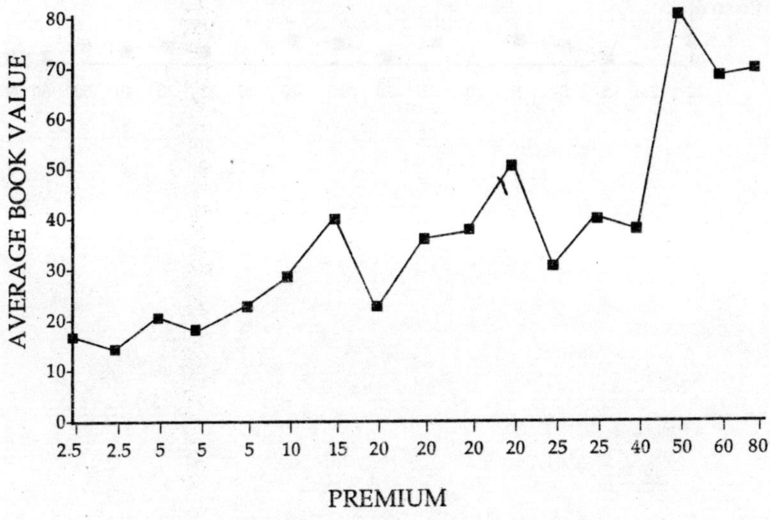

Diagram Displaying Relationship Between Premium and Issue Size

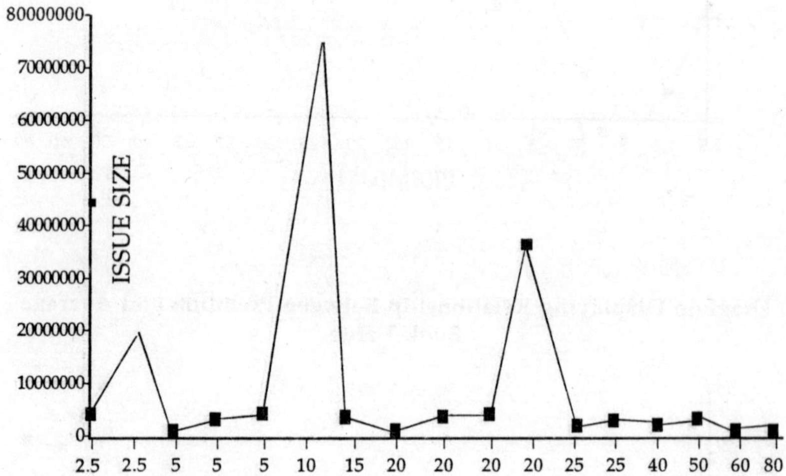

Statistical Interpretation

The equation which provides estimate of the dependent variable (Premium from values of the independent variables is given as under:

$$Y=-22.019+1.38\,X_1-0.0000001\,X,-0.032\,X,+0.157\,X,+\ 0.021\,X_5 \quad \text{.........} \text{ model 1}$$

Using this relationship between premium and independent variables one can estimate the value of premium for different sets of independent variables.

Another inference which is drawn from the statistical result is the value of standard error for each independent variable. The standard error of estimate measure the dispersion about the average line, called the regression line. The standard error of estimate measure the accuracy of the estimated figures. It is found that the estimated coefficients are statistically significant in case of average book value, PAT and average EPS. The coefficient related to issue size is of rights sign but statistically insignificant. Promoter's stake is also found to be statistically insignificant. As can be observed in our case, the value of standard error for each of the independent variable was obtained to be very small.

The coefficient of multiple determination in this case has come out to be 0.87 which indicates that 87 per cent of the variation in the dependent variable is explained by the independent variables included in the regression equation. The model therefore appear to have a good fit.

Using the estimated equation obtained above the value of premium for all the seventeen companies was evaluated and its relationship with the fair price was assessed as shown below:

The correlation coefficient between fair price and the price calculated on the basis of regression equation has came out to be 0.87 which is quite high. However, in order to further increase the degree of accuracy, some other variables which could affect the fair price have been explored. The variance of fair price from the actual price charged is given as under:

TABLE 4.2

S. No.	Name of company	Premium actual	Premium evaluated charged	Fair Price using model 1	Price as per model 1
1.	Sambandam Spinning Mills Ltd.	40.00	34.08	33.75	44.08
2.	Sri Nachammai Cotton Mills Ltd.	60.00	57.47	49	67.47
3.	The Rai Saheb Rekhchand Mohota Spinning & Weaving Mills Ltd.	80.00	70.11	107.50	80.11
4.	Acknit Knitting Ltd.	5.00	3.84	11	13.84
5.	Spice Island Apparels Ltd	25.00	19.60	24	29.60
6.	Valson Synthetics Ltd.	20.00	7.74	9.75	17.74
7.	Prakash Woollen Mills Ltd.	20.00	-.56	11	9.44
8	Tuni Textile Mills Ltd.	2.50	4.60	13.5	14.60
9.	Pranavaditya Spinning Mills Ltd.	5.00	33.56	18	43.50
10	Anjani Synthetics Ltd,	5.00	27.11	27.75	37.11
11	York Exports Ltd.	15.00	49.03	49	59.03
12.	Sunil Industries Ltd.	20.00	5.31	8.50	15.31
13.	Akai Impex Ltd.	50.00	18.41	15	2841
14.	Arihant Threads Ltd.	2 50	16.08	33	26.09
15.	Bhilwara Spinners Ltd.	10.00	8.41	21.50	18.41
16.	Towels India Exports Ltd.	25.00	27.84	31	37.84
17.	Coimbatore Spinning Mills Ltd.	20.00	20.27	29	30.27

TABLE 4.3

Name of Company	Actual Price	Fair price	% Variance
Sambandam. Spinning Mills Ltd.	50	33.75	-32.50
Sri Nachammai Cotton Mills Ltd. 70	49	-30	
The Rai Saheb Rekhchand Mohota Spg. & Wvg. Mills Ltd.	90	107.50	19.44
Acknit Knitting Ltd.	15	11	-2666
Spice Islands Apparels Ltd.	35	24	-31.42

Tuni Textile Mills Ltd.	12.5	9.75	-22
Pranavaditya Spinning Milte Ltd.	15	11	-26.66
Anjani Synthetics Ltd.	15	13.50	-10
York Exports Ltd.	25	18	-28
Sunil Industries Ltd.	30	27.75	-7.5
Akai Impex Ltd.	60	49	-18.33
Arihant Threads Ltd.	12.50	850	-32
Bhilwara Spinners Ltd.	20	15	-25
Valson Synthetics Ltd.	30	33	10
Coimbatore Spinning Mills Ltd.	20	21.50	7.5
Towels India Exports Ltd.	35	31	-11.42
Prakash Woollen Mills Ltd,	30	29	-3.33

As can be observed from the table 4.3, most of the ISSUES HAVE BEEN OVERPRICED because the variance have appeared with negative signs. The reasons for such variances were investigated through interactions with 5 merchant bankers and other issue management intermediaries.

Following factors were attributed to these variances

1. Promoter's experience.
2. Time gap between the date of issue and the commencement of commercial production.
3. Difference in Net Profit Margin earned by the company in pre-issue period and proposed to be earned by the company in post issue period.
4. Reserves of the company.
5. Number of equity shares to be issued.
6. Extent of term loan in the financing of the project.

It was stated by various merchant bankers that the above factors are not given due importance while fixing the premium on new issue in the normal course. But, most of them expressed their importance and suggested that the premium calculation should involve the above factors too. The importance of the above mentioned factors and the manner in which they may affect the premium on new issue is discussed below.

1. Promoter Experience

The promoter experience has important role to play in successful operations of the company. The larger the experience of the promoter, the greater the chances of success of the project. The experience of the promoter is always mentioned in highlights of the issue to attract the investors to apply for shares. The risk of investment in case of projects being managed by the experienced promoter is comparatively lesser than those being managed by the first generation promoters. Thus, the experience of promoters is also taken into account by primary market investors while evaluating their investment proposals.

2. Time Gap Between the Date of Issue and the Commencement of Commercial Production

This is another important factor which affects the quantum of premium. The projects which are likely to start in near future are preferred over these which are likely to start after considerable period of time from the date of issue. The uncertainities in respect of profitability and commissioning of the project in case of projects which are likely to start late are more as compared to the ones which are likely to start sooner. Thus, it has been observed that primary market investors prefer those projects where time gap between their investment and commencement of commercial production is small because in case where commercial production is likely to start later, problems such as cost escalation takes place which affect the profitability of the project.

3. Difference in Net Profit Margin being Earned by the Company and Proposed to be Earned

Net profit margin is used as very effective tool in investment analysis. It enables investors to assers reliability of projections made by a company, and also in projecting the profitability of the company. It has been observed in various cases that a company makes financial projections with net profits which are significantly different from the net profit margins being earned by the company while in operations. The achievement of finanical projection in such cases is doubtful and the investors accordingly discount the prices of shares of such companies. Thus, while fixing up the premium the merchant bankers should take due care that the difference is net profit margin earned by a company in the issue period and post issue period should not be widely different otherwise it would reflect a very optimistic and unrealistic financial projection by a company.

4. Reserves of the Company

Reserves of a company as mentioned is the audited financial information of company has also been relationship with the amount of premium to be charged. As the reserves are used to evaluate the book value per share of a company, therefore they are also considered by the investors of primary market while evaluating their investment decisions because the company with high reserves compared to its paid up equity capital has chance of announcing bonus issues.

Thus, Reserves as an absolute figure may not convey any important information to the primary market investors but their size in relation to the paid up equity capital enables investors of primary market to make judicious decision in their investment proposals. The company with a higher value of (Reserves/Equity) is in comfortable position to charge higher premium against the company with lower value of (Reserves/ Equity).

5. Number of Equity Shares to be Issued

The number of equity shares to be issued by a company is one of the most important factors which is considered by primary market investors. Keeping in view the other factors related to the company, the investor concentrates on the number of equity shares to be allotted to general public so as to ascertain his chances of getting allotment of shares. Where the investor feels that the chance of allotment of shares are remote, the may not like to apply in such company for allotment of shares as his funds would get tied up and he may have to forego some other better investment opportunity. Secondly, where number of equity shares allotted are small, the chances of capital appreciation are more because the price of shares like other commodities is also a function of supply and demand. But it would be more logical if the number of share to be allotted are analysed in relation to the paidup equity capital of a company. The company having lower value of (number of equity shares to be issued/paidup equity capital) has greater ability to maintain its share price in the secondary market. Therefore, the value of (No of equity shares to be allotted/Paid up equity capital) should also be given consideration while evaluating premium of a company.

6. Extent of Term Loan in Financing of the Project

The proportion of term loan in the capital mix to finance the project also determines the amount of premium to be charged on new issues. Large amount of term loans exposes a company to high financial risk due to fixed financial burden imposed on a company on borrowing a loan to finance its project. Thus, higher interest payments affects the bottomlines of a company and thereby reduces earning per share which may not be preferable to any investors. Thus a company with lower proportion of term loan in its capital structure is in a better position to charge higher premium against a company having higher content of term loan in its capital structure.

The aforesaid variables for all the seventeen companies under consideration are summarized in Table 4.4.

TABLE 4.4

S.No	*Name of Company*	*Variance*	*C.P.*	*T.L.*	*RE.*	*DNP*	*R/E*	*N/E*
1.	Sambandam Spinning Mills Ltd	-32.50	6	0.43	20	5.41	0.99	0.028
2.	Sri Nochammdi Cotton Mills Ltd.	-30	15	0.27	20	2.92	0.71	0.016
3.	The Rai Saheb Rekhchand Ltd.	19.44	3	0.37	60	2.95	4.29	0.023
4.	Acknit Knitting Ltd.	-26.66	3	0	17	2.8	0.1	0.086
5.	Spice Island Apparels Ltd.	-31.42	4	0	15	-5.62	0.38	0.032
6.	Tuni Textile Mills Ltd	-22	1	0	30	2.95	0.18	0.055
7.	Pranavaditya Spinning Mills Ltd.	-26.6	4	0.25	50	2.12	0.3	0.25
8.	Anjani Synthetics Ltd.	-10	1	0.1	36.55	6.55	0.36	0.055
9.	York Exports Ltd.	-28	3	0	30	9.49	1.14	0.046
10.	Sunil Industries Ltd.	-7.5	1	0.25	30	0.5	0.55	0.052
11.	Akai Impex Ltd.	-18.33	6	0.249	20	0.87	1.82	0.027
12.	Arihant Threads Ltd.	-32	6	0.16	0	17.37	0	0.048
13.	Bilwara Spinners Ltd	-25	1	0	30	0.559	0.35	0.055
14.	Valson Synthetics Ltd.	10	6	0.31	10	2.81	0.42	0.025
15.	Coimbatore Spinning Mills Ltd.	7.5	3	0.53	30	1.47	0.55	0.025
16.	Towels India Exports Ltd.	-11.42	1	0.21	50	9.5	0.13	0.037
17.	Prakash Woollen Mills Ltd.	-3.33	0	0.314	15	4.97	0.82	0.045;

C.P: Time Gap Between allotment of Shares and Commencement of Commercial Production

T.L.: Extent of Term Loan

R.E.: Promoter's Experience

DNP: Difference in Net Profit Margins (Actual and Proposed)

R/E: Reserves/Post Issued paidup capital

N/E: No. of equity shares to be alloted/post issued paid up capital.

The coefficient of correlation was evalulated to assess the degree of relationship between the variance of actual price against fair price and these variables are given as under

Variance of Actual & Fair price	*Variable*	*Coefficient of correlation*
-Do-	C.P.	0.29
-Do-	T.L.	0.55
-DO-	P.E.	0.35
-Do-	DNP	0.129
-Do-	R/E	0.50
-Do-	N/E	0.26

Using Multiple regression analysis, equation was obtained with variance as' dependent variable and all the other variables as independent variables. The results obtained are as under:

Statistical Results

Intercept = -19.471

X coefficients	*Coefficient*	*Standard error of coefficient*
C.P.	- 1.9808	0.983
T.L.	51.827	2.0674
P.E.	0.1164	0.2898
DNP	-0.3056	0.6347
R/E	3.423	4.178
N/E	-72.810	70.277

Coefficient of Determination = 0.63837

Therefore the equation would be given as

$$CY = -19.47 - 1.98\,X_1 + 51.82\,X_2 + 0.11\,X_3 - 0.30\,X_4 + 3.42\,X_5 - 72.81\,X_6 \text{.....(EQ-1)}$$

The value of coefficient of determination implies that 63.83% of movement in dependent variable (variance) is explained through independent variables (all aforesaid six variables).

Using the equation (1), the new value of variance (%) are obtained which are given below:

Name of the Company	*Variance (%)*
Sambandam Spinning Mills Ltd.	-43.26
Sri Nachammai Cotton Mills Ltd.	-32.48
The Rai Saheb Rekhchand Mohota Spg. & Wvg. Mills Ltd.	-5.29
Acknit Knitting Ltd.	-29.012
Spice Islands Apparels Ltd.	-28.17
Tuni Textile Mills Ltd.	-26.32
Pranavaditya Spinning Mills Ltd.	29.62
Anjani Synthetics Ltd.	-28.39
York Exports Ltd.	-22.22
Sunil Industries Ltd.	-32.99
Akai Impex Ltd.	-28.10
Arihant Threads Ltd.	-38.69
Bhilwara Spinners Ltd.	-25.60
Valson Synthetics Ltd.	-41.88
Coimbatore Spinning Mills Ltd.	-52.065
Towels India Exports Ltd.	-29.04
Prakash Woollen Mills Ltd.	-32.32

The new values of variances are used to discount the prices obtained under Model 1 and new prices are obtained which are given under the heading Price Model 2 in Table 4.7

The correlation between the fair prices and price obtained under Model 2, i.e. premium evaluated through model 1 (discounted with variance obtained through equation 1, shown above) was evaluated and found to be 0.92. This shows that the methodology of calculating premium may be used to arrive at premium developed in the study to be charged on new issues. In order to achieve further accuracy in calculating the premium, the new values of discounting factors were calculated using the following variables.

1. Extent of term loan 2. Promoter experience 3. Reserves/ Equity.

Since the above mentioned variable have shown high degree of correlation with the variance (%) therefore multiple regression model was run using these three variables. The Statistical results obtained are as under:

Intercept == - 32.508

Y == - 32.508+ 42.29 X,+ 0.181 X,+ 4.28 X, ...(Equation 2)

Using the above mentioned equation the new value of variances have been obtained and are given below:

TABLE 4.6

Name of the Company	*Variance (%)*
Sambandam Spinning Mills Ltd.	-7.05
Sri Nachammai Cotton Mills Ltd.	-32.48
The Rai Saheb Rekhchand Mohota Spg &Wvg. Mills Ltd.	12.80
Anknit Knitting Ltd.	-30.21
Spice Islands Apparels Ltd.	-24.96
Tuni Textile Mills Ltd.	-22.25
Pranavaditya Spinning Mills Ltd.	-26.45
Anjani Synthetics Ltd.	-17.55
York Exports Ltd.	-24.27
Sunil Industries Ltd.	-7.07
Akai Impex Ltd.	-12.13
Arihant Threads Ltd.	-31.85
Bhilwara Spinners Lid.	-20.95
Valson Synthetics Ltd.	-15.36
Coimbatore Spinning Mills Ltd.	5.14
Towels India. Exports Ltd.	-9.91
Prakash Woollen Mills Ltd.	-3.44

The variances obtained above were used to discount the prices obtained through model 1 to arrive at prices under model 3 which is given in Table 4.6. The co-efficient of correlation between the fair prices and prices obtained using model 3 was observed to be 0.95 which is very high. The t-test has been used to assess the statistical differences between fair price and prices obtained through these three models mentioned above. It was found that the prices fixed by merchant bankers have shown significant differences from fair prices whereas the prices obtained through these models have shown insignificant differences from the fair prices at 5% level of significance. Thus the results have been statistically tested and found to be correct. Table 4.7

TABLE 4.7

S.No.	*Name of company*	*Price Merchant Banker*	*Fair Price*	*Price Model 1*	*Price Model 3*	*Price Model2*
1.	Sambandam Spinning Mills Ltd.	50	33.75	44.08	40.97	25.01
2.	Sri Nochammdi Cotton Mills Ltd.	70	49	67.47	45.55	43.57
3.	The Rai Saheb Rekhchand Mohota Spg.& Wvg. Mills Ltd.	90	107.5	80.11	90.38	75.87
4.	Acknit Knitting Ltd.	15	11	13.84	9.65	9.82
5.	Spice Island Apparels Ltd.	35	24	29.6	22.21	21.26
6.	Valron Synthetics Ltd.	12.5	9.75	17.74	13.79	13.05
7.	Prakash Woolen Mills Ltd.	15	11	9.44	6.94	6.64
8.	Tuni Textile Mills Ltd.	15	13.5	14.6	12.03	10.44
9.	Pranavaditya Spng. Mills Ltd.	25	18	43.5	32.95	33.83
10.	Anjani Synthetics Ltd.	30	27.75	37.11	34.48	24.86
11.	York Exports Ltd.	60	49	59.03	51.86	42.44
12.	Sunil Industries Ltd.	12.5	8.5	15.31	10.43	9.38
13.	Akai Impex Ltd.	20	15	28.41	22.45	21.13
14.	Arihant Threads Ltd.	30	33	26.09	22.01	15.16
15.	Bhilwara Spinning Mills Ltd.	20	21.5	18,41	19.35	8.82
16.	Towels India Exports Ltd.	35	31	37.84	34.09	26.85
17.	Coimbatore Spinning Mills Ltd.	30	29	30.27	29.22	18.67

PART-B

FURTHER ISSUES

The misutilisation of free pricing is found to be more prevalent in case of further Issues of Companies which are already listed on one or the other recognised Stock exchange.

The price behaviour of Scrips of various Companies before and after the closer of the further Issue clearly indicates the price rigging of scrips with a view to charge unreasonable and unjustified premiums by the companies.

The price rigging exercise of the company starts almost a year before the time of issue. The companies were observed to rig the price to the extent of about double the price at which they offer shares to the general public. The prevailing market price against the price at which the shares were being offered to the price rise and many investors to apply in the further issue of the company. But, the expectation of the investors gets belied when they find that the share price falls significantly below the price at which it is offered to them. Thus, the investors expectation for making gains on allotment of shares to them from the market are not get fulfilled. However one reason could be increase in supply of shares due to further allotment of shares leading to decrease its price but the other and realistic factor is withdrawal of company's interest from maintaining the price of its scrip at a certain level or it may be off loading of scrips by the company itself in the market which depreciate the price heavily.

Although Sec. 77 of the Companies Act prohibits company from buying its share but the companies finds one may or the other by appointing broker agencies so as to keep control on their share price. SEBI has also taken various steps to curb these kind of practices but investors would also have to get cautious against such practice so that they do not get trapped by fly-by-night operators.

The pricing mechanism in the case of further issues of companies includes prevailing market price of scrips of the company apart from other factors previously discussed in case of pricing of new issues of companies. Intact, the prevailing market price and the floating stock of the company play a dominant role in estimation of premium on further issues of companies.

It has been observed in case of various companies that the price of scrips shows continuous upward trends till the issue gets oversubscribed and finally it drops down significantly without any logical reason. This has severally hurt the Investor's confidence and eroded the common investors from the securities market.

The common investors who are putting in their hard earned saving in premium issues expect a marginal increase in the value of their investment in the scrips of the company at least immediately after the allotment of shares. But, this has rarely happened in the case of further issues. Rather, the investment value goes significantly down by the time shares are allotted and received by the investors. A company is required to enlist its shares on all the stock exchange proposed in its prospectus within. 70 days of the closure of issue. A company usually allots shares after expiry of 55 days from date of closure of issues after finalisation of basis of allotment with the concerned regional stock exchange. After the allotment the shares are despatched to the investors who have been allotted shares. The undertaking by the company or its registrar regarding dispatch of share certificates to all the allottees is required before the listing of shares of the company on a stock exchange.

Therefore, it is very clear that the decrease in share price of a company immediately after date of closure of issue is due to selling pressure of shares which are already listed on the stock exchange as unlisted shares cannot be sold on a stock exchange.

It also reflects that the prices are deliberately maintained by operators to such a level that the issue can comfortably get subscribed.

The case studies of some companies (named below) conducted during the course of research work displays the important financial parameters which can help in estimating a fair premium to be charged on further issues.

1. Sharda Textiles Ltd.
2. Gimar Fibres Ltd.
3. Rajasthan Polyester Ltd.
4. Somani Swiss (India) Ltd.
5. Banswara Syntex Ltd.

The price behaviour of these shares before and after the date of Issue alongwith its relationship with the premium charged has also been studied to estimate the accuracy of the calculated premium.

The premium should be arrived at keeping in view the qualitative as well as quantitative factors related to a company. The information which may have bearing upon the premium is discussed separately for all companies under reference.

BANSWARA SYNTEX

Brief History of the Company

The Company was initially promoted by Shri R.L. Toshniwal and Rajasthan State Industrial Development & Investment Corporation Limited (RIICO) in joint sector. The company was incorporated on 5.5.1976 as a Public Limited Company for manufacture of synthetic blended yarn. It received certificate of commencement of business on 27th September, 1976. Later on it was converted into Private Sector, RIICO originally subscribed to 4,69,293 shares, of Rs. 10/- each. In terms of the buy-back agreement, shares disinvested by RIICO has been bought back by the promoters, their friends and relatives at price ranging from Rs. 12/- to Rs. 57/- per share. The company is now working as private sector undertaking. At present RIICO is holding only 12,000 shares of the company.

The Company started its operations in April, 1978 with 12500 spindles at Banswara (Rajasthan) which is a backward area. The Company's performance has considerably improved in the year 1987-1988 onwards. Performance during the year 1993-94 has been excellent. The turnover of the company has increased substantially during 1993-94 to Rs. 9453/- lacs from Rs. 9100/- lacs (for fifteen months) of previous year recording an annualised growth of 30%. The company in fact is one of the market leaders in fancy spun yarn.

Main Objects of the Company

The main object of the company as set out in its Memorandum and Articles of Associations of the Company is as under:

To carry on all or any of the traders or business of preparing, spinning, doubling, weaving, scouring, sizing, bleaching, colouring, dyeing, printing and finishing, working or manufacturing in any way whatever cotton, linen, wool, silk, flax, hemp, jute, artificial silk, rayon, leather, cloth, manmade and other fibrous articles, chemicals or synthetic or textile substances, to treat and utilise and deal in any waste arising from any such operations and also of makers of vitriol and of bleaching, dyeing and furnishing materials and the buying and selling of and dealing in all of any of the aforesaid substances.

Particulars of the Issue Object

1. To part finance the cost of the expansion project being implemented at the existing location at Industrial Area, Dohad Road, Banswara, Rajasthan.
2. To modernise the existing plant and machinery.
3. To meet long term working capital requirement of the Company.
4. To lease out certain machinery & equipment to Banswara Textile Mills Limited where fabric of the company is processed.
5. To meet the expenses of present issue.

Project

The Project is to expand the spinning/weaving capacity of the company to produce Synthetic spun yarn and fabric respectively. The Company propose to install 3660 Spindles and 27 Shuttles Looms thus taking the total capacity of the spindles of 43632 and 72 Shuttless Looms.

Schedule of the Implementation

Particulars	*Date of Commencement*	*Date of completion*
Acquisition of land	—On Existing —	
Development of land	—Completed—	
Construction Work	September. 1994	February 1995
Order Placement of Machineries	October 1994	January 1995
Delivery of Equipments	January 1995	End May 1995
Commencement of Commercial Production	Full Production by End June '95	

Jurisdiction of Premium

The proposed premium has been justified on the following grounds:

1. Track Record

BSL is an existing, profit making, dividend paying company. The dividend declared by the company in the year 1991, 1992, 1993 and 1994 were 9%, 9%, 12.5% and 18% respectively.

2. Past Performance

Year ended	*31.03.91*	*31.03.92*	*30.06.93*	*30.06.94***
EPS (Rs.)	6.73	0.93	5.00	16.08*
Book Value (Rs.)	57.64	55.70	55.33	59.33*

* Annualised

** For fifteen months

3. Projected EPS and Book Value

Year ending 30th June	*1995*	*1996*	*1997*
EPS (Rs.)	17.65	14.94	14.59
Cash EPS (Rs.)	2340	19.40	18.95
Book Value (Rs.)	42.49	55.67	68.50

The offer price of Rs. 50/- per share discounts the projected EPS for 1994-95, 1995-96 and 1996-97 of Rs. 17.65, Rs. 14.95. Rs. 14.59 by 2.83 times, 3.35 times and 3.42 times respectively. As against the above, the current price/earning (P/E) for the industry textile - (synthetic/blended) units is 17.4.

(*Source:* Capital Market, Volume IX/15 dated 23rd October, 1994)

4. Current Market Price

The company's share is currently quoted at Rs. 67.50 (at BSE on 31.1.95)

Apart from the reasons mentioned above, the company

and the Lead Manager (s) to the issue, in consultation with whom the premium was decided, are of the opinion that the premium is reasonable and justified.

II Capital Structure of the Company

		Amount of Capital	*Total Amount (including premium)*
A. AUTHORISED			
78,00,000	EQUITY SHARES OF Rs.10/- each	7,80,00,000	
20,000	Redeemable Cumulative Preference Shares of Rs. 100/- each	20,00,000	
		8,00,00,000	
B. ISSUED, SUBSCRIBED AND PAID UP CAPITAL			
36,59,213	Equity Shares of Rs. 10/- each	3,65,92,130	
	Less calls in arrears	2,38,098	
	Paid-up Capital	3,63,54,032	
C. PRESENT ISSUE			
20,00,000	Equity Shares of Rs.10/- each at premium of Rs. 40 per share	20,00,000	8,00,00,000
12,19,738	Equity share of Rs. 10/- each at a premium of Rs. 30 per share on rights basis to the existing shareholders of the company (hereinafter referred to as right issue) through a separate letter of offer in the ratio of '1' new share for '3' existing shares held on 28.02.95 (Record date).	1,21,97,380	4,87,89,520
D. OUT OF (C) (I) ABOVE			
4,00,000	Equity Shares of Rs. 10/- each for cash at a		

	premium of Rs. 40/- per share are reserved for firm allotment to Unit Trust of India as Financial Institutional	40,00,000	2,00,00.000
3,00,000	Equity Shares of Rs. 10/- each for cast at a premium of Rs.40/- per share are reserved for preferential reservations to Domestic Mutual Funds	40,00,000	1,50,00,000
4,00,000	Equity Shares of Rs. 10/- each for cash at a premium of Rs. 40/- per share are reserved for firm allotment to a group of NRIs/OCBs on repatriation basis	40,00,000	2,00,00,000
1,00,000	Equity Shares of Rs. 10/- each for cash at a premium of Rs. 40/- per share are reserved for preferential allotment to permanent employees including working directors of the company	10,00,000	50,00,000
E. NET OFFER TO INDIAN PUBLIC			
8,00,400	Equity Shares of Rs. 10/- each for cash at a premium of Rs. 40/- per share	80,00,000	4,00,00,000
F. PAID-UP CAPITAL AFTER THE PROPOSED ISSUE			
68,78,951	Equity Shares of Rs. 10/- each	6,87,89,510	18,94,47,442

Details of Promoter's Holdings in Equity Capital

Date of allotment	*No. of Shares*	*Type of issue*	*Month when the shares were made fully paid*	*% to post issue capital*	*Lock-in period*
11.07.77	6,000	Original allotment	Oct. 1977	0.09	Nil
21.03.77	3,000	Original allotment	Jul. 1977	0.03	Nil
11.08.90	92,000	Original allotment	Dec. 1990	1.33	Nil
13.11.90	3,54,271	Rights Issue' 90	Feb. 1992	5.15	Nil
12.04.94	10,06,512	Rights Issue '94	Sep/Oct 1994	14.63	5 years
	3,20,185			4.66	Nil
On diff. dates between 12.9.77 to 1.4.94	3,58,710	Purchased from others and from RIICO under buy-back arrangements	Purchased fully paid	5.21	Nil
To be allotted	7,13,226	From present Right issue	—	10.37	*5 years

* Out of the promoters holding 17,19,738 Equity Shares representing 25% of post-issue paid-up capital of company shall remain locked in for a period of 5 years from the date of allotment in Public issue/start of commercial production whichever is later.

5) The allotment to employees shall be for a maximum of 200 shares per employee. The No. of permanent employees including working Directors is 2089.

Assets and Liabilities

(Rs. in Lacs)

	30th June. 1994			*30th November, 1994*		
	Rs.	*Rs.*	*Rs.*	*Rs.*	*Rs.*	*Rs.*
	(1)	*(2)*	*(3)*	*(1)*	*(2)*	*(3)*
A. ASSETS						
Fixed Assets						
Gross Block		3408.48			3992.40	
Less: Depreciation		1399.57			1746.51	
Net Block			2008.91			2515.89
Investment			9.07			9.07
(Unquoted at cost)						
Current Assets, Loans and Advances						
Inventories		1962.78			2456.10	
Sundry Debtors		1372.95			1706.44	
Cash & Bank Balances		194.88			229.43	
Loans & Advances		629.00			610.94	
		4159.61			5002.94	
Less: Current Liabilities and Provisions						
Current Liabilities	2371.54			3056.75		
Provisions	78.29	2449.83		45.00	3101.75	
Net Current Assets			1709.78			1901.16
Total Assets			3727.76			4426.12
Less: Loan Fund						
Secured		2305.55			2591.29	
Unsecured		207.09	2512.64		383.40	2974.69
			1215.12			1451.43
B. REPRESENTED BY						
Share Capital Paid up						
1626317 Equity Shares of Rs. 10/- each			162.63			162.63
2032896 Equity Shares of Rs. 10/- each			203.29			203.29

Less: Allotment money due for payment by 11.7.94						
From Directors	20.95			0.13		
From others	80.17			0.91		
	101.12	101.12	102.17	2.04	2.04	201.25
			264.80			363.88
RESERVE AND SURPLUS						
Capital Reserve (Central Cash Subsidy)		16.76			31.76	
Share Premium		20.43			40.25	
Revaluation Reserve		32.44			289.21	
General Reserve		478.00			478.00	
Investment Allowance Reserve		43.50			43.50	
Surplus in Profit & Loss A/c		85.26			224.52	
		964.39			1107.24	
Less: Miscellaneous Expenditure to the extend not written off		14.07	950.32	19.69	1087.55	
			1215.12			1451.43

Profit and Loss Account

(Rs. in lacs)

Particulars	*31-3-*	*31-3-1990*	*31-3-1991*	*30-6-1992*	*30-6-1993*	*For the 1994 (15 months) from 1.7.94 to 30.11.94*
A. INCOME:						
Sales	3515.41	4116.95	5412.51	8661.05	8879.93	4330.89
Job Spinning Charges	190.35	127.80	62.52	438.65	573.15	257.81
Export Incentives	37.15	38.24	30.96	29.63	66.96	86.83
Other Income	16.89	22.72	35.25	46.92	74.71	16.01

Increase (Decrease) in Stock	(169.99)	140.29	148.97	206.15	308.89	312.97
	3589.81	4446.00	5690.21	9382.40	9903.64	5004.51
EXPENDITURE						
Material Cost (B)	2060-14	2688.63	3581.54	5561.33	5325.51	2631.14
Manufacturing Expenses	445.33	579.97	768.76	1341.13	1519.89	805.57
Payment to and Provision for Employees	279.24	303.74	336.91	511.87	504.99	204.88
Administrative & Selling Expenses	180.90	189.99	245.60	422.50	523.14	253.22
Financial Expenses	230.40	248.25	339.11	596.53	610.53	278.02
Excise Duty	240.83	196.82	276.27	690.58	971.15	608.68
Prior Period Adjustments (Net)	0.11	-	0.36	30.24	4.77	1.76
	3436.95	4207.40	5548.55	9154.18	9459.98	4819.27
Profit before Depreciation and Taxation	152.86	238.60	141.66	228.22	443.66	185.24
Depreciation	85.58	90.33	127.26	167.18	80.22	45.72
Profit before Taxation	67.26	148.27	14.40	61.04	363.44	139.32
Provision for Taxation	-	-	-	10.00	35.0	-
Profit after Taxation	67.28	148.27	14.40	51.04	328.44	139.52
NOTES						
1. Multi shift depreciation for earlier years	164.26	-	-	-	-	-

2. Debts written off	66.73	-	-	-	13.97	0.26
3. Excess Investment allowance reserve withdrawn	-	-	-	105.00	-	-
A) Includes						
i) Sales of Scrap and Misc. receipts	7.43	9.56	12.17	13.94	11.99	5.59
ii) Rent received	0.93	1.06	1.04	1.51	1.20	0.64
iii) Claims received	4.09	5.88	6.40	10.50	19.78	0.03
iv) Liabilities no longer required written back	0.20	0.03	2.26	2.03	20.64	-
v) Sales Tax Rebates	3.43	6.20	10.72	14.79	19.52	5.83
vi) Gain on exchange rate	-	-	-	3.99	(0.29)	3.92
vii) Profit on sale of Fixed Assets	0.08	-	-	0.16	1.87	-
viii) Debit/Credit Balance Written off	-	-	2.66	-	-	-
ix) Sale of Import Licence	0.73	-	-	-	-	-
B. Includes purchase of						
Cloth	215.12	291.15	416.14	890.72	486.11	589.50
Yarn	48.15	3.52	29.06	16.83	173.05	266.34
Fibre	11.61	22.02	14.35	46.44	19.79	4.11
Textile Store	-	2.18	6.01	7.70	4.04	0.42

Price behaviour of share of the company-before and after the date of issue

PRE AND POST ISSUE PRICE BEHAVIOUR OF SHARE OF THE COMPANY

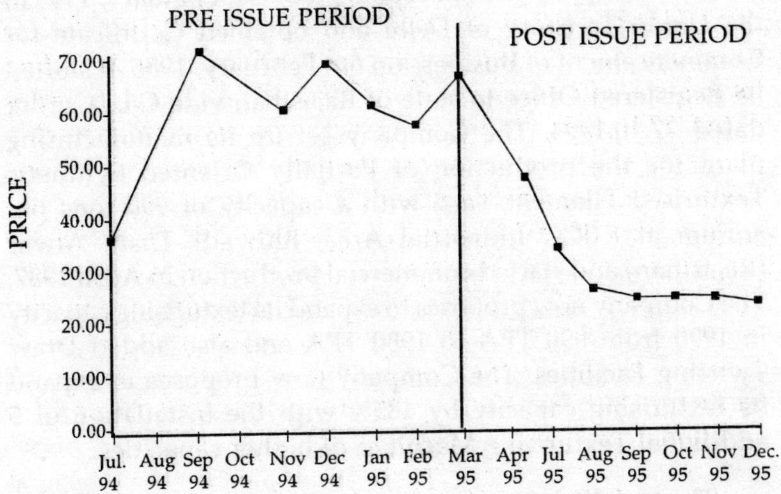

RAJASTHAN POLYESTER LIMITED

History and Business of the Company

The Company was incorporated on 31st January, 1985 in the Union Territory of Delhi and obtained Certificate for Commencement of Business on 6th February, 1986. It shifted its Registered Office to state of Rajasthan vide C.L.B. order dated 27.10.1994. The Company set up its manufacturing plant for the production of Partially Oriented Synthetic Texturised Filament Yarn with a capacity of 990 tons per annum at RIICO Industrial Area, Bhiwadi, Distt. Alwar (Rajasthan) and started commercial production in April 1987. The Company now proposes to expand its texturising capacity in 1990 from 990 TPA to 1980 TPA and also added Draw Twisting Facilities. The Company now proposes to expand its texturising capacity by 185% with the installation of 5 additional Texturising Machines of higher capacities.

The installed capacity after expansion shall be 5987 TPA as against the existing 2100 TPA on 350 days working on 80 denier basis.

Main Objects of the Company

The main objects of the Company as set out in the Memorandum of Association are as follows:

1. To carry out trade or business in all kinds of yarn like synthetic yarn, natural fibre yarn, worsted yarn, nylon yarn, nylon filament yarn, viscose rayon yarn, other rayon yarn, blended yarn of all types, viscose staple fibre, all other kinds of manmade fibres, chemicals and synthetics substances, polyester filament yarn, nylon tyre yarn and cord, various fibers.
2. To design, erect and provide consultancy and management services for synthetic yarn manufacturing plants and related units in India or Abroad.

II. Capital Structure of the Company

		Nominal Value	*Issue Price*
A. AUTHORISED			
1,47,50,000	Equity Shares of Rs. 10/-	14,75,00,000	
25,000	13.5% Redeemable Cumlative Preference Shares of Rs. 100/- each	25,00,000	
5,00,000	10% Cumulative Convertiable . Preference Shares of Rs. 60/- each	3,00,00.000	
		18,00,00,000	
B. ISSUED. SUBSCRIBED AND PAID UP CAPITAL			
18,62,500	Equity Shares of Rs. 10/- each	1,86,25,000	
C. PRESENT ISSUE			
a) Rights Issue			
3,72,500	10% Cumulative Convertible Preference Shares of Rs. 60/- each being offered to existing Shares Holders of the Company on Rights basis through a separate Letter of Offer	2,23,50,000	2,23,50,000
b) Public Issue			
29,80,000	Equity Shares of Rs. 10/- each for cash at a premium of Rs. 5/- per share are being offered to the Public	2,98,00,000	4,47,00,000
D. OUT OF THE PRESENT ISSUE TO PUBLIC			
7,45,000	Equity Shares of Rs. 10/- each for cash at a premium of Rs. 5/- per share are reserved for		

	allotment for Promoters, Directors, their friends, relatives & Associates (including Associate companies) (hereinafter referred to as Promoters)	74,50,000	1,11,75,000
1,30,000	Equity Shares of Rs.10/- each for cast at a premium of Rs. 5/- per share are being reserved on firm allotment basis for ICICI Asset Management Company Ltd.	13,00,000	19,50,000
1,00,000	Equity Shares of Rs.10/- each for cash at a premium of Rs.5/- per share are being reserved on firm allotment basis for Canbank Investment Management Services Ltd.	10,00,000	15,00,000
1,00,000	Equity Shares of Rs. 10/- each for cash at a premium of Rs. 5/- per share are being reserved on firm allotment basis for CRB Assets Management Company Ltd.	10,00,000	15,00,000
1,17,000	Equity Shares of Rs. 10/- each for cash at a premium of Rs. 5/- per share are being reserved on firm allotment basis for Apple Assets Management Services Ltd.	11,70,000	17,55,000
E. NOW OFFERED TO THE PUBLIC IN TERMS OF THIS PROSPECTUS			
17,68,000	Equity Shares of Rs. 10/- each for cash at a premium of Rs. 5/- per share (hereinafter referred to as Equity Shares).	1,78,80,000	2,68,20,000

OUT OF WHICH RESERVED FOR PREFERENTIAL ALLOTMENT

37,000	Equity Shares of Rs. 10/- each for cash at a premium of Rs. 5/- per share are reserved for preferential allotment to the permanent employees (including Indian working Directors)/Workers of the company	3,76,000	5,64,000

NET OFFER TO THE INDIAN PUBLIC

17,50,400	Equity Shares of Rs. 10/- each for cash at a premium of Rs. 5/- per share	1,75,04.000	2,62,56,000

F. EFFECT OF THE PRESENT ISSUE ON CAPITAL AND SHARE PREMIUM RESERVE

		Share Capital	*Share Premium Reserve*
a. At present			
18,62,500	Equity Share of Rs. 10/- each	1,86,25,000	
b. After the present issue			
48,42,500	Equity Share of Rs. 10 each	4,84,25,000	1,49,00,000
3,72,500	10% Cumulative Convertible Preference Shares of Rs. 60/- each	2,23,50,000	
c. After the conversion of CCPS after three years from the of allotment			
70,77,500	Equity Shares of Rs.10/- each	7,07,75,000	

7. The present and post-issue equity shareholding of the Promoters shall be as under:-

Shares	*No. of Shareholding*	*% of*
Present equity holding	10,45,000	5612%
Post-issue equity holding after Public issue of Equity Shares and Rights Issue of CCPS but prior to conversion of CCPS'	17,90,000	25.29%
Post-issue equity holding after conversion of CCPS	30,44,282	43.01%

Profit and Loss Account

(Rs. in lacs)

1990	*For the year ended 31-3-1991*	*For the year ended 31-3-1992*	*For the year ended 31-3-1993*	*For the year ended 31-3-1994*	*For the year ended 31-3-1994*	*For the year ended 31-7-*
A. INCOME						
Sales	1416.24	2175.58	2844.23	2912.82	3082.89	1110.25
Job charges	—	50.28	64.06	37.17	20.53	0.00
Other Income	1.74	4.80	4.75	11.68	6.52	9.50
Increase/(Decrease) in stock of finished/process stock	(6.42)	142.79	163.66	(170.87)	(98.81)	76.33
TOTAL "A"	**1411.56**	**2373.45**	**3076.70**	**2790.80**	**3011.13**	**1196.00**
B. EXPENDITURE						
Raw Material Consumed	1185.97	1994.50	2552.46	2222.00	2288.38	535.93
Excise Duty Paid	—	—	—	—	103.35	434.70
Manufacturing and other expenses	117.82	210.30	296.97	309.58	375.20	142.63
Interest and Finance charges	38.09	58.78	103.15	134.82	114.40	39.70
Depreciation	26.21	48.84	58.46	66.35	29.08	9.78
TOTAL "B"	**13S8.0S**	**2312.42**	**3011.04**	**2732.75**	**2910.41**	**1162.74**
Profit before Taxation (A-B)	43.47	61.03	65.66	58.05	100.72	33.34
(Less): Provision for Taxation	4.77	-	-	-	17.50	-
Add: Balance Profit/ (Loss) brought forwarded from previous year	(14.00)	12.27	7.40	27.02	50.83	94.25
Profit available for appropriation	24.70	73.30	73.06	85.07	134.05	127.59
APPROPRIATIONS						
Income tax for earlier years	-	-	-	1.29	-	-
General Reserve	.	3.05	3.28	5.00	10.00	-
Provision for divided	12.43	24.10	27.94	27.94	29.80	-

Investment Allowance	-	38.74	14.82			
Reserve Balance carried over to be Balance Sheet	12.27	7.41	27.02	50.84	94.25	127.59
	24: 70	73.30	73.06	85.07	134.05	127.59
SOURCES OF FUND SHAREHOLDER FUND						
Share Capital	123.90	186.14	186.23	186.24	186.25	186-25
Reserve & Surplus	27.27	64.20	101 91	14573	199.15	232.49
LOAN FUND						
Secured Loan	246.38	473.36	517.56	567.53	487.04	1029.74
Unsecured Loan	56.27	33.37	24.76	26.30	234.61	407.18
APPLICATION OF FUND						
FIXED ASSETS Gross Block	361.57	538.64	599.29	716.47	722.07	723.14
Less: Depreciation Net Block	79.27	128.12	186.58	252.93	282.01	291.79
Net Block	282.30	410.72	412.71	463.54	440.06	431.35
Capital work in progress including advances and preoperative expenses	11.28	21.57	45.65	4.26	142.31	885.63
	293.57	432.20	458.36	467.80	582.37	1316.98
INVESTMENT	-	0.07	0.17	0.21	0.21	
CURRENT ASSETS,						
LOANS &						
ADVANCES						
Inventories	72.69	211.89	427.84	227.80	134.13	188: 56
Sundry Debtors	60.02	186.28	157.67	211.03	285.73	240.68
Cash & Bank Balance	13.89	25.29	39.30	28.09	27.61	49.80
Loans & Advances	60.93	29.86	59.03	74.30	202.98	244.85
	207.53	453.32	683.84	541.23	650.45	723.89
Less:						
CURRENT LIABILITIES						
AND PROVISIONS	53.08	134.40	318.67	89.11	131.89	190.89
NET CURRENT ASSETS	154.45	317.92	365.17	452.12	518.56	533.00
Miscellaneous expenditure	5.80	6.86	6.86	5.71	5.91	5.47
(to the extent not written off)	453.82	757.07	830.46	925.80	1107.05	1855.66

Promoters & Their Background

The Company has been promoted by Shri G.M. Ganeriwala, Shri Ramnarain H. Dave and Shri A.K. Ganeriwala, Shri G.M. Ganeriwala, aged 34 years, is a Commerce Graduate (Hns) from Shri Ram College of Commerce, Delhi University. He has an experience of approximately 13 years in business and industry. Before promoting this Company, he was engaged in trading Synthetic Filament Yarn, Diamonds. PVC, Brass Scrap and Copper.

He is the main promoter of Rajasthan Polyesters Limited. The initial project was implemented under his supervision and control which was appraised and financed by two State Level Institutions i.e. Rajasthan State Industrial Development and Investment Corporation (RIICO) and Rajasthan Financial Corporation (RFC) in 1987.

Project Detail

The Company now proposes to expand its capacity by installing three Texturising Machines of 216 Spindles (machine speed of 700 mtrs./minute). As a result of "the proposed expansion, the Company would have an aggregate texturising capacity of 5987 TPA (on 80 denier basis).

Marketing and Selling Arrangement

The main markets for RPL's products are Surat and Bombay. The Company markets its products through a marketing network with sales office at Delhi, Surat and Bombay and selling agents at various other places. The sales to the weavers are made through agents/brokers. The Company currently has 20 agents. The agents handled the actual sale through a network of brokers. The Company pays the agents 1.5% on sales of which the agents generally pass 0.5% to the brokers.

The Company has already initiated efforts to market the additional production. About 8-10 additional agents are proposed to be appointed in Bombay and the relatively new markets at Ludhiana, Amritsar and Kanpur.

The Company's yarn is well accepted and hence no problem is envisaged in the marketing of additional production.

Schedule of Implementaiton

The detailed implementation schedule is as under:

a) As per ICICI appraisal

S.No	*Particulars*	*Commencement*	*Expected date of completion*
1.	Acquisition of land	Already/Acquired	
2.	Development of site	Already Developed	
3.	Civil Works Factory	September, 1993	April 1994
4.	Technical Arrangement	N.A.	
5.	Plant & Machinery		
	Order Indigenous-		
	Texturising Machines		
	Delivery	August, 1993	August, 1994
	Texturising Machines		
	Misc. Equipment	September 1994	February 1995
	Order	January 1994	March 1994
	Delivery	April 1994	June 1994
6.	Erection of Equipment	August 1994	February 1995
7.	Commissioning	August 1994	February 1995
8.	Trial Runs	Septermber 1994	February 1995
9.	Commercial Production		
	On two machines from	October 1, 1994	
	On two machines from	January, 1 1995	
	On One machines from	March 1, 1995	

Justification

The Company has fixed the premium of Rs. 5/- per share in consultation with Lead Managers to the Issue and is based on the following reasons:

i) The Company: is an exisiting profit making and dividend paying Company. The key financial data of the Company for the last three years and projections for the next four years are as follows:

	1992	*1993*	*1994*	*1995*	*1996*	*1997*	*1998*
Income	2844	2913	3083	5369	8328	8951	8951
PAT	66	58	53	197	285	305	309
Equity	186	186	186	484	484	484	707
EPS	3.53	3.12	4.46	5.05	5.43	5.84	4.37
Book Value	15.10	17.52	20.37	17.70	23.13	28.97	24.20

ii) The present expansion ensures optimum utilization. Book Value as at 31st March, 1994 was Rs. 20.37 and Earning per share at 31st March, 1994 stood at Rs. 4.46.

iii) As per the formula laid down by erstwhile CCI, the fair value of Company's share at 15% capitalisation of Rs. 19.19 per share.

PRE AND POST ISSUE PRICE BEHAVIOUR OF SHARE OF THE COMPANY

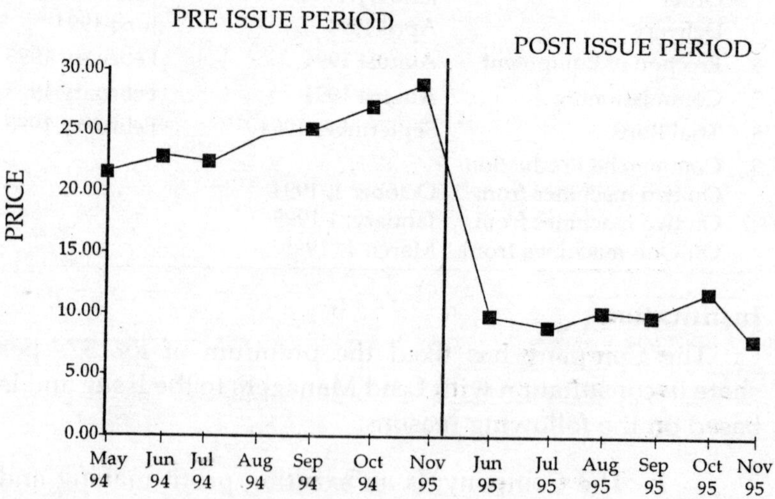

SHARDA TEXTILE MILLS LTD.

History and Present Business of the Company

Sharda Textile Mills (India) Ltd. was incorporated on 27th September, 1985 as a Private Limited Company and was converted into a public Limited Company on 3rd March, 1986. STML has set up a plant for processing of textiles i.e. Dyeing of Synthetic and Cotton fabrics with an installed capacity of 100 lac metres per annum. STML went public in April, 1986 with a public issue of 5,00,000 shares of Rs. 10 each for cash at par aggregating to Rs. 50 lacs and the same was oversubscribed by 25 times. The Company commenced commercial production in September, 1986.

STML further increased its capacity from 200 lacs to 300 lacs meters per annum in 1990-91 and the project was funded by Term loan from ICICI and internal accruals.

Main Objects of Company

The main objects of the Company, as stated in the Memorandum of Association of the Company, are:

1. To carry on the business of manufacturing, folding, decandizing, calenalering, including running hand and power process house, buying selling, importing, exporting, distributing and dealing in textiles, cotton, woollen, synthetics fibres, polyste, polymide, acrylic poly propylene, polynisic, poly methane, poly acrylic and other synthetic fibre, including running of a manufacturing units either unitary or composite and to undertake dyeing, bleaching, sanforizing, of cotton, yarn, cloth, silk, rayon, wool, jute, hemp and other fibre and/or their blends, fabrics of textile products whether on handlooms or in textile mills or other factories.
2. To carry on the business of textile and to act as exporters, manufacturers, brokers in textile and piece goods on wholesale or retail basis.

Capital Structure of the Company

A. AUTHORISED CAPITAL			
60,00,000	Equity Shares of Rs. 10/-	60000000	—
B. ISSUED, SUBSCRIBED AND FULLY PAID UP			
17,25,000	Equity Shares of Rs. 10/- each for cash at par	17250000	—
C. RIGHTS ISSUE (1: 1)			
17,25,000	Equity Shares of Rs. 10/- each for cash at a premium of Rs. 20/- per share to the existing share holders of the company in the ratio of 1: 1 through a separate letter of offer	17250000	51750000
D. PRESENT ISSUE			
19,50,000	Equity Share of Rs. 10/- each for cash at a premium of Rs. 25/- per share	19500000	68250000
E. NOW OFFERED TO PUBLIC FOR SUBSCRIPTION IN TERMS OF THIS PROSPECTUS			
19,50,000	Equity share of Rs. 10/- each for cash at a premium of Rs.25 per share	19800000	62850000
OUT OF ABOVE			
2,70,000	Equity Shares of Rs. 10/- each for cash at a premium of Rs.25 each to Kothari Pioneer Mutual Fund, Madras	2700000	9450000
40,000	Equity Shares of Rs. 10/- each for cash at a premium of Rs. 25 each to UTI Bank Ltd., Bombay	400000	1400000
50,000	Equity Shares of Rs. 10/- each for cash at a premium of Rs.25 each to United India Insurance Company Ltd., Madras	500000	1750000

40,000	Equity Shares of Rs. 10/- each for cash at a premium of Rs.25 each to The New Oriental Insurance Co. Ltd., Delhi	400000	1400000
50,000	Equity Shares of Rs. 10/- each for cash at a premium of Rs. 25 each to The New India Assurance Company Ltd., Bombay	500000	1750000
4,68,000	Equity Shares of Rs. 10/- each for cash at a premium of Rs. 25 each to Group of Non-resident Indians (NRIs) Overseas Bodies (OCBs) on reparation basis	4680000	16380000
II RESERVED FOR PREFERENTIAL ALLOTMENT:			
1,20,000	Equity Shares of. Rs. 10/- each for cash at a premium of Rs. 25 per share reserved for preferential allotment to Indian Mutual Funds (IMFs) on competitive basis	1200000	4200000
2,10,000	Equity Shares of Rs. 10/- each for cash at a premium of Rs. 25 per share reserved for preferential allotment to Indian Financial Insttt. (IFIs)/Schedule Banks on competitive basis	2100000	7350000
F. NET OFFER TO THE RESIDENT INDIAN PUBLIC			
7.02,000	Equity Share of Rs. 10/- each for cash at a premium of Rs. 25/- per share	7020000	24570000
G. PAID UP CAPITAL AFTER THE PRESENT ISSUE			
Existing	1725000 Equity Shares	17250000	
Right Issue (1:1)	1725000 Equity Shares	17250000	34500000
Public Issue	1950000 Equity Shares	19500000	48750000
Total	5400000 Equity Shares	54000000	83250000

Notes

1. Authorised capital of the company has increased from Rs. 4 crores by creation of further 20 lacs equity shares of Rs. 10/- each vide special resolution passed in the Annual General Meeting held on 30.09.94.
2. The Equity Shares remaining unsubscribed, if any, out of those reserved under category E II(a) & (b) above will be added back to the offer to the Resident Indian Public under F above.
3. Unsubscribed portion, if any, out of those reserved under category E1 the firm allotment shall be taken up by the promoters and in such an event, the share taken up by the promoters shall be locked in form three years.
4. The shares already allotted/to be allotted to the Promoters, Directors and their friends, relatives and associates are as under:

Allotment Date	*No. of Shares*	*Issue Price*	*% to Post Issue Capital*	*Lock in Period*	*From*
20/01/86	320000	Rs. 10	5.92	—	—
31/07/86	397500	Rs. 10	7.36	—	—
01/08/88	347500	Rs. 10	6.44	—	—
01/08/88	142500	Rs. 10	2.64	2 Years	*
Proposed (Right)	1207500	Rs. 30	22.36	5 Years	**

* Commences from the date of allotment in the present Public Issue.
** Commences from the date of allotment in the Right issue.

5. All past allotments as shown above have been for cash.
6. The Company has obtained the permission from the Reserve Bank of India for Issue of Equity Shares to NRIs/OCBs/FIIs on a repatriation basis vide

their letter No. PC.CO.FID (ii) 8487/ 10.02.40 (5559) /94-95 dated 02.01.1995.

7. NRI/OCB/FII applicants may please note that only such applications as are accompanied by payment in free foreign exchange will be considered for allotment under the reserved category. Payments can not be made through NR (0) account by such applications.
8. Prior to the proposed issue the promoters held 1207500 Equity Shares constituting 70% of the Issued, Subscribed and Paid-Up Capital. After the Proposed Right Public Issue the promoters shall hold 2415000 Equity Shares constituting 44.72% of the post issue capital.
9. In view of the new basis of allotment procedure, in the event of oversubscription, the issue size and the post-issue capital may increase by a maximum of 10% of the Net Public Offer.

Promoters

The company has been promoted by Dr. Ramesh S. Kagzi, a qualified Physician. He took his M.S. (Post Graduate) Degree in 1978 from Bombay University. Thereafter for sometime he worked with K.E.M. Hospital, Bombay. However, in 1979, he resigned from the job and joined the family business of textiles. In 1985, he promoted this company for processing of synthetic and cotton fabrics. He is having more than 14 years experience in the Textile Industry.

Out of the initial three promoters namely Shri S.N. Kagzi, Shri K.B. Kagzi and Dr. Ramesh S. Kagzi, first two promoters transferred their equity stakes in the company to Dr. Ramesh S. Kagzi in the year 1993. Dr. Ramesh S. Kagzi who is the Managing Director of the company since inception, continued. The provisions of Rule 40A & 40B are not applicable to the above.

Prior to the proposed issue the promoters (and family) / their companies held 1207500 Equity Shares constituting 70% of the Issued, Subscribed and Paid-up Capital. After the proposed Right Public Issue the promoters shall hold 2415000 Equity Shares constituting 44.72% of the pose issue capital.

There is no other pending litigation, dispute, defaults, non-payment of statutory dues or any proceedings initiated for economic offence against the promoters except following litigation.

One suit on behalf of the Textile Commissioner and two suits on behalf of Factory Inspectors have been filed against the promoter Dr. Ramesh S. Kagzi. Discharge applications have been filed and are to be heard.

The company has not revalued its assets since inception.

Project Details

The company intends to increase its present dyeing proceeding capacity from existing 300 lacs meters to 400 lacs meters p.a. and also intends to add value added processing of printing of textiles. The printing capacity will include Screen Printing tables, Flat Bed Printing Machines and Rotary Printing Machine which will enable printing sarees, dress materials and other fabrics. The total printing capacity of 170 lacs meters per annum is proposed to be commissioned by April 1995. The company also proposes to export Readymade Garments.

Market and Selling Arrangement

About 10000 million meters of fabric are processed every year in the country. Even then the per capita consumption is low as compares to other developing countries. Thus, there is ample scope for increased cloth production given the population level and higher standard of living.

Special Features for Marketing and Selling Arrangement

1. The company has already established itself in the market in Textile Processing. It has very good reputation in the market.
2. Lower utilities cost as compared to Bombay based Process Houses.
3. The place is in close proximity to main market i.e. Bombay.'
4. The place is well connected by road and railway services.
5. A notable feature of the textile trade is that a large number of textile dealers/ mills, either do not have any processing facilities or have inadequate facilities to meet their requirement. Therefore, it is a widely prevalent practice to get grey fabric processed from outside process houses. In fact the new comers to the textile trade who wish to sell fabric under their own name start by buying the grey fabric from the market and getting it processed on job basis.

The company is well known in the Textile Market and hence there will be no dearth of orders to utilise the full extended capacity. No Special marketing arrangement or strategy is called for, particularly in view of the fact that the company is already established in the textile processing industry. The company is having regular demand commitments from leading weaving concerns in the Bombay Market.

STML is in the textile trade since last 10 years and has been concentrating on its own products. With consistency in quality. STML has been able to get repeated job work from weavers through brokers. STML has been able to establish its products in view of the quality processing and control on purchases. The fabrics are mostly sold through brokers.

There is good potential for export of readymade garment. STML intends to market the garments either by establishing contacts through indentors or through commission agents.

Schedule of Implemention

The expansion comprising of the addition of the printing tables and flat bed Printing machine was completed with the finance from IDBI under equipment finance scheme, which is operating from September/October 1994. The remaining machines and equipments are standard made and are readily available on placing firm orders. The installation and commissioning will take above a month as the building is ready. As such, STML is confident of moderising its existing dyeing capacity from 300 lacs to 400 lacs will taken up simultaneously and is expected to be completed by July, 1995. Detailed schedule of Implementation is as under:

	Commencement (Month & Year)	*Completion (Month & Year)*	*Amount Spent till 31.12.94*	*Extent Completed (%)*
Acquisition of land	Existing			
Development of land	Existing			
Civil Works	The machine will be erected at existing building therefore no additional civil work is involved			
Plant & Machinery			Rs. 188 Lacs	28.66%
a) Indigenous order placement				
- Printing	Sept, 94	Mar, 95		
- Dyeing/Processing	Feb, 95	Mar, 95		
b) Delivery at site	Sept, 94	May, 95		
Arrangements for power	Being made			

Arrangement for water	Exisiting	
Erection and		
Commissioning of equipments		
- Printing	Sept, 94	Mar, 95
- Dyeing Processing	May, 95	Jun, 95
Trial Run		
- Printing	Sept, 94	Mar. 95
- Dyeing/ Processing	Jun, 95	Jun, 95
Commercial Production		
- Printing	Sept, 94	Apr., 95 -
Dyeing/ Processing	Jul, 95	Jul, 95

The company has already spent an amount of Rs. 188 lacs on the proposed project comprising Rs. 179 lacs for Plant & Machinery and Rs. 9 lacs for Erection and installation.

There has been no delay in implementation, as per schedule indicated in the appraisal report. The company has already applied for sanction of additional working capital to its regular bankers Union Bank of India.

Justification of Premium

The premium of Rs. 25/- on Equity share of Rs. 10/- each has been fixed taking into consideration the following parameters:

i) Track Record

The company is making profits since inception and is paying dividends. The company has strong fundamentals and the company's products have been well accepted in the market.

ii) Past Performance

Year ended March 31	*1991*	*1992*	*1993*	*1994*	*Apr-Oct.94 (7 months)*
Total Income	2018	2712	2785	2978	1823
PBIDT	159	181	194	247	162

Operating Profit	81	92	71	87	83
Net Profit	81	92	71	87	83
Dividend Rate	16.00%	16.00%	16.00%	16.00%	
Equity share capital	172.50	172.50	172.50	172.50	172.50
Reserve & Surplus	191	255	299	358	441
Book Value per share	21.07	24.78	27.33	30.75	35.59
EPS (Rs.)	4.70	5.33	4.12	5.04*	8.23
Cash EPS (Rs.)	5.62	7.07	6.20	7.36*	10.73

* Annualised

ii) Projected Performance

Year ended March 31	*1995*	*1996*	*1997*	*1998*
Total Income	3075	7333	8952	9673
PBIDT	332	839	994	1091
Operating Profit	161	473	561	669
Net Profit	154	375	418	484
Dividend Rate	20%	20%	25%	25%
Equity share capital	419	540	540	540
Reserve & Surplus	1030	1596	1879	2228
Book Value per share	34.60	39.56	44.80	51.25
EPS (Rs.)	7.58	6.94	7.74	8.96
Cash EPS (Rs.)	10.57	8.55	9.65	10.87

(Basis: *Capital Market* - October 1994)

The offer price of Rs. 35/- per share represents a P/E multiple of 3.81 based on the average E.P.S. of Rs. 7.88 projected for the next three years as compared to the industry P/E ratio of 14.10.

iv) The Stock Market high and low for the last three years and monthly high and low for the last six months are given in the section Stock Market Data. The average for last six months high and low market price works out to Rs. 62.75

and present market price (quoted on Bombay Stock Exchange as on 28.02.95) is Rs. 68/-.

There is no other material development having bearing on the company/ promoters etc.

Investors attention is drawn to the notes under the financial highlights before making the investments in the issue.

One the basis of the above factors, the company and the lead managers, are of the opinion that the Premium charged is reasonable and justified.

B. Financial Information

I. INCOME						
Processing Charges (Inclusive of Excise Duty)	1182.68	918.08	1783.08	1048.67	828.05	192.75
Cloth Sale	1278.74	1096.71	921.69	1724.92	2138.61	1617.42
Other Income	6.65	3.60	6.90	11.43	11.78	12.67
Increase/Decrease in Stock	23.78	(98.18)	44.07	109.12	52.45	(9.23)
Total	2491.75	1920.21	2755.74	2894.14	3030.89	1813.64
EXPENDITURE						
Raw Material	1648.89	1350.10	1406.10	1993.52	2118.53	1412"34
Manufacturing Expenses	208.96	185.31	608.44	175.07	164.13	93.62
Expenditure on Employees	40.01	24.43	35.94	47.00	50.47	31.92
Admn. & Other Expenses	28.70	29.22	24.34	21.90	26.00	25.69
Selling Expenses	61.35	45.14	72.99	46.13	41.13	20.70
Interest	127.36	61.50	59.43	86.52	120.17	53.89
Depreciation	47.28	15.62	30.23	35.68	39.61	2536
Preliminary Expenses w/o	1 28	1.28	1.46	1.46	1.46	—
Excise Duty	255.49	126.55	425.12	415.47	382.12	67.31

Total (Rs. In lacs)	2389.63	1839.15	2664.05	2822.75	2943.62	1730.83
YEAR ENDED	30.06.90	31.03.91	31.03.92	31.03.93	31.03.94	31.10.94
Profit before Tax	102.12	81.06	91.69	71.39	87.27	82.78
Profit for the Year	102.12	81.06	91.69	71.39	87.27	82.78

The Assets and Liabilities of the Company as at 30/06/90, 31/03/91, 31/03/92, 31/03/94 and 31/10/94 are set out betow. The Assets and Liabilities have been arrived at after making such regrouping as are in our opinion appropriate.

Assets as at	*30.06. 90*	*31.03. 91*	*31.03. 92*	*31.03.3 93*	*1.03. 94*	*1.10. 94*
1. Fixed Assets	447.62	538.54	711.66	783.41	902.06	1043.81
Less Depreciation	141.71	157.05	187.10	222.78	262.39	287.75
Net Stock	305.91	381.48	524.56	560.63	639.67	756.06
2. Investment (at cost)	0.25	0.25	0.25	0.25	0.25	2.10
3. Current Assets, Advances & Loans						
a) Inventories	350.03	251.85	295.91	405.03	457.49	448.26
b) Sundry Debtors	343.76	507.37	615.83	519.11	531.48	599.11
c) Cash & Bank Balances	7.77	38.03	42.01	43.27	13.69	18.90
d) Loans & Advances	33.67	44.32	28.41	27.53	37.03	49.04
	735.23	841.57	982.16	994.94	1039.69	1115.31
LIABILITIES AND PROVISIONS						
a) Secured Loans	592.76	662.64	754.46	816.21	811.20	845.46
b) Unsecured Loans	66.60	59.62	142.25	150.58	212.57	25671
c) Current Liabilities and Provision	87.10	144.88	190.45	123.98	129.82	162.50
	746.46	867.14	1087.16	1090.77	1153.59	1264.67

NET ASSETS	294.93	356.17	419.81	465.05	526.02	608.80
Add: Misc. Expenses to						
to the extent w/o	7.93	6.97	7.42	5.97	4 66	4.66
TOTAL ASSETS	302.86	363-14	427.23	471.02	530.68	613.46
REPRESENTED BY						
Equity Share Capital	172.50	172.50	172-50	172.50	172.50	172.50
Reserve & Surplus	130.36	190.64	254.73	298.52	358.18	440.96
302.86	363.14	427.23	471.02	530.68	613.46	

III. Dividend declared by the Company in respect of last two years are as follows:-

Year Ended Shares	*No. Equity Dividend*	*Rate of Dividend*	*Amount of*
31.03.1993	1725000 of Rs. 10/- each	16%	2760000.00
31.03.1994	1725000 of Rs.10/-each	16%	2760000.00

Notes

1. Figures have been rounded up regrouped and rearranged wherever necessary.
2. Fixed assets are stated at cost including transportation charges and other incidental expenses incurred in relation to acquisition and installation of the same.
3. The company has provided depreciation on straight line method @ prescribed in schedule XIV of the Companies Act, 1956 except,, for the depreciation on machinery which has been provided at single shift working instead of multiple shift working.
4. Income on investment have been accounted on accural basis.
5. Interest on term loan from financial institution has been capitalized to plant and machinery.
6. Stock are taken on cost or market value whichever

in slower as taken/valued are certified by the management of the company.

7. Contigent liabilities have not been provided for in respect of excise demand deputed by the company departments the like amount as per the order of the Supreme Court in Company's favour.

PRE AND POST ISSUE PRICE BEHAVIOUR OF SHARE OF THE COMPANY

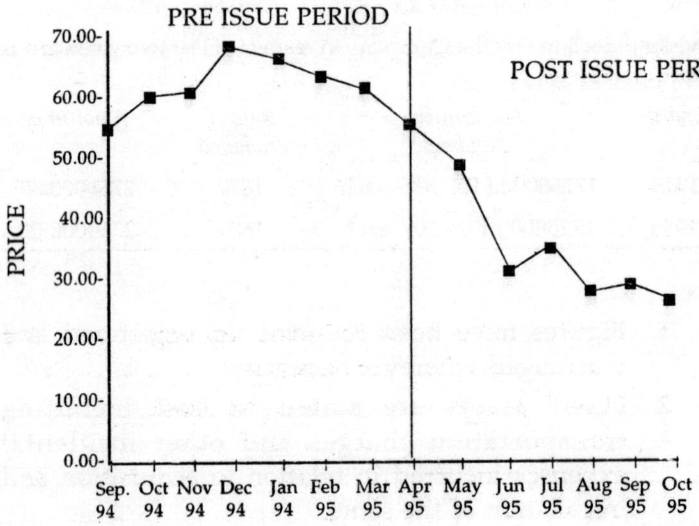

SOMANI SWISS INDUSTRIES LTD.

History and Present Business of the Company

Somani Swiss Industries Ltd. (SSIL) was incorporated 'as a Public Limited Company under the name of Ashish Investments Ltd. on 18th February, 1974, and w.e.f. 4th February, 1993, the name of the company has been changed from Ashish Investment Ltd. to Somani Swiss Industries Ltd.

The Company was incorporated as investment company in the year 1974 and subsequently acquired the running business in the same year of Star Rolling Mills at Guwahati (Assam) from Kumar Iron & Steel Co., a partnership firm.

The Company presently engaged in the manufacturing of Cold twisted deformed (CTD) Bars and Rods of prime quality with an installed capacity of 34,800 MT per annum. The Company's products are confirmed to BIS (Formerly ISI) specification. The company is the commercial agent for Tata Iron & Steel Co. Ltd. and Steel Authority of India Ltd.

The company came out with a public issue of 74,750 equity shares of Rs. 10 each for cash at par aggregating to Rs. 7,47,500 for providing finance required for the company's investment business. The issue was fully subscribed.

The Promoters

The company was promoted by Mr. Mahendra Kumar Somani in the year 1974. Presently Mr. Ashish Somani holds the controlling interest in the company. The promoters are holding 25% out of the existing issued Equity Share Capital and their holding after the present issue will be 18.82% excluding the Equity participation of Foreign collabarators.

Mr. Ashish Somani, aged 27 years is now the chief promoter of the company. He is a Commerce graduate from the Delhi University. He is young and experienced in the field. Mr. Ashish Somani is the Managing Director having control on the overall activities of the company under the supervision of the Board of Directors. He, with his family business background, has gained good business and industry exposure. He is widely travelled in India and abroad and familiar with the needs of modern business and therefore is committed to integrate the Company with the global economy by creating world class, world scale manufacturing facilities which will be internationally competitive.

Main Objects of the Company

The main objects of the company as set out in the the memorandum of Association include inter-alia as under: -

1. To carry on all or any of the business of financiers of industrial, commercial and other enterprises and general financiers money lenders, sahukars, trustees, real estate owners, landlords, real estate agents, builders underwriters, guarantors, hire-purchase dealers, Chit-fund organisers, investors, promoters, brokers and dealers of and in shares.
2. To carry on all or any of the business of buyers, sellers, traders, indentors, brokers, agents, manufacturers, producers and dealers of all kinds of iron and steel, metals, rods, wires, pipes, tubes, bars, angles, plates, strips, minerals chemical stones and stone-chips, sands, structure material of all kinds, steel & metal furnitures, wooden furnitures, forest products, raw materials, stores machineries and other materials required in connection therewith.

Schedule of Implementation

The company require about 24 Months to implement the Project from the zero date (July 1994). The company has identified the land, technology, Plant & Machinery and equipment etc. The possession of the land is expected by

January, 95 and the civil work is expected to start by February 95. Orders in respect of import of Plant as a package deal with technical and basis engineering detail are placed with EMS-INVENTA AG., Switzerland Baring unforeseen circumstances, the company expects to start commercial production by April 1996. PA

S.No.	*Activities*	*Commencement*	*Expected completion*
1.	Acquisition of land	Decembher 94	January 95
2.	Development of site	January 95	February 95
3.	Civil Works	February 95	December 95
4.	Technical Arrangement for know how	Completed	
5.	Plant & Machinery		
-	Imported		
	Order	Already placed	
	Delivery	April 95	October 95
-	Indigineous		
	Order	January 95	March 95
	Delivery	June 95	December 95
6.	Erection of Equipment	June 95	February 96
7.	Trial Runs	March 96	April 96
8.	Commercial Production	April 1996	—

The company has deployed a sum of Rs. 21.07 crores on this project till 31st August, 1994. As per appraisal the project would be completed within 18 months. The amount spent on each item as stated above are as under:

	Nature of Amount Spent Rs.	*(in crore)*
1.	Advance against acquisition of land	5.33
2.	Advance against imported plant & Machinery	15.14
3.	Miscellaneous Fixed Assets	0.06
4.	Pre-operative Expenses	0.55

The company has submitted it's working capital to its banker, for the requirement of additional working capital of Rs. 23.17 crores for the project. The company's bankers are yet to assess the working capital requirements.

Capital Structure

		Nominal Amount	*Issue Amount*
A. AUTHORISED CAPITAL			
7,00,00,000	Equity Shares of Rs.10/-	700000000	
B. ISSUED, SUBSCRIBED AND PAID UP CAPITAL			
5,80,000	Equity Shares of Rs.10/- each	5800000	—
C. PRESENT ISSUE			
6,80,00,000	Equity Share of Rs.10/- each for cash at a premium of Rs. 8/- per share	680000000	1224000000
D. OUT OF WHICH			
i) Rights Issue			
3,71,20,000	Equity Shares of Rs. 10/- each for cash at premium of Rs.8/- per share for share-holders of the company in the ratio of Sixty four new Equity Shares for every one equity shares held on 12th December 1994 with a right of renunciation thereunder	371200000	668160000
ii) Public Issue			
3.08,80,000	Equity Shares of Rs. 10/- each for cash at a premium of Rs. 8/- per share	308800000	555840000
E. OUT OF D (ii) ABOVE			
1,04,98,000	Equity Shares of Rs. 10/- each for cash at a premium of Rs.8/- per share are		

	reserved for firm allotment to Promoters, Directors, their friends, relatives & Foreign Collaborators	104980000	188964000

F. NOW OFFERED TO PUBLIC IN TERMS OF THIS PROSPECTUS

2,03,82,000	Equity share of Rs. 10/- each for cash at a premium of Rs.8/- per share	203820000	366876000

OUT OF WHICH:

16,50,000	Equity Shares of Rs. 10/- each for cast at a premium of Rs.8/- per share reserved for NRI/OCB/FII on firm allotment basis	16500000	29700000
23,17,000	Equity Shares of Rs. 10/- each for cash at a premium of Rs.8/- per share are reserved on preferential allotment basis for NRIs/OCBs/FIIs with repatriation benefits on competitive basis	23170000	41706000
40,76,400	Equity Shares of Rs. 10/- each for cash at a premium of Rs.8/- per share reserved for preferential allotment to Indian Financial Institutions on competitive basis	40764000	73375200
25,000	Equity Shares of Rs. 10/- each for cash at a premium of Rs. 8/- per share reserved for preferential allotment to employees of the company	250000	450000

G. NET OFFER TO THE INDIAN PUBLIC

82,37,200	Equity Shares of Rs. 10/- each for cash at a premium of Rs. 8/- per share	82372000	148269600

H. PAIDUP CAPITAL AFTER THE PRESENT ISSUE

(*Rs. in Lacs*)

	Share capital	*Share premium*	*Total*
Existing	58.00	—	58.00
Right Issue	3712.00	2969.60	6681.60
Sub Total	3770.00	2969.00	6739.60 ·
Public Issue	3088.00	2470.40	5558.40
TOTAL	6858.00	5440.00	12298.00

The pre & post equity holding of promoters are as under

PREISSUE HOLDING

Total No. of Shares	Promoters No. of Shares)	Percentage holding	
a) Present Paidup Capital 580000	145000	25%	
b) Out of the Present Issue			
i) 37120000 (Rights)	9280000	25%	
ii) 30880000 (Public)	*10498000	34%	
Subtotal 68000000	19778000	29.08%	
Post Issue Holding (A+ B)			
Total	68580000	19923000	29.05%

*Out of which 8384000 equity share are to be alloted to foreign collaborators at same premium at which the issue is made.

Profit and Loss

(Rs. in lacs)

Particulars	*1989-90*	*1990-91*	*1991-92*	*1992-93*	*1993-94*	*1.4.97 to 31.8.94*
A. INCOME:						
Sales	245.91	187.79	215.11	1244.12	2477.56	1031.12
Other Income	50.42	31.95	51.00	69.15	84.54	32.97
Increase in stocks of finished goods & others	—	23.02	—	63.89	20.32	54.70
TOTAL	296.33	242.76	266.11	1377.16	2582.41	1118.79

EXPENDITURE						
Purchase of finished semi-finished goods	106.18	42.73	67.72	853.33	1535.76	668.33
Manufacturing & other expenses	172.42	191.76	171.94	487.17	974.72	418.02
Decrease in stock of finished goods & others	6.48	—	12.44	—	—	—
Depreciation	4.82	5.00	5.41	5.41	10.30	4.29
Interest	4.09	2.56	4.60	5.30	18.21	7.61
TOTAL	293.99	242.05	262.11	1351.21	2538.99	1098.26
Profit before investment						
Allowance Reserve & Taxes	2.34	0.71	4.00	25.95	43.43	20.53
Investment Allowance Reserves	1.76	0.34	—	—	—	—
Profit before taxes	0.58	0.37	4.00	25.95	43.43	20.53
Provision for taxes	—	—	—	—	—	—
Profit after taxes	0.58	0.37	4.00	25.95	43.43	20.53

B. ASSETS AND LIABILITIES

	As at 31.03.90	*As at 31.03.91*	*As at 31.03.92*	*As at 31.03.93*	*As at 31.03.94*	*As at 31.08.94*
I. SOURCES OF FUNDS						
1. Share Holder's Fund						
a) Capital	33.00	58.00	58.00	58.00	58.00	58.00
b) Reserve & Surplus	30.54	31.25	167.34	183.82	217.78	234.37
c) Advance against issue of shares					51.60	2107.03
	6.544	89.25	225.34	241.82	327.38	2399.17
2. Loan Funds						
a) Secured Loans	31.22	25.81	16.26	90.89	142.47	12650
b) Unsecured	3.22	3.22	3.27	3.27	3.27	3.27
TOTAL	97.98	118.28	244.87	335.98	473.12	2529.17

II. APPLICATION OF FUNDS						
1. FIXED ASSETS						
a) Gross Block	71.86	73.87	220.56	230.48	281.39	281.39
b) Less Depreciation	29.62	34.62	49.50	64.37	84.13	92.37
c) Net Block	42.24	39.25	171.06	166.11	197.26	189.02
d) Capital work in progress	—	—	—	—	51.60	2107.03
	42.24	39.25	171.06	166.11	248.86	2296.05
2. INVESTMENTS	8.26	8.26	8.26	8.26	8.26	8.26
3. CURRENT ASSETS, LOANS & ADVANCES						
a) Inventories	47.43	63.57	75.89	125.41	189.32	222.04
b) Sundry Debtor (unsecured)	33.19	15.14	20.72	43.03	53.85	54.70
c) Cash & Bank Balance	2.07	3.49	1.38	9.20	7.85	7.50
d) Loans & Advances (unsecured)	27.12	66.98	63.27	85.89	110.97	108.86
Less: Current Liabilities & Provisions						
a) Liabilities	47.12	71.75	77.00	74.71	116.03	131.08
b) Advances from Customers	15.21	6.66	16.71	27.21	29.96	37.16
	62.33	78.41	95.71	101.92	145.99	168.24
NET CURRENT ASSETS	47.48	70.77	65.55	161.61	216.00	233.12
TOTAL	97.98	118.28	244.87	335.98	473.12	2529.17

(Rs. in lacs)

	As at 1989-90	*1990-91*	*1991-92*	*1992-93*	*1993-94*	*31.3.94*
Profit after tax	0.58	0.37	4.00	25.95	43.43	20.53
Equity Capital	33.00	58.00	58.00	58.00	58.00	58.00
Reserve & Surplus (Excluding						

Revaluation Reserve)	30.54	31.25	35.26	61.20	104.63	125.16
Book value	19.25	15.39	16.08	20.55	28.04	31.58
EPS	0.18	0.06	0.69	4.47	7.49	'8.50
Dividend	—	—	—	—	—	—

*Annualised

Notes

1. Face value of equity share is Rs. 10/- each.
2. Reserve & Surplus include Revaluation Reserve of Rs. 132.08 lakhs in 1991-92 and 122.62 in 1992-93, which is net of depreciation (Rs. 9.47 lakhs in each year) on the amount added on revaluation and transferred to Profit & Loss Account.
3. Though the Assets of Company had been revalued in the year 1991-92. The depreciation debited to the Profit & Loss Account in 1991-92 and 1992-93 was Rs. 5.41 lakhs in each year instead of Rs. 14.87 lakhs. The difference of 9.47 lakhs in the depreciation has been adjusted by transferring from Revaluation Reserve to Profit 251 and Loss Account.

Future Projections (For next Five years)

(Rs. in lacs)

	1994-95	*1995-96*	*1996-97*	*1997-98*	*1998-99*
Profit after tax	45.91	1361.56	2719.65	3134.36	3244.44
Equity Capital	58.00	6858.00	6858.00	6858.00	6858.00
Reserve & Surplus (Excluding Revaluation Reserve)	150.54	1407.36	3034.46	4797.22	6396.74
EPS	7.91	*2.02	3.97	4.57	4.73
Book Value	35.96	19.98	22.35	24.93	27.26
Dividend (%)	—	—	16%	20%	24%

* Weighted & Annualised

Notes

1. Face value of Equity Share is Rs. 10/- each.

The Lead Managers confirm that the premium has been decided by the company in consultation with them and they are of the opinion that the premium decided is reasonable and justified considering the present performances and future prospects of the company.

Justification of Premium

The Premium of Rs. 8/- per share has been determined taking the following factors into consideration.

— Present and projected earnings per Share
— Present and projected Net Asset Value
— Business prospects of the Company's products

The Objects of Issue are

1. To part finance the cost of Project under diversification programme for manufacture Speciality Polyset Filament Yarn and also Commodity POY (Partially Oriented Yarn).
2. To augment the long term resources of the company.
3. To meet the part expenses of the issue.

Project

The company proposes for diversification programme in high growth industry for setting up a project for the manufacturing of 9.975 MT per annum of Polyester Filament Yarn (PFY) in technical collaboration with world leader M/s EMS-INVENTA A.G., Zunch. The plant is being setup at village Bhiwadi, Distt. Alwar, Rajasthan.

PRE AND POST ISSUE PRICE BEHAVIOUR OF SHARE OF THE COMPANY

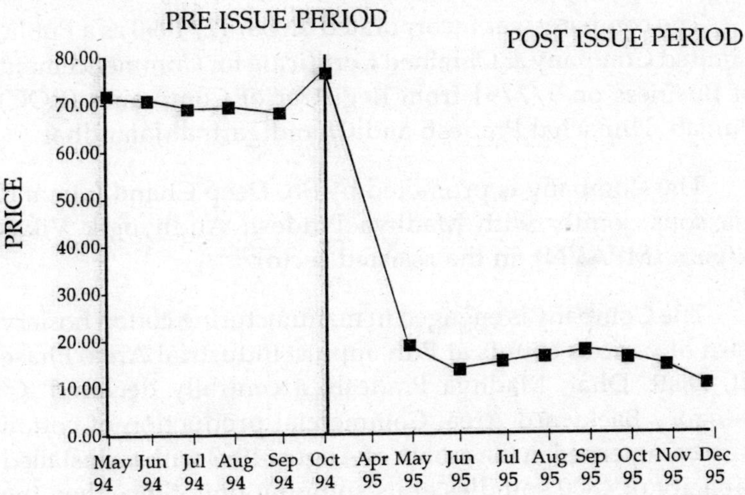

GIRNAR FIBRES

History, Main Objects and Present Activities of the Company

History and Present Activities of the Company

The company was incorporated on 06/12/1990 as a Public Limited Company & Obtained Certificate for Commencement of Business on 9/7/91 from Registrar of Companies (ROC) Punjab, Himachal Pradesh and Chandigarh at Jalandhar.

The Company is promoted by Sh. Deep Chand Jain and his sons, jointly with Madhya Pradesh Audhyogik Vikas Nigam (MPAVN), in the assisted sector.

The Company is engaged in manufacturing cotton hosiery yarn of various counts at Pithampura Industrial Area, Phase III, Distt. Dhar, Madhya Pradesh, a centrally declared 'C' category Backward Area. Commercial production of cotton yarn commenced in the month of August 1993 with an installed capacity of 4800 spindles at its spinning unit. Since then the Company has installed all the 12480 spindles as envisaged in the initial project in a phased manner.

Promoters & their Background

Girnar Fibres Limited was promoted by Mr. Deep Chand Jain and his sons Mr. Jatinder Jain, Mr. Satish Kumar Jain, Mr. Raj Kumar Jain and Mr. Gulshan Kumar Jain jointly with MPAVN in the assisted sector. The private promoters have long experience in the Hosiery Industry since 1956. Shri Deep Chand Jain, B.A. aged 61 years, having overall experience of about four decades in the hosiery industry is also the promoter of Gimar Fabrics (India) Pvt. Ltd. (GFIPL), Girnar Hosiery Works (GHW), and Girnar Capital Trust Ltd. (GCTL). Sh. Jatinder Jain, a Commerce Graduate has overall experience of about 12 years in Hosiery and Textile Industry. Shri Satish Kumar Jain, B.A. aged 42 years having overall experience of 20 years in the hosiery industry is a partner of GHW and Director of GFIPL. Shri Raj Kumar Jain, B.A. aged 36 years, with an overall experience of 14 years in the hosiery industry, is presently a director of GFIPL. Shri Gulshan Kumar Jain, B.A. aged 41 years having about 20 years experience in the hosiery industry is a Director of GFIPL.

MPAVN is a State Development Institution of Madhya Pradesh State Government. MPAVN has been actively assisting entrepreneurs in setting up industrial ventures in the state of Madhya Pradesh by providing them with the Financial Assistance by way of Equity Participation and term loans.

Main Object of the Company

The main objects of the Company as set out in the memorandum of association are as under:

1. To cany on the business of ginner, spinners, weavers, knitters, combers, manufacturers, producers, bleachers, dyers, pressers, printers, processors, importers, exporters, buyers, sellers of and dealers in all kinds of yarns, fibres and fabrics.
2. To make, manufacture, produce, purchase, sell, import, export or otherwise deal in all types of raw materials, stores, goods, products including carprolactam hexam ethylene-diamine. adipic, acid dimethye tere-phthaiate acryionitrile and other allied chemicals required for the manufacture of the textile products.
3. To carry on the business of dress makers, clothiers, tailors, outfitters, costumers makers of garments, wearing apparel, lingarie and trimmings of every kind, corset makers, glovers, lace manufacturers, leather dressers.

Project

Girnar proposed to expand its capacity with the installation of 14,440 additional spindles, at the existing location for the manufacture of cotton combed hosiery yarn of 25s and 30s counts on the basis of the market demand. After the installation of the proposed additional spindles, the company is expected to produce 4090 tons of cotton yarn per annum at the optimum level.

Schedule of Implementation

Activities	*Starting Date*	*Expected Completion Date*
*Site Development	Jan '95	Completed
*Construction of factory building	Jul '95	November '95
*Placement of Orders For Machinery	August '85	September '95
*Receipt of Machinery at site	Oct '95	March '96
*Trial Runs	March '96	March '96
*Commencement of Commercial Production	April '96	—

Marketing

The textile industry has made considerable progress in domestic and export market, particularly, the exports which include cotton fabrics, cotton yarn, knitting and woollen products and hosiery fabrics. The cotton production, as per Directorate of Cotton Department (DCD) increased from 97.59 lacs bales in 1991 to 120.67 lacs bales in 1992-93, while the consumption of cotton by mills increased from 107.57 bales to 112.81 lacs bales during the same period. During the current year, the mill consumption is estimated at 1.17 lacs bales against estimated production of 129 lacs bales against estimated production of 129 lacs bales.

The company proposes to manufacturing combed cotton hosiery yarn to 25s and 30s count partly for the existing customers and partly for the outside market where the demand is on the rise.

Export Prospects

Recently the Company has started selling its yarn to

merchant exporters in Calcutta and its quality has been approved and very well accepted in the export market as well. Now the Company is also planning to enter the Export Market directly during the current year.

Capital Structure of the Company

A. AUTHORISED CAPITAL			
2,50,00,000	Equity Shares of Rs.10/-	250000000	
B. ISSUED. SUBSCRIBED AND PAID UP			
81,25,700	Equity Shares of Rs.10/- each fully paid-up	81257000	—
C. PRESENT ISSUE			
1,30,77,150	Equity Share of Rs. 10/- each for cash at a premium		
OUT OF WHICH			
1. Rights Issue			
40,62,500	Equity Shares of Rs. 10/- each for cash at premium of Rs. 2.50 per share on Right basis in ratio of 1: 2 to the existing Shareholders on Record Date by a separate letter of offer	40628500	10157125
2. The Public Issue			
90,14,300	Equity Shares of Rs. 10/- each for cash at a premium of Rs. 5/- each	90143000	45071500
D. OUT OF THE PRESENT ISSUE C (2) ABOVE			
10,14,300	Equity Shares of Rs. 10/- each for cash at a premium of Rs.5/- per share are reserved for firm allotment to Promoters. Directors, their friends, relatives & associates	10143000	5071500
E. NOW OFFERED TO PUBLIC IN TERMS OF THIS PROSPECTUS			
80,00,000	Equity share of Rs.10/- each for cash at a		

	premium of Rs.5/- per share	80000000	40000000
OUT OF WHICH:			
16,00,000	Equity Shares of Rs. 10/- each for cash at a premium of Rs. 8/- per share are reserved on preferential allotment to Indian Mutual fund on competitive basis	16000000	8000000
19,20,000	Equity Shares of Rs. 10/- each for cash at a premium of Rs. 5/- per share reserved for preferential allotment to NRI's and FII's including OBCs on competitive & repatriation basis	19200000	9600000
16,00,000	Equity Shares of Rs. 10/- each for cash at a premium of Rs.5/- per share have been reserved for preferential allotment to FI's on competitive basis	16000000	8000000
NET OFFER TO THE RESIDENT INDIAN PUBLIC			
28,60,000	Equity Shares of Rs. 10/- each for cash at a premium of Rs.5/- per share		
PAID UP EQUITY CAPITAL AFTER THE PUBLIC ISSUE			
2,12,02,850	Equity Shares of Rs. 10 each	212028500	
	Share premium Account	55228625	

A. Qualitative Factors

1. Existing well established and profit making Company promoted by experienced promoters with about four decades of experience and hosiery and Textile industries.
2. The yarn produced by the Company is being ranked at par with the product of the country's market leaders quality wise and commands one of the best price in the market.

3. The company is eligible for exemption from the payment of Sales Tax for a period of seven years of deferment from the payment of Sales Tax for a period of nine years from the date of commercial production and power subsidy under the backward area concessons given by the Madhya Pradesh State Government to industry located in 'C' category district. The Company is also entitled for exemption under section 80 HHC of the income Tax Act. These exemption would enable Company's bottom line.

Quantitative Factors

1. The company achieved a turnover of Rs. 20.24 crores in the year ended 31.03.95 and furthermore the Company has already achieved a turnover of Rs. 5.75 crores during the first three months of the current year 1995-96.
2. The past and projected financial performance and financial indicators as appraised by IFCI are as follows:

Particulars	*For the year ended*					
	31/3/94 (7 Months)	*31/3/95*	*31/3/96*	*31/3/97*	*31/3/98*	*31/3/99*
Total Income	366.24	2024.00	1972.00	3537.00	3760.00	3984.00
Net Profit	(-) 42.13	44.22	285.00	410.00	486.00	572.00
Capital	812.57	811.22	2120.29	2120.29	2120.29	2120.29
EPS (Rs.)	—	.55	1.34	1.93	2.29	2.70

3. The average EPS over the next three year works out to Rs. 2.23 per share Considering the price earning (PE) multiplier of 12, the expected market price works out to approximately Rs. 26 per share against which the Company is offering shares at Rs. 15/- per share.

Apart from reasons mentioned above, the company and

the lead managers to the issue in consultation with whom the premium has been decided, are of the opinion that the premium is reasonable and justified.

Audited Financial Data

Profit and Losses

(Rs. in lacs)

Particulars	*Period Ended 31.03.1994*	*Period Ended 31.03.1995*	*Period Ended 31.06.1995*
1. INCOME:			
Sales	36327846	201717461	57346460
Other Income	296425	666571	232000
Total	36624271	202384032	57578460
2. EXPENDITURE			
Cost of Goods consumed/sold	19196995	153824211	36797247
Manufacturing Expenses	4423241	14006624	6344786
Personnel Expenses	2154328	5716995	787348
Administrative & Other Expenses	2276275	3997782	667684
Financial Expenses	5144199	15822986	5922003
Selling Expenses	967253	1835320	390401
Excise Duty	1350923	6195956	421341
Preliminary & Public Issue Expenses	654938	654938	—
Total	40836898	202054812	51330810
Depreciation	4658837	10222147	2586527
NET PROFIT/LOSS AFTER DEPRECIATION	(-) 4212718	4422587	3661123
NET PROFIT/LOSS B/F	—	(-)4212718	209869
Balance carried to Balance Sheet	(-) 4212718	209869	3870992

Note: The figure of Profit & Loss Account in respect of the years ending on 31.03.93, 31.03.92 and 31.03.91 are not being given as the Company started commercial production in year 1993-94.

Particulars	Period Ended 3009.91	Period Ended 31.03.92	Period Ended 31.03.93	Period Ended 31.03.94	Period Ended 31.03.95	Period Ended 31.03.96
1. SOURCES OF FUNDS						
A. Shareholder Fund	78110	5303110	44200000	81115500	81122500	81122500
- Share Application Money						
(Pending Allotment	8193150	18703150	37060750	—	—	—
- Reserve & Surplus	—	—	—	—	209869	3870992
2. Loan Fund						
a) Secured Loans	—	-	23400000	106063934	126748005	123008811
TOTAL	8271260	24006260	104660750	187179434	208080374	208002303
II. APPLICATION OF FUNDS						
1. Fixed Assets						
a) Gross Block	—	2635111	34848835	121112916	168572260	165872260
b) Less Depreciation	—	2375	51129	5016709	15238856	17825382
c) Net Block	—	2632736	3797706	116096207	150633404	148046878
d) Capital Work in Progress	—	4315682	44656959	18676882	8984747	8984747
e) Project Development Exp. (Pending Allotment)	54551	1084655	5250301		4780561	5005819
f) Advance on Capital Account	5721769	6014955	—	15439296	1349134	4058985
Total	5776320	14048028	56704966	150212385	165747846	166096249
2. Current Assets. Loans & Advances						
a) Inventories	—	—	—	9033707	30031628	38681630
b) Sundry Debtors	—	—	—	12944147	19939616	28625666
c) Cash & Bank Balance	2380544	9651351	49686458	9882908	2169960	1500124
e) Investments	—	—	—	300000	300000	300000
	2469170	9960020	50397113	35747230	56161319	-
Less: Current Liabilities						
& Provisions	31230	209848	7146491	8887338	19068292	36287698
TOTAL	2437940	750172	43250622	26859892	37093027	36666373
3. Misc. Expenditure						
(To the extent not written off or adjusted)						
a) Preliminary Expenses	57000	154500	154500	139050	123600	123600
b) Share issue Expenses	53560	4550662	5755389	5115901	5115901	
TOTAL	57000	208060	4705162	10107157	5239501	5239501
TOTAL (1)+ (2)+ (3)	8271260	24006260	104660750	187179434	208080374	208002303

Pre and Post Issue Price Behaviour of Share of the Compnay

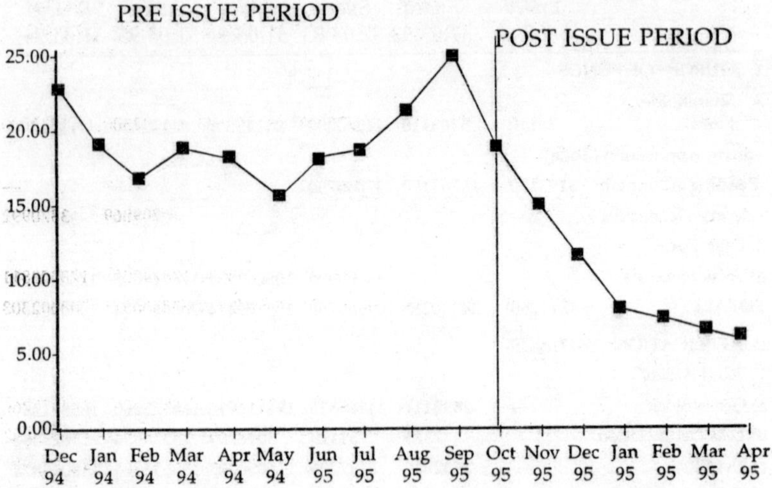

As can be observed from the price behaviours of shares in case of all the companies, the price of scrip has dropped below their offered price within a time frame of four months (approx) after the closure of the issue. The pro and post Issue price and their variance from the Issue price for all the companies is given below.

S.No.	*Name of Company*	*Issue price*	*Avg. price before issue*	*Avg. price after issue*
1.	Sharda textile Mills (India) Ltd.	35	62.50	21.50
2.	Girnar Fibers Ltd.	15	17.87	9.39
3.	Banswara Syntex Ltd.	50	58.22	29.20
4.	Somani Swiss (Industries) Ltd.	18	70.12	13.68
5.	Rajasthan Polyster Ltd.	15	24.38	9.50

BAR CHART

Model for fixing premium is case of further Issues of companies

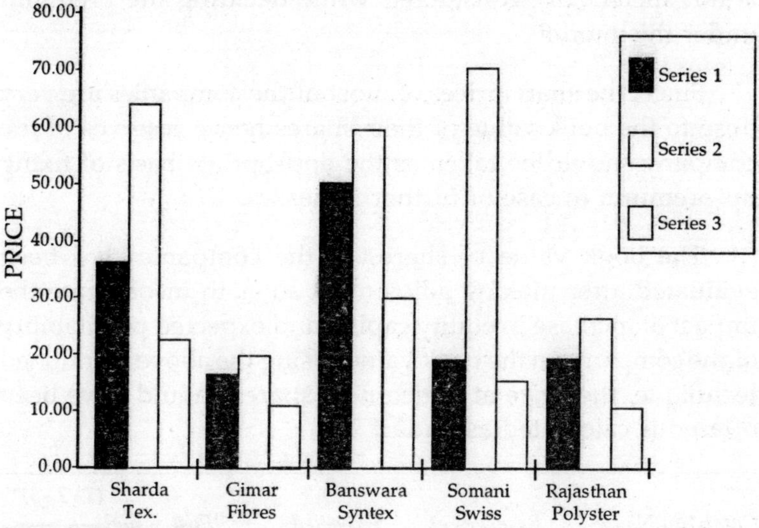

Series 1=issue price
Series 2=average price before issue
Series 3=average price after issue

The price of any security should reflect the expected earning of a company. In developing this mode!, the time horizon for expected earnings is taken as one year because the projections of profitability for more than one year are inherited with lot of subjective estimates and therefore they cannot be assessed with fair accuracy.

On the basis of profitability of the company during previous years, one can project the estimated profit for the next year. The estimated profit can be assessed with help of profit margin which the company has normally earned in the previous years and the expected turnover which the company is likely to make in the coming financial year. While, computing the expected turnover, impact of proposed project should also be taken into account. In case of further issues, the qualitative factors such as promoter track record marketing and selling arrangement has very little role to play because the effect of these factors are automatically included in the profit margins of the previous year. Therefore, their impact is not specifically considered while deciding the premium under this model.

Since, the share prices of most of the companies are very dose to the book value of their shares hence reserves of the company should be taken as the appropriate basis of fixing up premium in case of further issues.

The book value of shares of the companies has been evaluated after making adjustment so as to incorporate the impact of increase in equity capital and expected profitability of the company on the book value. Using the above mentioned technique, the price at which new shares should have been offered is calculated as under.

Company Name	*(1)* *Reserves as per latest audited results*	*(2)* *Expected increase in reserve proposed project*	*(3)* *Post issue paid up Capital*	*(1+2+3)** ——— *No Equity Share*
Somani Swiss Industries Ltd.	234.37	0 (As the commercial production is due to start in April 96) it is expected .. that no profit would be transferred to the reserves	823.7	1058.07 ——— =12.85 82.37
Banswara Syntex Ltd.	1087.11	137 (Half year reserve)	687.89	10 x 7.11 +137+ 687.99= [27.79]

Rajasthan Polyster Ltd.	232.49	0 (As commer production expected to start in March i.e. last month of financial year)	484	14.79
Sharda Textiles mills (India) Ltd.	440.96	59.90 (for another five months (Keeping the same trend)	540.00	21.90
Girnar Fibers Ltd.	38.70	54	2120.28	10.43

*Model IV

The relationship among the prices under our model, average price after Issue price can be observed from the diagram drawn below.

S.No Price as per after issue		*Name of Company before issue*	*Issue price Model IV*	*Average price*	*Average price*
1.	Somani Swiss Industries Ltd.	18	13.68	70.12	12.85
2.	Banswara Syntex	50	29.20	58.22	77.79
3.	Rajasthan Polyester Ltd.	15	9.50	24.38	14.79
4.	Sharda Textile Mills (India) Limited	35	21.50	62.50	21.90
5.	Girnar Fibres Ltd.	15	9.39	17.87	10.43

DIAGRAM DISPLAYING RELATIONSHIP AMONG PRICES GIVEN IN TABLE SHOWN ABOVE

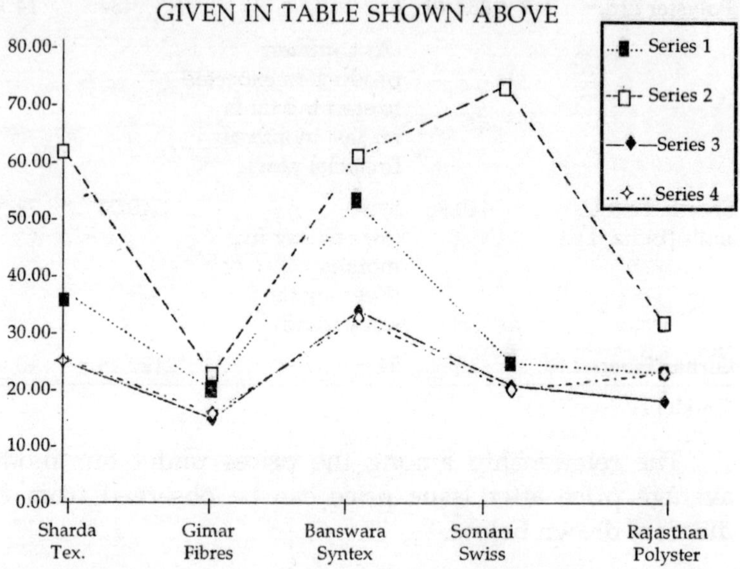

S1 = issue price *S2 = model price;*
S3 = average price afterissue *S4 = average price before issue*

The diagram drawn above displays close relationship between fair price and the model price which shows that the model can be used to reach at an approximate price in case of further issues.

Thus, we conclude that the prices yielded by the model can serve as base price which can be slightly adjusted to provide for effect of macro factors such as projected state of industry and capital market

As can be observed from the table, the price calculated according to the proposed model are more realistic as compared to those evaluated by merchant bankers.

The statistical results and analysis indicates that pricing can be made more effective by using the methodology discussed above. Although, it is very difficult to reach at a very accurate price but a close approximation can be easily

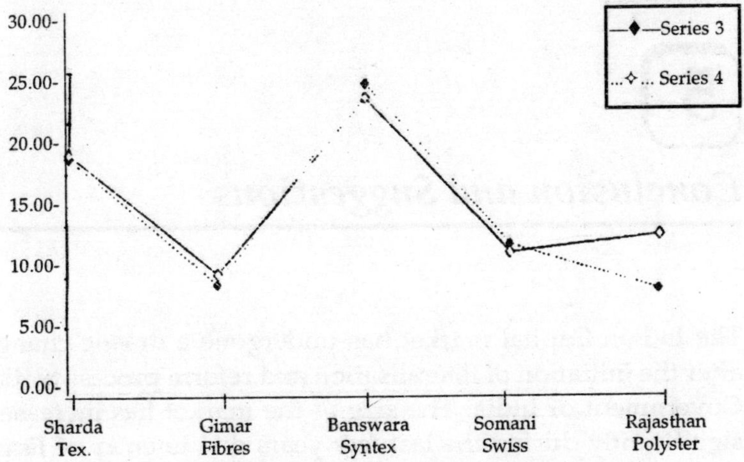

S3 = average price afterissue *S4 = model price*

made. It is due to this problem, the concept of Book Building is used. *Book building is a process of fixing the price for a share issue based on feedback from potential investors on how high they are willing to pick up shares within a given range of prices.*

With the help of the models discussed for further issues and new issue, one can easily calculate the range of price which can be offered in the book building process and finally arrive at a precise price of the issue. This would be more realistic phenomena of pricing the issues and it would be in the interest of investors as well as the company.

The problem relating to oversubscription, overpricing, development of issues would be solved if the pricing of new and further issues is made by use of the methodology developed in this study. The methodology would enable the merchant bankers to easily and systematically incorporate the effect of credentials of the company on the minimum price to be charged by investors. The merchant bankers would not face problems in quantifying the quantitative factors with the help of this model.

5

Conclusion and Suggestions

The Indian Capital market has undergone a drastic change after the initiation of liberalisation and reform process by the Government of India. The size of the market has increased significantly during the last few years due to entry of large number of investors, companies and various intermediaries such as Merchant Bankers, Registrars etc. According to reliable sources, the Investor population has grown from 9 million to over 16 million during the period 1992-93 to 1994-95. The average amount of investable per individual investor has risen from Rs. 3800 in 1991-92 to Rs. 5,000 in 1992-93. Such an increase can be attributed to abolition of CCI and emergence of free pricing in India. The Control on pricing of issue was regulated by Controller of Capital Issues through the Capital Issue (Control) Act, 1947 till 1992 when it was abolished after four and a half decades through an Presidential ordinance. The CCI methodology of pricing the issues was inherited with large number of limitations which were becoming obstacle for the companies approaching capital market to raise funds from Public. CCI used to compute fair values of shares which was average of the book value based on latest balance sheet and Profit Earning Capacity Value (PECV) based on the past profitability. The PECV was Capitalised at appropriate rates (8, 10, 12 or 15) depending upon market price of the shares, type of industry in which it was based, dividend received of the company etc. Thus, the methodology was based more upon the historical data of the company and had nothing to do with the future earning potential of the company.

Due to unrealistic pricing mechanism of CCI, most of the time Investors received Securities at a discount to their prevailing market prices. Thus, companies were not satisfied with the mechanism of CCI. The limitation was not only confined to further issue but also in case of new issues of companies. The issues were not properly priced as a result of which grey market was formed. The grey market is an unofficial capital market where investors who have applied for particular shares of a company through its public issue, sell their shares even before they are actually allotted to them. As the market doesn't have any Government recognition and legal sanctity, it is known as unofficial market. During the year 1992, the grey market was at its peak. Certain papers and periodicals were regularly publishing the price of shares in the grey market. The volume of business transacted in the grey market runs into hundreds of crores with large volume of business. As it involves frantic buying and selling by brokers many small investors were harmed. Nowadays, the size of grey market has reduced as only few scrips are traded in grey market. Due to origination of grey market, problems like multiple application and therefore massive over subscription cropped up. The over subscription is not desirable as it leads to blocking up of large amount of funds and therefore resist the process of capital formation. There were certain cases in which CCI had over priced the issue as it don't give any consideration to the size of issue. Keeping in view the aforesaid limitation associated with CCI methodology of pricing the issues, the Finance Minister in the year 1992 freed the capital market from Government Controls over capital issues and set the economy on new track to gain fresh momentum for growth. The abolition of CCI was hailed by corporate sector. The new issues and further issues flooded the market. During the period October 1992 and December 1992, over 86 companies entered the market to mobilise about Rs. 4000 crore by way of rights and rights-cum-public issues. About 40 companies entered the market in October 1992 to raise an aggregate amount of Rs. 2252.80 crore. This trend became more pronounced in the later years. SEBI laid down certain guidelines on pricing of issues and any company can approach capital market with any amount of premium as long as they comply with the guidelines. Unlike CCI, SEBI is not exercising direct control over issue pricing.

Immediately after the announcement of free pricing the corporate sector lined up to raise funds from primary market at their desired price. Share premium is perceived to be low cost fund and the companies can easily collect it by overpricing the issue. It has been observed that most of the companies issue bonus shares to its promoters a year before it plans to raise funds from public so that minimum promoter stake can be maintained even if promoters apply for less number of shares at high price being offered to the public at the time of Public issue. As a result of greed of corporate sector, many right, issues could not be subscribed during the period 1992-93. This is due to the fact, the rights issues are given to the existing shareholders at the considerably low price compared with prevailing market price of the scrip so that the shareholders may benefit through capital gain. But in the free pricing era this opportunity was no longer available to the shareholder as the companies charged high premium leaving no scope for capital gain to the shareholders. Public issues also had the same fate. During the month of April 1993, 73 companies approached the public with issues and only five could comfortably get subscribed. Many issues get undersubscribed and the liability was borne by underwriters. Finally, a stage reached when merchant banker had to put great efforts in arranging underwriters for the issues being managed by them.

In fact, some merchant banker have pointed out that world over, the issues are priced at a discount to market price but it is only in India where hefty premium are charged.

Thus, the equilibrium between investors and issuer got upset in the market and the issuer tried to take unfair advantage of free pricing. The phase was perceived as transition phase and it is expected that the system would attain stability gradually. In the light of abovementioned facts, SEBI has consistently made efforts to weed the limitations attached with the system.

SEBI has required companies coming out with issues, investors, merchant bankers, registrars, etc. to play a completely different rote than what they used to perform prior to abolition of CCI. The companies entering the market will have to adequately fix the price of its shares. In fact most of the companies are of the view that charging of higher premium is not only in the interest of the company but also shareholders. Premium is a low cost fund which helps a company in not resorting to borrowing and thus keeps away the company from the high interest burden. Therefore it helps a company in increasing its profitability. But some of the financial analyst are of the view that higher premium does not imply low cost of capital for a company. Moreover, the shareholder would forego higher earning rate on the amount contributed as premium. Therefore, while charging premium a company must assess the opportunity cost of funds from the shareholders point of view because that will enable company in achieving its main aim i.e. shareholder's wealth maximisation.

It is also necessary on the part of merchant bankers and underwriters not to involve themselves with the company charging unjustifably high premium without any basis of fundamentals. Hence companies coming out with issues must decide their issue price not only on the basis of historical records but also keeping in view the future growth potential of the company.

SEBI has required investors also to play a very cautious role in the free pricing era. Investors must acquaint themselves about the company in which they are investing their funds by going through its prospectus and other financial newspapers and measures. They may also consult capital market experts, management consultancy agencies and portfolio managers to get insight of the problem and to take effective investment decision. Shareholder must attend all the meeting and should participate in the meeting by interacting with the management of the company. It has also been observed that investors are getting mature and development of some issues are consequence of it.

SEBI has laid down tremendous responsibilities on the part of merchant bankers. They should not work under the influence of the company as it would affect their reputation in the lay run. Moreover, SEBI has made it compulsory for merchant bankers to be registered with them and on the basis of networth, certain categories of merchant bankers are required to act as lead manager to the issue. Recently SEBI has also given up task of vetting the prospectus and the responsibility has been put on the Merchant bankers.

Therefore, it would be in the interest of merchant bankers to spare themselves from offering higher premium simply to get business and they should base their decision on the true financial position and growth potential of a company.

SEBI itself has taken number of steps to eradicate the problems associated with the free pricing. SEBI has made mandatory for all companies to provide all disclosures which are likely to affect the investment decision of investors. SEBI is making consistent efforts towards investor protection and it may come out with further guidelines to completely weed out the existing problems. Y.H. Malegam Committee has proposed the idea of banning companies from making future projections. According to amendments made in the guidelines of SEBI, only those companies which have a track record of paying dividends for at least 3 years out of the proceeding 5 years will be allowed to float public/rights issue. Manufacturing companies which do not have a dividend paying track record can access the primary market provided their projects have been appraised by financial institutions or a scheduled commercial bank and the appraising body is participating in the project either by way of subscribing to the equity or by providing loans which should be minimum 5% of the project cost. SEBI has introduced the norm that in case of public/right issue there should be 5 public share holders for every one lakh of fresh issue of capital and 10 share holders in case of every one lakh of offer for sale.

The aforesaid discussions clearly reveals that a traditionary phase of free pricing is undergoing and various steps would have to be taken from time to time to completely streamline the method. The primary market interemediaries alongwith companies approaching capital market and the investors would be required to play a constructive role in it.

The theoretical basis of equity valuation should also be taken by companies and merchant bankers while pricing an issue.

This study has been done with an idea to find out limitation in CCI methodology of pricing and the state of free pricing in India. The merchant banker and other primary market intermediaries were interacted during the course of study to explore the variables which are being used in pricing of issue and also to find a method to further streamline the process of pricing.

The study has been done for new issues and further issues separately. In case of new issues data of seventeen companies operating under textile industry is used to arrive at the methodology of pricing whereas in case of further issues, data of five companies operating under textile industry was used.

The basic parameters which most of the merchant bankers consider while pricing an issue are: promoter's track record; projected book value per share; projected earning per share, issue share; and projected profit after tax. The relationship between premium and the aforesaid variable was evaluated and finally regression equation using these variables was determined. The fair price was assumed to be average price of shares for six months from the date of listing. An attempt is made to develop a model which can yield us price close to the fair price, as defined above. Three models have been developed for new issue pricing. Model I is based upon regression equation obtained between premium as dependent variable and Average Book Value, Average Profit after Tax, Issue size, Promoter's stake and Average Earnings per share as independent variables. The price obtained using model, have shown close relationship with the fair price adopted in the study, in order to attain further accuracy, the variable causing variance between fair price and the price estimated by a merchant banker have been found through interaction with different primary market intermediaries. The variables which have been referred by most of the Intermediaries are Promoter's experience, time gap between allotment of shares and accrual of profit, reserves/equity. Number of shares to be allotted, Extent of term loan in the capital structure and difference in actual and proposed net profit margin. The relationship between the percentage of variance and these variables was observed using coefficient of correlations. It was found that three variable namely, Reserves/Equity, Extent of Term loan and promoter's experience have shown high degree of correlation among all the above mentioned variables. A regression equation was estimated between percentage variance as dependent variable and all the six variables as independent variables. Using the estimated equation, new values of variances are obtained which have been used to discount the prices obtained under Model 1. The prices so obtained are referred to as price obtained under Model II. The prices obtained under Model II has shown higher degree of correlation with the fair price as compared to price obtained under Model I. Another regression equation was developed between percentage variance as dependent variable and the three variables which have shown high degree of correlation as independent variables. The equation is used to derive new set of values for the percentage variance which are subsequently used as discounting factor to arrive at new price under Model III from Model I. The prices obtained under Model III have shown very close relationship with fair price.

In case of further issues, the book value of the company subsequent to allotment of further shares alongwith effect of expected profit on the reserves of the company is taken as basis of pricing the issue. The prices have been evaluated using the above mentioned method and compared against the fair price. A very dose relationship was observed between them.

Finally, it has been concluded that one cannot achieve the exact value of fair price but a close approximation can be made and finally preciseness can be obtained by book building method. Book Building is a new concept in India. It has arisen because of inefficiencies related with present capital market. The problems such as high cost of raising funds, unrealistic pricing of the issues on account of wide gap between date of final pricing and date of opening of issue. The basic objective of book building is to determine the optimum price for share keeping in view the demand level so as to arrive at proper allocation decision. The whole issue is divided into two parts-Public portion and placement portion. Public portion should be decided of keeping in view that at least 25% of paid up equity must be offered to public so as to obtain enlistment of shares on stock exchanges. Placement portion is that portion of the issue which is offered to the members of syndicate of underwriter to the issue on a firm basis and does not form part of public issue. In the event of undersubscription of the public portion, the underwriters would take it up.

Initially, a company appoints a book runner who prepares preliminary prospectus and files it with SEBI for vetting. A preliminary prospectus contains all details like in a usual prospectus but does not contain issue price, number of shares to be offered and the amount to be raised. The book runner also forwards the copy of preliminary prospectus to the syndicate of underwriters and also mentions the price range in it. The syndicate of under writers mainly comprising of FIs, MFs etc. forward the copy to clients and collect orders from them for the quantity of securities required by them at various prices at which they are comfortable. On receipt of the offer from the potential subscriber, the book runner and the issuer determine the price at which the securities will be offered to the public.

Therefore, with the help of methodology, which is outcome of the study, one can very easily estimate a price close to the fair price and accordingly a range can be evaluated. The range can be used by book runner, who is usually category I merchant banker, to arrive at precise price for offering shares to the public.

Thus, the methodology obtained under the study would help considerably the merchant banker in calculation of accurate premium and justifying their role in the free pricing era. It would also help other primary market participants such as investors, companies, underwriters in diligently performing their role and would make free pricing of issue successful in India.

Bibliography

BOOKS

Dennis E. Logue, *Efficiency of the Market for First Public Offerings of Common Stock,* Cornell University, U.S.A. 1971.

Frank K. Reilly, *Investments,* The Dryden Press, 1988.

J.N. Dhankar, *Capital Issues—Listing and Merchant Banking,* Skylark Publications, New Delhi, 1989.

R. Davies, *Valuation of Shares,* The Macmillan Company, Great Britain.

R.L. Sidey, *Valuation of Shares,* The Law Book Company, Great Britain, 1950.

Merret, Howe and Newould, *Equity Issues and the London Capital Market,* Longmans, 1967.

Fischer and Jordan, *Security Analysis and Portfolio Management,* Prentice Hall of India private Ltd. 1992.

E. Bruce Frederikson, *Frontiers of Investment Analysis.*

Donald E. Varghn, *Survey of Investments.*

Herbert B. Mayo, *Investments an Introduction.*

Timothy Johnson, *Investment Principles.*

Edwin Elton/Martin Gruber, *Modern Portfolio Theory and Investment Analysis.*

William F. Sharpe/Gordon J. Alexander, *Investments.*

Daniel S. Aheam, *Investment Management and Economic Research.*

Benjamin Graham/Charles McGolrick, *The Interpretation of Financial Statements.*

Benjamin Graham/David L. Dodd/Sidney Cottle, *Security Analysis Principles and Technique.*

Lawrence J. Gitman, Machael D. Joehnk. *Fundamentals of Investing,* Harper and Row Publishers.

Burton G. Matkiet. *Random Walk down Wall Street,* W.W. Norton and Co. 278

H. Parker Willis, Jules Bogen, *Investment Banking,* Harper Brothers Publications, 1936.

Investment Bankers Association of America, *Fundamentals of Investment Banking,* Englewood Cliffs, New Jersey, 1949.

M. Keeley, *Raising Equity—The Problem of Setting the Issue Price; Issues in Finance,* Philip Allan Publishers Ltd., Great Britain, 1986.

Elton, E.J., and Gruber, M.J. *Modern Portfolio Theory and Investment Analysis.* New York: John Wiley and Sons. 1987.

Cochran, W.G. *Sampling Techniques.* New Delhi: Wiley Eastern Limited, 1977.

Morkowitz, H., and Wright, G.P. *Statistics for Management and Economics.* Columbus: Charles E. Merril Publishing Company, 1985.

Archer, Stephen H. and Charles A.D. Ambrosio, *The Theory of Business Finance: A Book of Readings,* third edition, Macmillan Publishing Co. Inc., New York.

Jarraw Robert A., *Finance Theory,* Prentice Hall Inc.. Englewood Cliffs, New Jersey.

Blume, M.E. and J.P. Friedman, *The Complete Guide to Investment Opportunities,* The Free Press, Macmillian Inc., New York.

Haung, Chi Fu and R.H. Litzenberger, *Foundations for Financial Economics,* North Holland, New York.

Levy Haim and Marshall Sarnat, *Capital Investment and Financial Decisions.*

Chandra, Prasanna (1978), *Valuation of Equity Shares in India,* Sultan Chand, New Delhi.

Nabhi SEBI Guidelines on Capital Issues and Merchant Banking.

Prospectus of all the Companies studied in the course of research.

Kulkarni, S.N. "Share Price Behaviour in India: A Spectral Analysis of Random Walk Hypothesis, *Sankhya*, XL, series D, part 2, 1978, 135-162.

ARTICLES

Deepak S. Raja, Equity pricing: *The Bottomline.* Mon 22 Feb 1993.

Dr. M. Thripalraju, 'E.P.S. and P.E.R.: The much abused ratios' Thursday 14 Jan 1993, *The Economic Times,* New Delhi.

Deepak S. Raja, Equity Evaluation and Pricing. Mon. 7 Dec. 1992. *The Economic Times:* New Delhi.

J. Malraj, Are Earnings Per Share Computed Correctly, Mon. 14 Dec. 1992. *The Economics Times,* New Delhi.

T.N.T. Nair, Underwriters Playing Traunt. Nair *The Economic Times,* New Delhi, Mon 15 March 1993.

S.D. Naik and B.G. Shirsat, Export Earnings to Go up. *The Economic Times,* Research Bureau.

S. Venkitaraman, "Disclosure of Parameters for Justification of Premium in Offer Documents Chartered Secretary, February, 1996.

S. Ramesh, "Free Pricing of Issues," *Chartered Secretary,* November, 1992.

B. Banerjee, "Free Pricing of Capital Issues", *Chartered Accountant,* March, 1993.

Business World. "The Great Primary Market Rip-offs," June/ July, 1995.

Chaudhuri, S.K., "Short-run Share Price Behaviour: New Evidence on Weak Form of Market Efficiency," Vikalpa, XVI, 4.

Foster, George, "Asset Pricing Models: Further Tests", *Journal of Finance and Quantitative Analysis,* XIII, 1, (March 1978).

Rao V. "Anatomy of Security Market Indices -1", *Fortune India* (October 1992).

Zahir, M.A. "Factors Affecting Equity Prices in India. *The Chartered Accountant*, March 1992.

Sharma, Ratan K. (1989), "Factors Affecting Relative Prices of Equity Shares —An Empirical Analysis", *The Chartered Accountant*, Vol. 38.

Krishan, Bal (1984), "Determinants of Equity Prices in India," *Management Accountant*, Volume 19.

Chawla, D. & G. Srinivasan (1980) "Security Prices and Monetary Variables," *Chartered Accountant*, Vol. 29.

Ojha, P.R. (1976) "Impact of Earnings, Retained Earnings and Dividends on Share Prices", *Indian Management*, Vol. 15.

Author, "Quantitative Analysis," *Indian Economic Journal* Vol. 12.

Chen, Naifu, Richard Roll (1986), "Economic Forces and Stock Markets," *Journal of Business*, Vol. 59.

Appendix

QUESTIONNAIRE-1

Name of the Lead Manager:

Name of the Official:

Designation:

Questions

1. Why CCI had been abolished?

2. What factors are being considered by various Merchant Bankers in estimating the premium of issue?

3. Do you think free pricing is justified in India?

4. What suggestions would you recommend to further improve the system of free pricing in India?

5. What are the Limitations in the system?

QUESTIONNAIRE-II

Name of the Lead Manager:

Name of the Official:

Designation:

Questions

1. Why most of the Issues are overpriced nowadays?

2. What reasons can be attributed for overpricing of issues?

3. What should be the fair price at which securities should be offered in the primary market?

4. Who is responsible for overpricing of issues — Merchant bankers or the companies approaching capital market to raise funds?

5. How one can overcome the problems associated with inadequate pricing of equity issue?

Index